SECRET LIVES

—— OF ——

GREAT FILMMAKERS

ACKNOWLEDGMENTS

The author would like to thank Michael Carney for his assistance in researching this book.

Library of Congress Cataloging in Publication Number: 2009937589

ISBN: 978-1-59474-434-1

Printed in China

Typeset in TradeGothic

Designed by Doogie Horner
Illustrations by Mario Zucca
Production management by John J. McGurk

Distributed in North America by Chronicle Books
680 Second Street
San Francisco, CA 94107

10 9 8 7 6 5 4 3 2 1

Quirk Books
215 Church Street
Philadelphia, PA 19106
www.irreference.com
www.quirkbooks.com

SECRET LIVES

OF

GREAT FILMMAKERS

WHAT YOUR TEACHERS NEVER TOLD YOU ABOUT THE WORLD'S GREATEST DIRECTORS

QUIRK BOOKS

PHILADELPHIA

BY ROBERT SCHNAKENBERG

ILLUSTRATED BY MARIO ZUCCA

CONTENTS

INTRODUCTION

"When the legend becomes fact," John Ford famously counseled, "print the legend." There are a lot of legendary stories told about famous film directors—and many of them are true. In the pages of *Secret Lives of Great Filmmakers*, we'll attempt to sort out the facts from the fables, keeping in mind Ford's dictum and allowing for the large amount of mythologizing (self- and otherwise) that goes on in Hollywood and in capitals of cinema around the globe. Welcome to a world where the booze flows freely, the "casting couch" is open for business 24/7, and your ability to finance your next masterpiece is limited only by the budget you've allotted for blow.

Movie directors have been called the last cowboys, likened to gods, and analogized to chefs, CEOs, and Peeping Toms. From the earliest days of the medium, they assigned themselves tremendous power over the casts, crews, and creative content of their pictures while assuming few of the accompanying responsibilities. Producers ponied up the money to make their artistic visions come to life, but at the end of the process they were often left quite literally holding the bag—an empty one that once was filled with the cash of a thousand Pasadena dentists. This business model has generated some remarkably good—and some stunningly bad—movies and supplied the fodder for a thousand great director anecdotes, many of which we retell here. From such imperious tyrants as Cecil B. DeMille to public provocateurs like Spike Lee, directors have always had a knack for bullying their subordinates, feuding with their rivals, and stirring up trouble with the suits.

Also in the mix are the personal quirks, weird habits, and pathological predilections that are par for the course for every fabulously successful creative person. Between these covers lurks one of the strangest collections of cross-dressers, toe suckers, germophobes, control freaks, and sex addicts ever assembled. Here you'll find the answers to a thousand trivia questions you can use to confound your movie-mad friends: Which famous director was obsessed with croquet? Who devoted an entire room in his mansion to books about Napoleon? Is it really true Alfred Hitchcock had no belly button?

If film directors truly are like voyeurs, using their cameras to show us aspects of the human experience we might not otherwise see, then it's only fair that we turn the tables on them. Let's peep into *their* rear windows for a change, look in *their* celluloid closets, debunk a few urban legends, and find out what makes the great modern mythmakers tick. Like a stag reel you pull out of the shoebox and screen for special friends, these secret lives should be shared with anyone who can handle a walk on the wild side of movie history. And so, without further ado . . . Dim the lights! Roll 'em!

D. W. GRIFFITH

JANUARY 22 1875–JULY 23, 1948

NATIONALITY:
AMERICAN

ASTROLOGICAL SIGN:
AQUARIUS

MAJOR FILMS:
BIRTH OF A NATION (1915), *INTOLERANCE* (1916)

WORDS OF WISDOM:

"ACADEMY OF MOTION PICTURE ARTS AND SCIENCES? WHAT ART? WHAT SCIENCE?"

D. W. Griffith was the George Washington of film directors—the "founding father" of auteurs—a man whose imperious manner and grand appetites set the standard for every moviemaker who came after him. With his straw hat and oversized megaphone, he is also the physical template for the "director" archetype. Fortunately, most of the filmmakers who came after him saw fit not to emulate his other defining characteristic: a racism so pernicious it taints the undeniable technical brilliance of his trailblazing silent features.

David Llewelyn Wark Griffith was born in La Grange, Kentucky, a small farm town just outside of Louisville. He was one of seven children. His father was Colonel Jacob Wark Griffith, known as "Roarin' Jake" to his friends, a gold prospector, plantation owner, and all-around bullshit artist who occasionally dispensed medicine without a license. Roarin' Jake—who claimed to be descended from Welsh warrior kings—had made a name for himself during the Civil War. In 1861, after his house was burned down by Union guerrillas, he joined the Confederate cavalry and rose to the rank of lieutenant colonel. According to legend, he once suffered a broken hip courtesy of a Union cannonball, but refused to give up his command. Unable to walk or ride, he simply commandeered a horse and wagon and led his men into battle from a seated position. For the rest of his life, Roarin' Jake kept his officer's saber hanging above his mantel—a constant reminder to the young D. W. of the "Lost Cause" for which the South had fought.

Besides teaching D. W. the rebel yell, Roarin' Jake also instilled in him a love for great literature. He introduced the boy to Shakespeare, Poe, Dickens, and Longfellow and took him to his first "magic lantern" show—a nineteenth-century precursor to motion pictures in which slides depicting classic stories were projected onto a large screen. He also instructed D. W. in the time-honored traditions of southern racism. Once, when one of his African American servants gave D. W. a haircut he didn't like, Jake accused the elderly barber of "ruin[ing] my best-looking son," cursed at him, and chased him around the yard with his beloved saber. D. W. Griffith later said that his father was "the one person I really loved most in all my life."

When D. W. was ten, his father died suddenly. The old rebel had spent a lazy spring evening on the front porch guzzling whiskey and eating home-made pickles straight from the barrel. The overindulgence proved to be fatal for a man with a stapled stomach. After scarfing down no fewer than eight gherkins and several tin cups of booze, Roarin' Jake keeled over. Doctors determined that the unusual combination of food and drink caused the stitches in an old war wound to rupture. He passed away a few hours later.

In 1890 the Griffith family moved to Louisville. There Griffith worked at a series of odd jobs—elevator operator, bookstore clerk, reporter for the *Louisville Courier-Journal*—before settling on a career in the theater. Performing under the stage name Lawrence Griffith, he appeared in a variety of minor roles in stock company stage productions. He also worked behind the scenes as a prop man for Sarah Bernhardt. Pay was abysmal, and Griffith harbored dreams of becoming a writer, so he lit out for the coasts. Settling first in California and later in New York City, Griffith finally gained a foothold in the nascent movie industry. He directed his first film, *The Adventures of Dollie*, in 1908, with his wife, Linda, in the lead.

Over the next seven years, Griffith made movies at a dizzying pace. At one point, he was cranking out four fifteen-minute shorts a week. Most were adaptations of classic tales or dramatizations of historical and biblical events. Often they featured members of his growing repertory company, such as Mary Pickford, Lillian Gish, and Mack Sennett. As Griffith's reputation grew larger, so did his cinematic ambitions. His 1915 full-length feature *Birth of a Nation* was epic in scope—moviemaking on a scale no one had yet attempted. It cost $110,000 to make and yielded a gross of $19 million—of which Griffith reportedly received ten percent.

It was also undeniably, unapologetically racist. Reflecting Griffith's Confederate upbringing, *Birth of a Nation* (an adaptation of Thomas Dixon's 1905 novel *The Clansman*) made the Ku Klux Klan into the heroes of the post–Civil War era. African Americans were depicted as rampaging savages bent only on raping white women. (Unwilling to sully his celluloid by casting any black actors, Griffith simply had white performers in blackface play their roles.) Although the film screens as repugnant today, when released it represented mainstream opinion on matters of race. It was in fact the first film ever shown in the White House, where President Woodrow Wilson—himself

a Southern racist—gave it his seal of approval. Griffith's film, he gushed, was "like writing history with lightning." As late as the 1970s, the Ku Klux Klan was still using *Birth of a Nation* as a recruiting tool.

Griffith followed up with another historical epic, *Intolerance*. This time Jews were the objects of Griffith's vilification, although the fact that the film bombed at the box office mitigated its cultural impact. The 1920s saw the director's fortunes dim considerably. He began to drink heavily, engaged in a series of extramarital affairs, and lost most of his riches in various ill-advised business ventures. "He spends his money rapidly and moodily," *Time* magazine euphemistically reported. By the time of his first sound film, 1930's *Abraham Lincoln*, Griffith's career was circling the drain. Contemporaries like Charlie Chaplin and John Ford were running rings around him artistically, and he hadn't scored a hit in fifteen years. Griffith lived the last two decades of his life in virtual seclusion, emerging from his alcoholic stupor only occasionally to polish somebody's screenplay or accept an award honoring his contributions to film. He died of a brain hemorrhage in Hollywood on July 23, 1948.

> **TERRIFIED OF LOSING HIS HAIR, THE TYRANNICAL D. W. GRIFFITH WORE CUSTOM-MADE STRAW HATS DESIGNED TO LET THE SUNLIGHT NURTURE HIS FOLLICLES.**

* * *

BOWERY BOY

During his days as a young actor trying to make it in New York, Griffith spent most of his off-hours cruising the Bowery for skanky prostitutes. Although it has long been considered Manhattan's fetid armpit, the Lower East Side held a strange fascination for Griffith, who called it a "steaming, bubbling pot of varied human flesh." "The skin of the Bowery women was of every known hue," he rhapsodized in his memoirs. "After the age-old manner of the siren, they chanted in many languages and accents the one hymn to lust." The ladies may have been for sale, but that didn't stop Griffith from working overtime to impress them. On the contrary, he styled himself quite the playa. An evening on the town would start with a quick shoe shine, followed by the selection of a dapper chapeau ("set . . . at a rakish angle," he records). Then it was off to the local beer hall, where Griffith would chat up the "working girls" with grandiose tales of his own accomplishments. Typically he would claim to be an English lord, or a duke, and was surprised when he left the establishment with no one on his arm. "How often was I assured that I would never get out of those grimy streets!" he lamented.

MR. HEINZ
Griffith was such a wolf that one of his actresses, Mae Marsh, took to calling him "Mr. Heinz" behind his back (for the "fifty-seven varieties" of women he liked to have at his disposal at all times). Another actress, Miriam Cooper, tells of being sexually harassed in the back seat of Griffith's limo. After a long day of shooting, Griffith offered Cooper a ride home, and then, while she wasn't looking, planted a wet, sloppy, gross-tasting kiss on her mouth. ("He smelled of butter: We'd had corn on the cob for lunch," Cooper reports helpfully.) Uninterested in her director's corny advances, Cooper managed to fend him off—though afterward she lived in fear of being fired.

HAIRBRAINED SCHEMES
Though most of his contemporaries rated him as strikingly handsome, Griffith was extremely insecure about his physical appearance. As a young man, he spent hours looking at himself in the mirror, studying what he considered to be his many flaws. As he got older, he lived in mortal terror of going bald. He developed a theory that sunlight on the scalp promoted hair growth, so he had his trademark straw hats made with a special wide mesh to let the rays caress his follicles. He even started shaving his head in the absurd belief that doing so would prevent him from losing his hair.

THERE'S SOMETHING ABOUT MARY
The first time he met Mary Pickford, Griffith was decidedly unimpressed. "You're too little and too fat," he told her, "but I might give you a job." She went on to become one of the biggest stars of the silent era.

DORK CALLING ORSON
Griffith was well aware of his place in motion-picture history—maybe a little too aware. Asked his opinion of Orson Welles's *Citizen Kane*, Griffith said he "particularly loved the ideas he took from me."

FEWER JEWS, MORE SLAVE GIRLS!

As anyone who's seen *Intolerance* can attest, the crucifixion of Jesus sequence is rife with anti-Semitism. Jews gathered around the cross are depicted as snarling, hook-nosed savages. But it could have been much worse. Responding to the objections of some outside organizations that there were *too many* Jewish extras in the scene, the studio ordered Griffith to reshoot the sequence with more Romans and fewer Jews. Griffith burned the existing footage and happily complied. But he wasn't so obliging when studio bosses decided that the film needed "more sex" and asked him to add some scenes of seminude slave girls. Another director was brought in to shoot that sequence.

LUSH LIFE

Toward the end of his life, Griffith was a falling-down drunk. After an afternoon of boozing, he would emerge from his bedroom only to grab another bottle from the liquor cabinet. During the day, he would haunt various watering holes, where he was known to get into fistfights with bartenders or to buttonhole people he knew and subject them to long, rambling disquisitions on his glorious film career. Griffith, a writer for the *New Yorker* observed, "gets crocked and insults women in the cocktail bars daily." Another writer, whom Griffith solicited to do a profile on him, found him "slobbering" in his hotel room, nearly insensible. On one occasion, Griffith invited a friend over for dinner, forgot that he had done so, and then kicked the man out for trying to steal his food. The next week, he forgot the incident had ever occurred and invited the same person over again.

AND THE AWARD FOR GROSS INSENSITIVITY GOES TO . . .

He may have been an alcoholic, an adulterer, and a vicious racist, but never let it be said that D. W. Griffith wasn't honored in his native country. In 1953, the Directors Guild of America began handing out a D. W. Griffith Award for distinctive achievement in film direction. In 1975, the U.S. Postal Service honored Griffith with his own postage stamp. For forty-six years, the Griffith Award would remain the guild's highest honor, until a groundswell of protest over the great auteur's early "race films" led to a much-needed name change. Declaring that Griffith's contemptible films "helped foster intolerable racial stereotypes," the Guild rechristened the prize the DGA Lifetime Achievement Award in 1991.

CECIL B. DEMILLE

AUGUST 12, 1881–JANUARY 21, 1959

NATIONALITY:
AMERICAN

ASTROLOGICAL SIGN:
LEO

MAJOR FILMS:
THE TEN COMMANDMENTS (1923), *THE GREATEST SHOW ON EARTH* (1952)

WORDS OF WISDOM

"GIVE ME ANY TWO PAGES OF THE BIBLE AND I'LL GIVE YOU A PICTURE."

The stereotype of the imperious, bullying director may have been invented by D. W. Griffith, but Cecil B. DeMille perfected it. His kingly affectations knew no bounds. His office was outfitted with stained-glass windows and bearskin rugs. Antique firearms lined the walls. The desk was elevated, like a throne. The same pomp and circumstance followed him onto the studio lot, onto which he swaggered like a pasha in riding boots and breeches, a huge retinue of attendants catering to his every whim. A violinist was kept on retainer to provide appropriate mood music for his comings and goings. A Filipino houseboy followed DeMille around wherever he went; his sole job was to carry a chair behind the great director at all times. Even DeMille's physical flaws took on an added magnificence. "He wore his baldness like an expensive hat," actress Gloria Swanson once observed, "as if it were out of the question for him to have hair like other men."

DeMille's greatness was largely self-made. His playwright father, whom he idolized, died of typhus when he was twelve years old. After his death, DeMille's mother started a theatrical company. Show business was in the boy's blood. He wrote and performed for the stage and later used his mother's contacts to collaborate with the Jesse L. Lasky Feature Play Company, one of America's earliest movie studios. DeMille's debut film for the company, 1914's *The Squaw Man*, was the first feature film made in Hollywood. It was an enormous success, as nearly every one of DeMille's films would be. In all, DeMille directed more than seventy films—only six of which failed to earn a profit at the box office.

He was an uncanny arbiter of public taste, giving the people biblical epics when they wanted them during the silent era, switching over to Westerns as soon as the religious pictures started losing money, then back to biblical epics again in the late 1940s. Always his specialty was the spectacular, with the Oscar-winning circus extravaganza *The Greatest Show on Earth* being perhaps the prime example. The consummate showman, DeMille (or "C. B.," as he liked to style himself) became one of America's first filmmaker/celebrities, paid homage to in films like *Sunset Boulevard* (in which he played himself) and in song by the likes of Bob Dylan (whose "Tombstone Blues" name checks DeMille alongside Beethoven, Ma Rainey, and Jack the Ripper). An active supporter of the blacklist, DeMille was also one of Hollywood's most outspoken conservatives, earning the ire of organized labor with his anti-union organization, the DeMille Foundation for Political Freedom.

More feared than loved, DeMille never inspired the loyalty and reverence enjoyed by other directors of his era, such as John Ford and Howard Hawks. Had he lived longer, he would have seen the kind of grand-scale epics he loved to make pass totally out of fashion. When he died of heart failure on January 21, 1959, many newspapers devoted more space to the killing that same day of *Our Gang* star Carl "Alfalfa" Switzer than to the passing of one of America's most successful directors.

THIS SIDE OF PARADISE

Befitting a man who staged movie epics on a grand scale, DeMille liked to add theatrical flourish to his parties, most of which took place at "Paradise," his secret hideaway in the Santa Monica Mountains. There DeMille indulged his predilection for "dressing up," striding around the property clad only in a white, yellow, or black cloak. And that *was* a pistol in his pocket. C. B. routinely packed heat, which he claimed was for shooting the rattlesnakes that sometimes turned up on the grounds. Invited male guests were required to wear special costumes that DeMille provided: silk Russian blouses with oversized cummerbunds. Women could wear as much (or as little) of whatever they pleased. If you were lucky, DeMille took you aside and shared some of his vast collection of European erotica, which included an exquisite privately printed three-volume illustrated edition of the works of François Rabelais. If you were *really* lucky, the director summoned you over to his bungalow-style "boom boom room," where naked women danced the seven veils to the beat of Ravel's "Bolero" and, in the words of one guest, "catered to the gastronomical desires" of the menfolk.

THOU SHALT WHAT?

DeMille may have directed *The Ten Commandments*, but that doesn't mean he followed them. Take the proscription against adultery, for instance. Although he remained married to his wife, Constance, for more than fifty years, DeMille didn't let that stop him from shagging other women whenever he pleased. At one point, he was carrying on with two mistresses at the same time: actress Julia Faye and screenwriter Jeanie MacPherson, whom he conveniently installed in the office next door to his. Constance DeMille was well aware of her husband's affairs, but seemed willing to let him stray to his heart's content as long as he provided for her and their children.

C. B.'S LEGACY

Speaking of *The Ten Commandments*, when it came time to promote his second version of the biblical epic in 1956, DeMille hit upon a novel publicity stunt. He had stone tablets of the commandments installed at courthouses and other government buildings across the United States. Today, many of those monuments still stand—and several have become the targets of lawsuits filed by groups advocating the constitutional separation of church and state.

GRIN AND BEAR IT

Some directors have the casting couch. DeMille had the polar-bear-skin rug of love. The enormous hide, which covered most of his office floor, was well known in Hollywood as the setting DeMille preferred to use for "creative conferences" with female screenwriters. He told one aspiring scribe he would be glad to hear her story pitch, but only after they had "got[ten] to know each other better" and developed the "real relationship" he felt was key to a successful writer–director collaboration. The woman took one look at the rug and fled DeMille's office in horror.

PUT YOUR FEET UP

DeMille had a raging foot fetish that became the stuff of Hollywood legend. He was initially attracted to one of his long-term mistresses, Julia Faye, after reading a magazine article that claimed she had "the prettiest feet and ankles in America." Another of his lovers, the actress Bebe Daniels, revealed that they never actually had intercourse. DeMille preferred to lick her feet while he masturbated instead. And when Paulette Goddard wanted the fe-

male lead in DeMille's 1940 film *North West Mounted Police*, she "auditioned" by walking into his office and lifting one of her bare feet onto his desk. She got the part. Fittingly, it was DeMille who suggested to impresario Sid Grauman that he immortalize the Hollywood elite by having them leave their footprints in wet cement outside his Chinese theater.

MADMAN LIBRARIAN

In addition to his passion for tootsies, DeMille had a mania for order. He insisted on arranging all the books on his shelves in descending order by height.

MACHO MAN

DeMille was one of the first of the hypermacho directors—a breed that would come to include Howard Hawks, Sam Peckinpah, William Friedkin, and others. "Cecil was like a young bull: dynamic, male, determined, and sassy," his niece Agnes observed. His tolerance for pain was legendary. "He had the courage of a lion," said Gloria Swanson. While filming *The*

> DID THIS GUY HAVE A FOOT FETISH OR WHAT? WHEN PAULETTE GODDARD WANTED THE LEAD ROLE IN A CECIL B. DEMILLE FILM, SHE "AUDITIONED" BY WALKING INTO HIS OFFICE AND LIFTING ONE OF HER BARE FEET ONTO HIS DESK.

Plainsman in 1937, DeMille directed Jean Arthur (who was playing Calamity Jane) to practice her bullwhip technique on him, repeatedly whacking him in the wrist until she cut him rather badly. He said it was because he didn't want to waste money and lose an extra until she was ready to execute the trick in front of the cameras. In 1956, the then seventy-three-year-old DeMille suffered a massive heart attack while climbing a 107-foot ladder on the set of *The Greatest Story Ever Told*. He ignored his doctor's orders and was back on the job within a week.

Nothing pleased DeMille more than to see his actors rise to match his own level of bravery. When Gloria Grahame refused to let a stand-in take her place for a scene in *The Greatest Show on Earth* in which an elephant nearly steps on her face, DeMille was positively giddy. The enormous beast came so close to stamping on Grahame that it left a smudge on her nose with its foot.

On another occasion, DeMille offered forty dollars to an extra playing an Aztec warrior if he would slide down a wall buck naked. The man wound up with a badly flayed back, but he got his bounty.

Then there were the unfortunate actors who failed to rise to the occasion. In 1949, DeMille made the mistake of casting the timid and phobic Victor Mature as the male lead in the biblical epic *Samson and Delilah*. Mature was afraid of nearly everything—including water, heights, crowds, the toothless lion he was supposed to wrestle, the cardboard swords used in the battle scenes, and the on-set wind machine. At one point Mature retreated to his dressing room to escape all the things that petrified him. Incensed, DeMille ordered him to be hauled out and proceeded to dress him down in front of the entire cast and crew. "I have met a few men in my time," the director railed. "Some have been afraid of heights, some have been afraid of water, some have been afraid of fire, some have been afraid of closed spaces. Some have even been afraid of open spaces—or themselves. But in all my thirty-five years of picture-making experience, Mr. Mature, I have not until now met a man who was one hundred percent yellow!"

AIR CECIL

Although best known as a cinematic pioneer, DeMille left an outsized mark on aviation history as well. A licensed pilot, he founded his own airline—Mercury Aviation—in 1919. It was the first U.S. commercial airline to carry passengers on a regular schedule. In 1954, working on a commission from the secretary of the Air Force, DeMille designed the uniforms worn by cadets at the U.S. Air Force Academy. Those uniforms are still being worn today.

CHARLIE CHAPLIN

APRIL 16, 1889–DECEMBER 25, 1977

NATIONALITY:
BRITISH

ASTROLOGICAL SIGN:
ARIES

MAJOR FILMS:
THE GOLD RUSH (1925), *CITY LIGHTS* (1931), *MODERN TIMES* (1936)

WORDS OF WISDOM:

"I HAVE NO FURTHER USE FOR AMERICA. I WOULDN'T GO BACK THERE IF JESUS CHRIST WAS PRESIDENT."

One of the most impersonated men in movie history, Charlie Chaplin proved to be a poor imitation of himself. In 1915, he entered a Charlie Chaplin lookalike contest in San Francisco—and lost. In fact, he failed to even make the finals. A bummed-out Chaplin told reporters afterward that he was "tempted to give lessons in the Chaplin walk, out of pity as well as in the desire to see the thing done correctly." The fact that this anecdote still astounds is a testament to the level of celebrity achieved by the "Little Tramp," the unassuming English music-hall comedian who became, for several decades, the most famous man in the world.

How famous was Chaplin? At the height of his notoriety, he received more than 73,000 letters in two days during a visit to London in the 1920s. He was the first actor—not to mention the first director—to appear on the cover of *Time* magazine, and the first real-life entertainer to have a comic strip devoted to his exploits, the 1916 howler *Pa's Imported Son-in-Law*. His Little Tramp was the most recognizable fictional characters in history and made him a millionaire by the age of thirty. Yet long after he made his fortune, the tight-fisted auteur continued to live out of shabby hotel rooms, rarely changed his clothes, and kept his uncashed paychecks stuffed in a trunk for months. Legend has it that he based the Tramp on his own shambolic appearance as a youth growing up on London's East End.

Chaplin's parents separated shortly after his birth in 1889. His alcoholic father went on to drink himself to death, while his mother wound up in a mental institution. Before they flamed out, however, they made sure to introduce him to the world of the English music hall. It was to prove his means of escape from the grim gauntlet of Victorian orphanages to which he was consigned. Chaplin spent years treading the boards in Britain, honing his comedic personae (including various puffed-up city slickers and the ever-popular "comic Jew"), before embarking on a series of successful tours of the United States beginning in 1910. In 1913, producer Mack Sennett "discovered" Chaplin and put him to work making two-reel comedies in Hollywood. The Age of the Tramp, which would last until the character's final big-screen appearance in 1936, had officially begun. The character proved so wildly popular that by 1917 Chaplin was given total creative control over his own work.

With that creative control, Chaplin produced a string of masterpieces: *The Gold Rush* in 1925, *City Lights* in 1931, *Modern Times* in 1936. But a concomitant lack of control over his personal life complicated his legacy. Two shotgun marriages to much younger women ended in scandal and divorce. In 1943, a paternity suit filed against him by actress Joan Barry led to criminal charges of white slavery, on which he was later acquitted. And while Chaplin's womanizing (some would say borderline pedophilia) outraged the bourgeois decency police, his left-wing politics wound up causing him more trouble in the end. His refusal to support the United States in World War II, pro-Soviet views, and outspoken hostility toward industrial Capitalism attracted the attention of anti-Communist crusaders in Congress, who briefly considered hauling him before the House Un-American Activities Committee. They backed down only after Chaplin threatened to make a mockery of the hearings by showing up to testify in his Tramp costume. The McCarthyites got the last laugh, however, when they barred Chaplin from reentering the United States after a trip to Europe in 1952. The exiled auteur settled in Switzerland and did not return to his adopted country until 1972. After a long period of physical and mental decline, during which he worked on new scores for some of his classic movies, the great director died on Christmas Day, 1977.

ROBBING THE CRADLE

To say Chaplin liked his women young is an understatement. He married his first wife, Mildred Harris, in 1918 when she was sixteen and he was twenty-nine. She had tricked him into the union by claiming she was pregnant. She wasn't. She did become pregnant by him shortly after they got hitched, but the baby was born with severe birth defects and lived only three days. The tumultuous marriage wheezed on for another year before dissolving in a blizzard of scandalous accusations. Chaplin charged that Harris was sleeping with another woman behind his back; Harris claimed that Chaplin smacked her around in bed.

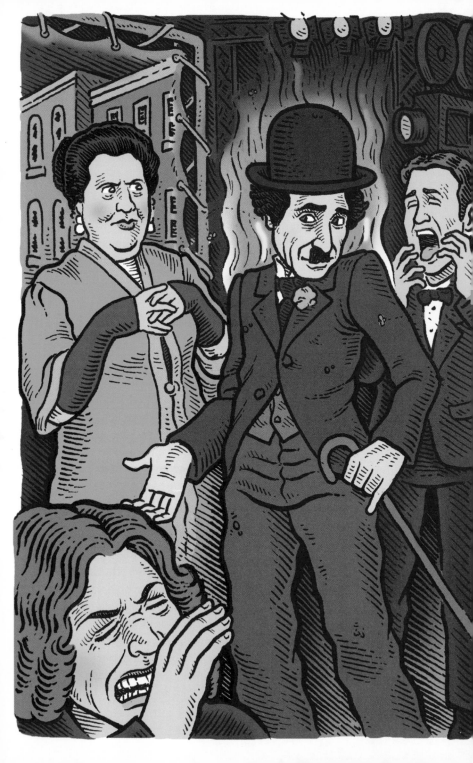

Undeterred, Chaplin tried again with another sixteen-year-old bride, actress Lillita McMurray. The model for the eponymous nymphet in Vladimir Nabokov's novel *Lolita*, McMurray adopted the stage name Lita Grey and took parts in several of Chaplin's best-known features. Chaplin first met her when she was fifteen and he was thirty-five. He immediately became "caught up in a sex-powered delirium," in the words of one biographer, and slept with her soon after. She got pregnant, and although Chaplin did everything he could to convince her to have an abortion, Lita's family blackmailed him into marrying her in 1924. In her 1927 divorce complaint, she alleged that he forced her to perform fellatio on him and had cheated on her with at least five prominent actresses, whom she threatened to name. To avoid additional negative publicity, Chaplin settled the case, relinquishing the then-exorbitant sum of $625,000. The director was so scarred by the split that he devoted just two lines to Lita in his autobiography.

As he aged, Chaplin grew at least a little wiser. He may or may not have married twenty-six-year-old actress Paulette Goddard on a trip to China in 1936, when he was forty-seven. Records aren't exactly clear on the mat-

AT THE PEAK OF HIS POPULARITY, CHARLIE CHAPLIN WAS ARGUABLY THE MOST FAMOUS MAN IN THE WORLD—DESPITE APPALLING PERSONAL HYGIENE AND A REPELLENT BODY ODOR.

ter, however, and in any case he had split with Goddard and was back to his old cradle-robbing tricks by 1943, when he married Oona O'Neill, the daughter of playwright Eugene O'Neill. She was seventeen at the time and had already had relationships with Orson Welles and future *Catcher in the Rye* author J. D. Salinger. (The sensitive Salinger was so peeved at being robbed of his girlfriend by the Little Tramp that he wrote Oona an angry letter describing in sordid detail his impression of her wedding night with Chaplin.) The marriage to Oona was Chaplin's most successful. They stayed together thirty-four years, until his death in 1977—at which point she promptly descended into alcoholism—proof, to some, of the stresses imposed on her by her marriage to Chaplin.

BIG BOX OFFICE, BIGGER BODY ODOR

He may have been beloved by the American public, but Chaplin was never very popular within the film community. According to Fatty Arbuckle's wife, Minta Durfee, there was good reason: Chaplin stunk. The Little Tramp had terrible body odor, the result of poor personal hygiene. "He was a very clever man, but he was plenty dirty," Durfee once observed. She was being kind. Chaplin was known to wear the same suit for two weeks straight without changing—right down to his shoes and socks. His B.O. was so heinous, Durfee reported, that at least one director refused to work with him because of the stench. The problem was most pronounced early in his career, before Chaplin grew rich and famous. A former assistant records that Chaplin believed he could save on wardrobe costs by simply buying one shirt, wearing it until it wore out, and then throwing it away. This caused some real consternation during the summer months. On the set of *Tillie's Punctured Romance* in 1914, Chaplin revolted his female costar, Marie Dressler, by leaving the same rancid chunk of banana on his collar through sixteen days of filming under the hot lights—in July. Dressler eventually had to complain to director Mack Sennett to get Chaplin to remove the offending piece of fruit.

THE NOT-SO-LITTLE TRAMP

If he reeked so much, why did Chaplin get so much play with the ladies? He had other attributes to compensate for his abysmal grooming habits. The first time she met him, the notorious gold-digger Peggy Hopkins Joyce reportedly tried to pick up Chaplin with the question: "Is it true what all the girls say—that you're hung like a horse?"

UNCLE CHARLIE

Spencer Dryden, the drummer for the seminal 1960s psychedelic rock band Jefferson Airplane, was Chaplin's nephew. In fact, Dryden often hung out on Chaplin's studio lot when he was a child. For years, however, Dryden kept their relationship a secret—even from his fellow band members—out of fear they would think less of him if they found out Charlie Chaplin was his uncle.

TRAMPS LIKE US

Is there an unspoken bond between comic buffoons? Count the Little Tramp among the many fans of the Dumb Kid. At an awards ceremony honoring Jerry Lewis in Berlin in 2005, Chaplin's daughter Geraldine told the story of the last time she saw her father alive. On his deathbed, Chaplin was watching a Jerry Lewis movie on television and yelling at no one in particular: "He's funny, that bastard! That bastard is funny! He knows how to take the audience!"

WHEN ICONS COLLIDE

Chaplin enjoyed a less-than-congenial relationship with another Hollywood legend. Marlon Brando was the leading man in Chaplin's last movie, 1967's *A Countess from Hong Kong*. The two men never meshed, and Brando emerged from the experience with considerable acrimony for the filmmaker he had once called "probably the most talented man the medium has ever produced." Chaplin, he revealed in his autobiography, was a "fearsomely cruel man," "an egotistical tyrant and a penny-pincher," and "probably the most sadistic man I'd ever met." "He harassed people when they were late," Brando charged, "and scolded them unmercifully to work faster." One time when Brando showed up fifteen minutes late to the set, Chaplin chewed him out in front of the entire cast and crew, berating him as a disgrace to the acting profession. (Brando subsequently demanded and received an apology.) Especially irksome was Chaplin's humiliating treatment of his forty-year-old son Sydney, who played Brando's sidekick in the film. In front of the assembled company, Papa Chaplin repeatedly mocked Sydney's intelligence and acting ability, at one point accusing him of not having brains enough to turn a doorknob. For his part, Chaplin said that working with Brando was simply "impossible."

SCAREDY CAT

Beneath his commanding exterior, Chaplin was a jumble of anxieties and bizarre phobias. One example: He was petrified of rubber and all products made from it. For whatever reason, he considered rubber "dirty" and refused to use rubber props throughout his movie career. He refused to wear a condom for the same reason—a possible explanation for the numerous unwanted pregnancies he initiated over the decades. Tasseled stocking caps also freaked him out, and it was said he would not speak to anyone who was wearing one. Warm milk was another no-no. The smell of unrefrigerated milk so revolted him (he claimed it reminded him of sex) that he avoided touching milk bottles entirely. Finally, Chaplin lived in mortal fear of being assassinated. He was so convinced that somebody would try to bump him off that he rarely appeared in public if he didn't have to—even refusing to have his photo taken at the dedication of his star on the Hollywood Walk of Fame.

STEALING CHAPLIN'S BODY

Maybe Chaplin should have worried less about getting killed and more about what might happen to him *after* his death. In March 1978, grave robbers in Vevey Switzerland absconded with Chaplin's two-month-old corpse, demanding a ransom of £400,000 for its return. It took Swiss police nearly three months to catch the corpse-nappers, during which time a number of unsavory rumors began circulating about the motivation for the crime. (One report suggested Chaplin had been dug up because he was a Jew buried in a Gentile cemetery—an odd allegation since Chaplin wasn't Jewish) In the end, the culprits turned out to be a pair of unemployed Bulgarian auto mechanics who were desperate for money and saw an opportunity. After their arrest, the men were charged with attempted extortion and disturbing the peace of the dead. The ringleader was eventually sentenced to four-and-a-half years of hard labor. Police had to use a mine detector to locate Chaplin's coffin because the bumbling criminals had forgotten where they'd stashed it. It was reburied that May in a high-security tomb lined with concrete. Of the ghoulish caper, Chaplin's widow Oona offered the most apt summary: "Charlie would have thought it ridiculous."

JOHN FORD

NATIONALITY:
AMERICAN

ASTROLOGICAL SIGN:
AQUARIUS

MAJOR FILMS:
STAGECOACH (1939), *THE SEARCHERS* (1956), *THE MAN WHO SHOT LIBERTY VALANCE* (1962)

WORDS OF WISDOM:

"IT'S NO USE TALKING TO ME ABOUT ART. I MAKE PICTURES TO PAY THE RENT."

Legend has it that John Ford got his first big break in Hollywood after producer Carl Laemmle watched the then–prop boy choreograph a thunderous charge by a group of cowboys on horseback. "Try Ford," Laemmle told a fellow producer who needed a director for a two-reel Western. "He yells loud."

Ford never stopped yelling. In fact, he bullied and badgered his way to Hollywood immortality, earning a well-deserved reputation as one of the movie industry's biggest tyrants. No actor was spared from "Pappy" Ford's abuse—from icons such as John Wayne (whose work he routinely denigrated despite employing him in more than twenty pictures) to the lowliest extra. That Ford remained beloved by so many who worked for him is a testament to the quality of the performances he managed to elicit.

There is no simple biographical explanation for all that anger. Ford wasn't beaten as a child; his upbringing doesn't even appear to have been all that difficult. He was born John Martin Feeney in Portland, Maine, on February 1, 1894 (although, in an early example of the self-mythologizing for which he would become notorious, he always claimed his given name was Sean Aloysius O'Feeney). His father ran a saloon out of the back of a grocery store, and his mother specialized in making children (eleven total over a twenty-year span beginning in 1876).

Ford was an indifferent student, preferring to spend his time in the back of the classroom drawing cowboys and Indians. As the star fullback on his high school football team, he earned the nickname "Bull" for his habit of lowering his leather helmet like a battering ram and charging through the defensive line. He pursued no education beyond high school, though he later claimed to possess several college degrees. (If they gave out credits for blarney, Ford would have had a Ph.D.)

Of his many siblings, Ford was closest to his older brother Francis. The black sheep of the family, Francis dropped out of high school, got a girl pregnant, ran away from home, joined the army, signed on with a vaudeville stage act, and moved to Hollywood to work in silent films, in roughly that order. He also changed his last name to Ford, after the auto company, he said. Eager to emulate his brother, John Ford skipped a few of the other steps and went right to the name change and acting career. In one of his first roles, he played a Ku Klux Klansman in D. W. Griffith's *Birth of a Nation*.

Ford also worked behind the scenes, as a gopher, prop boy, and jack-of-all-trades, learning the fundamentals of the film business. In 1917, he started directing, making his mark with a series of silent Westerns starring actor Harry Carey. In the 1920s, Ford earned a reputation as a filmmaker who always turned his pictures in on time, kept them under budget, and generally made money for the studio. On the set, he projected an air of authority—so much so that his crews dubbed him "Pappy," a nickname that stuck for the rest of his life.

Over the course of a nearly fifty-year career, Ford made 140 films and won four Oscars. His lush, painterly landscape shots—many of them composed on location in Utah's Monument Valley—defined the look of the classic movie Western and influenced a generation of filmmakers. Ford also helped make a star out of John Wayne, teasing strong performances out of the one-time B-movie cowboy through the use of mind games and bullying. (He referred to Wayne as "the big idiot" and was reputed to be the only man in Hollywood capable of making the Duke cry.) Despite numerous instances of unprofessional behavior (in 1954 he reportedly sucker punched Henry Fonda on the set of *Mister Roberts*) Ford commanded a level of respect and admiration unseen in the film community before or since. As a result, he was granted full autonomy to make pretty much any film he wanted until well into his sixties, at which point health problems started to overtake him. He died of stomach cancer in 1973, at age seventy-nine.

ONE-EYED JACK

Ford is famous for his trademark eyepatch—although he didn't start to wear it until relatively late in his career. The affectation dates to 1953, when Ford had surgery to remove some cataracts. The operation was successful, but he became so irritated by the bandages the doctors made him wear that he tore them off before he was supposed to. As a consequence, his right eye became extremely sensitive to light, and he went "on the patch" for the rest of his life.

KING OF PAIN

Actors who worked with Ford tend to use one word to describe him: sadistic. The director had a cruel streak a mile wide, and he delighted in pushing the buttons of those who worked for him. "Actors were terrified of him," said John Carradine, "because he liked to terrify them. He was a sadist." "He was an SOB. He was a demonical man," complained actress Dorris Bowdon. "You knew you were in trouble when he started rolling his head around," Ford veteran Harry Carey reported. "It looked like he was some sort of lizard. It was the sadism welling up in his body." Among the torments that Ford put his performers through: never complimenting them on their work; berating them in front of the entire crew in highly personal terms; and making them do multiple unnecessary takes of scenes for no other reason than to break them down and bend them to his will. Many days Ford would arrive on the set and command one of his actors to bend over so that he could literally kick him in the ass. African American actor Woody Strode was one of Ford's favorite punching bags—in every sense of the term. "He'd stomp on my feet, slug me, throw rocks at me," Strode remembered. Strode's race

TALK ABOUT YOUR BULLYING DIRECTORS: JOHN FORD WOULD OFTEN ARRIVE ON THE SET AND COMMAND AN ACTOR TO BEND OVER SO THAT HE COULD LITERALLY KICK HIM IN THE ASS.

provided an easy outlet for Ford's abuse. "Woody, you son of a bitch, quit niggering up my goddamned scene!" the one-eyed director screamed after Strode had misplayed a take. To be fair, Ford's bigotry toward blacks was pretty much par for the course for a white man of his time. He opposed segregation, hired a lot of minorities to work on his crews, and once claimed to an interviewer that all his best friends were black. But he wasn't above dropping the "n" word whenever he wanted to put someone down. (For the record, Ford was also an anti-Semite; he was known to address letters to Jewish friends "Dear Christ Killer.")

POWER LUNCH

Was one of the most avowedly macho directors in cinema history a closet homosexual? In her memoir *'Tis Herself*, actress Maureen O'Hara, a Ford regular, does more than hint that Pappy Jack was batting for the other team. She full-on outs him. O'Hara tells of how Ford filled up his sketchpad with drawings of penises during pre-production meetings on their 1955 film, *The Long Gray Line*. Then after filming began, O'Hara recalls walking into Ford's office after lunch one day to find him passionately kissing another man. (She doesn't say who, but the strong suggestion is that it was the film's star, bisexual actor Tyrone Power.) "I was shocked and speechless," O'Hara writes, adding that as soon as she discovered them the men were "on opposite sides of the room in a flash." Unsure how to process this information, O'Hara quietly withdrew from the room and pretended she hadn't seen anything. Later, the actor in question approached her on the set. "Why didn't you tell me John Ford was homosexual?" he asked. "How could I tell you something I knew nothing about?" O'Hara replied. If true, O'Hara's revelation casts a different light on some of the intense male–male relationships in Ford's films, as well as the director's well-documented homophobia. (According to John Wayne, Ford had once accused him of walking "like a fairy.") To his credit, Ford never showed any personal animosity toward homosexual friends and associates. "Doesn't everyone have a gay cousin?" he once remarked.

RED FACED

Now we know about Ford's sex life and his racial attitudes. What were his politics? Those are a little harder to pin down. Nazi filmmaker Leni Riefenstahl, whom he entertained at his home in 1938, came away convinced that he was a socialist. In 1947, Ford defined himself as a "State of Maine Republican," which in those days meant a moderate conservative. "God bless Richard Nixon," he famously pronounced in 1973 at a White House ceremony when he was awarded the Presidential Medal of Freedom, giving some credence to those who claimed he was a right-winger. And just to confuse matters further, during the blacklist in the 1950s, Ford took a strong stand in favor of civil liberties. At an emergency meeting of the Directors Guild to discuss the purging of suspected Communists from Hollywood, arch-conservative Cecil B. DeMille led the charge to compel directors to sign loyalty oaths to the United States and rat out crew members who may have attended Communist Party meetings. Ford remained silent throughout the four-hour meeting, which grew raucous with accusations of treason on both sides. Most members assumed that Ford would side with the conservatives, but when he finally chose to speak, he surprised everybody. "My name's John Ford," he said. "I make Westerns.

I don't think there is anyone in the room who knows more about what the American public wants than Cecil B. DeMille. In that respect I admire him. But I don't like you, C. B. I don't like what you stand for and I don't like what you've been saying here tonight." Ford then moved that DeMille and the entire board of directors resign and that a vote of confidence be issued for guild president Joseph Mankiewicz, a blacklist opponent. DeMille was humiliated. He called it one of the worst nights of his life. After that, whenever Ford found out someone was in danger of being blacklisted, he stood up for him. "Send the Commie bastard to me," he'd say. "I'll hire him."

NOW GO GET ME A CUP OF COFFEE
Ford ran a tight ship, refusing to allow writers or producers on his sets. "Don't you have an office?" he would bellow whenever one showed up unexpectedly. He brooked no interference from "the suits." One day, when a studio executive complained that Ford's current film was behind schedule, the director asked him how many days behind it was. "Four days," the chief replied. Without another word, Ford picked up the script and ripped out four pages at random. "Now we're back on schedule," he declared.

INDIAN BUMMER
Ford was famous for hiring Native Americans as extras in his Westerns—a departure from the standard Hollywood practice of casting swarthy Caucasians in the roles. He also employed Indians behind the scenes, as technical advisors. One of his favorites was "Old Fat," a Navajo medicine man whom Ford put on retainer during production of *Fort Apache* in 1948. Old Fat's job was to predict the weather and, wherever possible, pray for cloud formations that would look good on camera. The old man's daily weather reports proved so accurate that Ford started scheduling all his shots around them. One day, when Old Fat failed to report, Ford asked a Navajo tribesman for an explanation. "His radio broke," came the reply.

PAPPY'S GOT A BRAND-NEW SQUEEZEBOX
To herald his arrival on the set, Ford paid an accordion player to crank out one of his favorite traditional tunes, such as "My Buddy," "Red River Valley," or "Bringing in the Sheaves." The musician was instructed to stroll around the set all times, keeping the actors in the proper mood and creating a little appropriate Western atmosphere.

SERVICE RIVALRY

In his old age, Ford spent most of his leisure time watching television. A life-long trivia buff, he was a huge fan of *Jeopardy*. He also loved *Hogan's Heroes*, the lowbrow situation comedy starring Bob Crane as a wisecracking Army captain imprisoned by the Nazis. But he drew the line at *McHale's Navy*, a similarly themed show about hijinx on board a World War II PT boat. As an old Navy man, Ford was happy to see Army officers portrayed as buffoons, but not sailors.

HOWARD HAWKS

MAY 30, 1896–DECEMBER 26, 1977

NATIONALITY:
AMERICAN

ASTROLOGICAL SIGN:
GEMINI

MAJOR FILMS:
BRINGING UP BABY (1938), *TO HAVE AND HAVE NOT* (1944)

WORDS OF WISDOM:

"A GOOD MOVIE IS THREE GREAT SCENES AND NO BAD SCENES."

They don't make 'em any more macho than Howard Hawks. A two-fisted drinker, degenerate gambler, and shameless womanizer, Hawks practically invented the stereotype of the cool, conscienceless playboy director—for which his fellow satyrs Peter Bogdanovich, Roman Polanksi, and William Friedkin must be eternally grateful.

He didn't seem like a likely candidate for the Bad Boy Hall of Fame. Born in Goshen, Indiana on May 30, 1896, Hawks was raised in a devoutly religious household. His mother was a Christian Scientist, and Hawks himself was officially listed as a Christian Scientist on his high school entrance documents, though it's unclear how much he practiced his family's faith.

Hawks's formative years were defined by tragedy. When he was fifteen years old, his five-year-old sister Helen Bernice contracted enteritis after eating a piece of unripe fruit. In accordance with her religious beliefs, his mother elected not to seek medical treatment at a hospital, and Helen Bernice died. The funeral director was ordered to cremate the remains, the surviving family members concealed their grief, and the dead girl was rarely spoken about again. The same dismal pattern repeated itself some years later, when Hawks's sister Grace contracted tuberculosis. Once again Helen Hawks refused to send her ailing daughter to a sanitarium—and once again the girl died. This time Hawks and his younger brother Kenneth blamed their mother for their sister's death.

Hawks attended Cornell University, where his stated major was mechanical engineering but his true passions were drinking, gambling, and whoring. After college and service in the U.S. Army, Hawks pursued a career in Hollywood. He directed his first feature, *Road to Glory* (oddly enough, a paean to Christian Science), in 1926. The silent age was good to Hawks, and to Kenneth, who was also enjoying early success as a filmmaker. But it was not to last. On January 2, 1930, while filming a flying sequence for the movie *Such Men Are Dangerous*, Kenneth Hawks was killed in a midair plane crash over the Pacific. He was thirty-two years old. Howard Hawks never got over the death of his brother, whom he considered his superior as a director.

The tragedy pushed him to drive himself even harder to achieve success.

With the advent of talkies, Hawks's gift for dialogue—both crafting his own and seeking out screenwriters who could supply the kind of snappy, rat-tat-tat byplay he preferred—allowed him to thrive where other silent directors had failed. He specialized in two kinds of films: manly adventures, often in the Western, gangster, or war genres (such as *To Have and Have Not*, *The Big Sleep*, and *Red River*), and screwball comedies (*Bringing Up Baby* and *His Girl Friday*). He helped launch the career of Lauren Bacall (it was Hawks who suggested that she change her name from Betty to Lauren) and redefine the image of women in film to the style he preferred: assertive, tough-talking, and overtly sexual.

"Overtly sexual" was a term that could be applied to Hawks himself. He was married three times, and he cheated serially on each of his wives. An auto racing and motorcycling enthusiast, Hawks was also known to hunt, fish, and "roll the bones" at the craps table with reckless abandon. His compulsive gambling got so bad that he had to ask Warner Brothers to advance him thirty percent of his salary on *To Have and Have Not* to pay off his bookies. More than once, without his wife's consent, Hawks withdrew all the money from their joint bank account to bet on the horses. At one point the IRS was garnishing half his wages to pay off his back taxes.

Hawks continued to make films—and gamble and carouse and ride motorcycles—well into his seventies. His family was convinced he would live forever, but his German Shepherd had other ideas. On the evening of December 3, 1977, after drinking a couple of glasses of whiskey, a sloshed Hawks tripped over his dog at his home in Palm Springs, California, and knocked his head on the stone floor. He died of complications from a brain injury less than three weeks later.

THE GREY FOX

Hawks was a lifelong womanizer, nicknamed "The Grey Fox of Hollywood" by his friend John Ford for his relentless tomcatting. A proponent of the casting couch, Hawks slept with many of his leading ladies, including Joan Crawford, Ann Dvorak, Ann Sheridan, and Jean Harlow (who considered him a lousy lover). An unabashed adulterer, Hawks would often slink into bed next to his wife at four in the morning, literally with lipstick stains on his collar.

"Sex was simply a physical need that had no relation to the person he was with," his second wife, Slim Keith, reported. Well into his seventies, Hawks retained his roving eye for the ladies. He threw topless pool parties for bathing beauties at his Palm Springs mansion and once boasted to a friend about an anonymous sexual encounter he'd had with a young woman who showed up at his house by mistake. Even on his deathbed, Hawks was still trying to score some digits. Hospitalized following the fall at his home, he asked several of the nurses for their phone numbers and invited one back to his place to party with him.

MALLETS AFORETHOUGHT

When not chasing skirts, Hawks could often be found chasing a little wooden ball across a well-manicured lawn. He was obsessed with croquet. Together with his brother Bill, he dominated the game on the West Coast in the 1940s and '50s. Hawks even had a regulation croquet lawn installed on his property. There he whiled away entire afternoons swinging the mallet alongside fellow Hollywood croquet enthusiasts such as Darryl Zanuck, Joseph Cotten,

> MORE THAN ONCE, AND WITHOUT HIS WIFE'S CONSENT, HOWARD HAWKS WITHDREW EVERY PENNY FROM THEIR JOINT BANK ACCOUNT TO BET AT THE RACETRACK.

and Cesar Romero. In July 1946, Hawks even got a little East Coast/West Coast rivalry brewing when he hosted a grudge match pitting himself and Zanuck against East Coast powerhouses Moss Hart and Tyrone Power. The event was staged under specially installed floodlights and covered by *Life* magazine. Howard Hughes was among the spectators. For the record, the East Coast team prevailed, two games to one. In recognition of his contributions to the popularity of the sport, Hawks was inducted into the United States Croquet Hall of Fame in 1980.

SCIENCE CLASS

Long before stars like Tom Cruise and John Travolta used their celebrity to promote the teachings of Scientology, Hawks was spreading his own unconventional religious beliefs through his movies. His first feature, *The Road to*

Glory, was essentially a Christian Science propaganda film. In the movie, a blind woman forsakes medicine and relies instead on the healing power of prayer to save her lover after he is seriously injured by a falling tree. Amazingly enough, not only does *he* recover, but *she* regains her sight as well! Hawks later disavowed his work on the project, admitting he "was not in a very good frame of mind" when he wrote the screenplay.

BAD FOR THE JEWS

Hawks was a notorious anti-Semite. His outspoken hatred of Jews was so well known in Hollywood that Lauren Bacall kept her Judaism from him while filming *To Have and Have Not*, for fear that he might fire her. Once when the two were eating lunch in a café, orchestra conductor Leo Forbstein walked in. Hawks nearly popped his cork. "Do you notice how noisy it is in here suddenly?" he seethed. "That's because Leo Forbstein just walked in. Jews always make more noise!"

FISH STORY

Ernest Hemingway was the kind of "man's man" to whom the hypermacho Hawks could relate. The two often went on fishing trips together, and Hawks was always trying to get Hemingway to collaborate on a screenplay. "I don't want to go out to Hollywood," Hemingway complained during one such outing, off Key West in 1943. "I don't like it. I wouldn't know what to do." Hawks assured him they could work on scripts together from any location and proposed a challenge: Hawks would make a good movie out of Hemingway's worst novel. Which one was that, Hemingway asked. "That piece of junk called *To Have and Have Not*," Hawks replied. Hawks proceeded to refashion Hemingway's story to suit his own purposes, creating a minor classic he considered to be his own version of *Casablanca*.

SOUTHERN COMFORT

Another famous writer Hawks *did* entice out to Hollywood was William Faulkner. The unstable, alcoholic Mississippian shared Hawks's passion for hunting, flying—and bourbon. Although he never wrote a full script for Hawks, the director liked to keep Faulkner around the set as a kind of on-call dialogue jobber. "If I wanted a scene or a story, I'd call Bill up and get it," Hawks recalled. "He knew what I wanted." Most of the time, what Hawks wanted was someone to get wasted with. "Bill drank too much, but when he wasn't drinking he was awful good." Hawks and Faulkner often went hunting together as well. Screen legend Clark Gable once accompanied them on one of their expeditions. They made for an odd threesome, as Hawks later observed: "I don't think Gable ever read a book, and I don't think Faulkner ever went to see a movie." That premise was borne out by the subsequent conversation. As they were driving through Palm Springs on their way to the Imperial Valley, the talk turned to writing. Gable asked Faulkner who his favorite authors were, "Thomas Mann, Willa Cather, John Dos Passos, Ernest Hemingway, and myself," Faulkner replied, with characteristic modesty. Gable was taken aback. "Oh, do you write, Mr. Faulkner?" he asked. "Yeah," retorted Faulkner. "What do you do, Mr. Gable?"

TO DRINK AND DRINK NOT

One drunk to whom Hawks was less forgiving was Humphrey Bogart. A lush with a weakness for Scotch, Bogie showed up on the set of *To Have and Have Not* three sheets to the wind, staggering around like a blind man. "Bogie, you're not that good an actor that you can cope when you've got a few drinks in you," Hawks counseled. "Too bad," Bogart replied. "I like my drink." "Right," said the director "Then either I need a new actor or you need a new director." Bogart never indulged in a liquid lunch again.

VOICE LESSONS

To deepen Lauren Bacall's high nasal voice in preparation for her role as a sexy seductress in *To Have and Have Not*, Hawks drove her to a Los Angeles mountaintop and had her read passages aloud from the biblical epic *The Robe* out loud to him in the low, smoky tones he preferred.

CASABLANCA: THE MUSICAL

Hawks was offered a chance to direct *Casablanca*, but he turned it down after his wife told him the script was terrible. Of the finished film, directed by Michael Curtiz and now considered a classic, Hawks complained that it had an "awful musical comedy quality" because of all the singing scenes set in Rick's Café. "I never had any faith in my doing anything like that," he said.

Oscar Micheaux and Other Overlooked Directors from the Golden Age of Hollywood

N ot every great director becomes a household name. Here are four lesser-known filmmakers who still made an impact during the 1920s, '30s, and '40s.

OSCAR MICHEAUX (1884–1951)
Major Films: *Within Our Gates* (1920), *Body and Soul* (1925)

Say the words "African American indie filmmaking pioneer" and most people will think "Spike Lee." Six decades before *She's Gotta Have It*, however, Oscar Micheaux was using film as a medium for educating Americans about race—and following a D.I.Y. business plan that was light-years ahead of its time. The son of former slaves, Micheaux self-published novels and sold them door-to-door before raising enough money to finance his first feature in 1919. He personally bankrolled most of his films—traveling the country with a projector in hand to screen them wherever and whenever possible. His politically charged "race films" generated controversy both inside and outside the black community and helped till the soil for Melvin Van Peebles, Gordon Parks, and others.

WILLIAM DIETERLE (1893–1972)
Major Films: *A Midsummer Night's Dream* (1935), *The Hunchback of Notre Dame* (1939)

With Austrian ex-pats Erich Von Stroheim and Josef Von Sternberg, German-born William Dieterle was part of the Axis of Eccentricity, a trio of Teutonic directors who took Hollywood by storm in the 1930s. Like those two better-known geniuses, Dieterle had aristocratic affectations. He was famous for wearing white gloves on the set at all times—a fact that was played up by the studio publicists as emblematic of his "European" refinement. Nothing could be further from the truth. Dieterle came from a working-class background and the gloves were the byproduct of a skin allergy. His other quirks were less endearing. It was said that Dieterle never started work on a film until his astrologer gave him permission. The notoriously sadistic filmmaker also kept tiny scale models of his sets in his home so that he could move around his "actors," in the form of dried-up peas.

WILLIAM WELLMAN (1896–1975)
Major Films: *A Star Is Born* (1937), *Battleground* (1949)

A kind of junior-grade Howard Hawks, William Wellman is well regarded among classic film aficionados but sometimes gets lost in the shadow of his more celebrated contemporaries. A master of the action picture, "Wild Bill," as he was known, was himself something of an action hero. He was descended from Francis Lewis—one of the signers of the Declaration of Independence—but lived as if unburdened by the dignity of his family heritage. He was expelled from high school for dropping a stink bomb on his principal's head ("A direct hit!" he later exulted), he played professional ice hockey, and he was a World War I flying ace before embarking on a film career. He acted in silents, but saw his prospects dry up after he slapped one of his leading ladies—who also happened to be director Raoul Walsh's wife. Fed up with acting, which he considered "unmanly," he turned to directing, and while churning out his fair share of hack work he also occasionally produced a gem like *Battleground* or *The Ox-Bow Incident*. Upon his death, his body was cremated and the ashes strewn by airplane over the United Sates.

LEO MCCAREY (1898–1969)
Major Films: *Going My Way* (1944), *The Bells of St. Mary's* (1945)

Leo McCarey won three Academy Awards. (That's three more than Alfred Hitchcock, for those keeping score at home.) He was one of the most financially successful filmmakers of his era, and in 1944, he boasted the highest reported income of any U.S. citizen. Yet he is all but unknown today, with many of his most acclaimed movies relegated to the occasional rec room screening at the old folks home. But the man behind such sentimental favorites as *Going My Way* and *The Bells of St. Mary's* gets an undeserved bad rap. Though he longed to make serious melodramas, McCarey's real calling was comedy. He came up with the idea of pairing Laurel and Hardy, directed the Marx Brothers' best movie, *Duck Soup*, and helped kick-start the careers of W. C. Fields and Mae West.

FRANK CAPRA

MAY 18, 1897–SEPTEMBER 3, 1991

NATIONALITY:
AMERICAN

ASTROLOGICAL SIGN:
TAURUS

MAJOR FILMS:
IT HAPPENED ONE NIGHT (1934), *MR. SMITH GOES TO WASHINGTON* (1939), *IT'S A WONDERFUL LIFE* (1946)

WORDS OF WISDOM:

"BEHIND EVERY SUCCESSFUL MAN, THERE STANDS AN ASTONISHED WOMAN."

Frank Capra's trademark blend of patriotic sentiment and feel-good populism—dubbed "Capracorn" by his detractors—has influenced generations of middlebrow filmmakers, from Robert Zemeckis to Ivan Reitman to Ron Howard. Anytime anybody "goes to Washington" or learns how wonderful life is by the end of the movie, the Mark of Capra is showing. Audiences seem to have an endless appetite for such schmaltz. How would they feel if they found out that the real Frank Capra was a racist crypto-Fascist who worked in a brothel and once contracted an STD? It's a wonderful life, indeed.

Born in Sicily, Francesco Rosario Capra moved to the United States with this family when he was six years old. Settling in Los Angeles, he endured a typically hardscrabble immigrant upbringing. He learned English, got into scrapes with other kids, and worked hard to stay on the good side of his bickering, unhappily married parents. He took a job delivering newspapers but was subjected to repeated molestation by older, bigger boys—a searing experience that fueled his lifelong homophobia. While still in high school, Capra got his first show-business job, playing guitar in a whorehouse. The pay was one dollar a night, and Frank never sampled the wares, claiming he was too scarred by the experience of being molested. Sexual development for Capra would come much later, and when it did it scarred him for life. Literally.

When Capra was a sophomore in college, his father died horribly in an industrial accident. The elderly man was nearly severed at the waist after his coat was caught in the gears of a water pump at the lemon grove where he worked. Left without financial support from his family, Capra was given a loan by his school treasurer to pay his tuition—a small act of kindness that would inspire a scene in one of his greatest films, *It's a Wonderful Life*.

After graduating with a degree in chemical engineering, Capra served in the military in San Francisco during World War I. It was there that he first got involved in the movie business, answering a want ad in a Bay Area newspaper from an aging Shakespearean actor who wanted someone to film him as he recited poetry. Returning to Los Angeles, Capra landed jobs as a prop man for silent-film director Mack Sennett and a gag writer on Hal Roach's *Our Gang* comedies. (Among his *Our Gang* innovations was the development of a so-called nigger baby act featuring token black rascals "Sunshine Sammy" Morrison and Allen "Farina" Hoskins.) His big break came while directing comedies for silent comedian Harry Langdon.

In 1928, Capra began an eleven-year relationship with Columbia Pictures, during which he directed more than twenty-five films. He became a major money maker for the studio and a reliable font of prestige pictures as well. *Lady for a Day*, *Mr. Deeds Goes to Town*, *Lost Horizon*, *You Can't Take It With You*, and *Mr. Smith Goes to Washington* were all nominated for multiple Academy Awards, and *It Happened One Night* (1934) was the first film to win Oscars in all five major categories.

During World War II, Capra was commissioned a major and put to work making propaganda films for the U.S. Army—including the classic series *Why We Fight*. Returning to Hollywood in 1946, he directed one final masterpiece—the Christmas classic *It's a Wonderful Life*—and several forgettable comedies under his proprietary Liberty Films banner. In the 1960s, Capra's wholesome brand of all-American entertainment fell out of favor with the public, only to enjoy a resurgence in the "Morning in America" 1980s under President Ronald Reagan. *It's a Wonderful Life* in particular has become a yuletide perennial, inspiring numerous parodies and homages. Capra himself lived long enough to see his films come back into fashion. He died of heart failure at his home in Southern California in 1991, at the ripe old age of ninety-four.

WHY WE HATE

"Blacks have hate in their heart," Capra informed an interviewer in 1984. The fact that a man born in 1897 would harbor some racial and ethnic prejudices should come as no surprise. The fact that he kept trumpeting them publicly well into his eighties, after most educated Americans had put them aside or learned to keep them under wraps, is somewhat disturbing, especially given Capra's reputation as the cinematic tribune of apple pie American values. As a child growing up in Los Angeles, Capra was taught to hate "niggers," "cholos" (Mexicans), and "Japs" by his xenophobic immigrant parents. Capra and his friends used to take special delight in tormenting the local watermelon man, an Asian gentleman who used to bring his fruit to market in a horse-drawn wagon. If he wasn't vigilant about driving the boys off with his buggy whip, he would often find that they had run up behind him and destroyed his entire inventory. When Capra returned to his old high school in 1950 to pass out diplomas, he was mortified at the number of black graduates. Even as an old man, Capra claimed the only African-Americans he could tolerate were those, like professional baseball players, who had completely assimilated into white culture.

THE FIRST CUT IS THE DEEPEST

While in his early twenties, Capra contracted a raging case of gonorrhea after a one-night stand with a woman he met at a party in San Francisco. He sought treatment at an underground "clap shack" and appeared to have the problem under control until—wham!—another anonymous sexual encounter left him with a maddeningly itchy penis once more. This time, the quack doctor Capra consulted suggested a radical remedy: adult circumcision. "This guy wants to make a Jew out of me," Capra groused to a friend, before agreeing to undergo the procedure, which was conducted in a makeshift operating room with a shot of alcohol as the anesthetic. To Capra's dismay, the make-believe *mohel* proved a little too aggressive with the scalpel, removing not only his foreskin but every inch of flesh around the head of his phallus. "The son of a bitch cut everything off!" Capra later wailed. The operation left Capra hunched over in agony, bleeding into a rag—and sexually crippled for the rest of his life. "That finished women for me," he later admitted. "It practically wrecked my life." As a consequence of the botched surgical procedure, Capra had to endure excruciating pain with every erection. He also ejaculated prematurely. "I became a lousy lay," the director confessed. "I just go in and bang bang bang—there it goes, I can't hold it back. No woman likes to be fondled and then have somebody squirt all over her." Over the years, Capra consulted numerous doctors to try to overcome his sexual dysfunction. With some effort (and the saintlike patience of his second wife, Lucille) he was finally able to become "master of his domain," so to speak. "I finally learned how to do it and hold back," he said. "It took a lot of brainwork." By the time he was in his late eighties, he declared himself cured, telling interviewers that he never failed to perform in the bedroom. Better late than never.

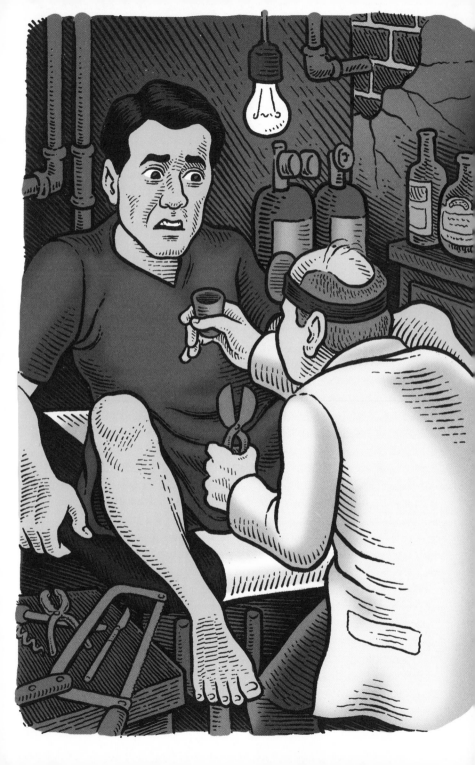

RIGHT FROM THE START

Thanks to films like *Mr. Smith Goes to Washington*, Capra has long been associated in the public mind with a scrappy brand of all-American populism and, by extension, with Franklin Delano Roosevelt's New Deal. Despite appearances to the contrary, however, Capra was no liberal. He was a lifelong conservative Republican who voted for the GOP candidate in every presidential election from 1920 until his death in 1991. Although charmed by Roosevelt personally, he loathed FDR's policies and derided him to newspapermen as "too big for the country's good." Capra's political heroes included Barry Goldwater, Gerald Ford (with whom he golfed regularly), and Ronald Reagan (to whom he sent a wire of congratulations upon his election to the presidency). He even excused Richard Nixon for his Watergate crimes on the grounds that he was just trying "to protect his friends." All of Capra's tub thumping on behalf of the right wing didn't keep him from being investigated by Senator Joseph McCarthy's red-baiting House Un-American Activities Committee, however. In the eyes of McCarthy, Capra's past

> FRANK CAPRA AGREED TO A RADICAL REMEDY FOR A CASE OF GONORRHEA: ADULT CIRCUMCISION AT AN UNDERGROUND "CLAP SHACK." THE PROCEDURE LITERALLY SCARRED HIM FOR LIFE.

associations with left-leaning screenwriters made him suspect. As a result, he was "greylisted" and a secret file on him remained classified until 1986.

ITALIAN HERO

Being a rock-ribbed Republican is one thing, but was Capra actually a dyed-in-the-wool Fascist as well? He certainly admired Generalissimo Francisco Franco, whose side he favored in the Spanish Civil War, and he was an early and ardent backer of Italian dictator Benito Mussolini as well. According to screenwriter John Lee Mahin, Capra kept an enormous oil painting of Il Duce on his bedroom wall well into the 1930s. "He adored him!" Mahin reports.

ALFRED HITCHCOCK

AUGUST 13, 1899–APRIL 29, 1980

NATIONALITY:
BRITISH

ASTROLOGICAL SIGN:
LEO

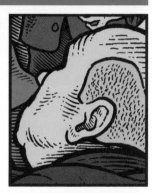

MAJOR FILMS:
REBECCA (1940), *VERTIGO* (1958), *PSYCHO* (1960)

WORDS OF WISDOM:

"THE LENGTH OF A FILM SHOULD BE DIRECTLY RELATED TO THE ENDURANCE OF THE HUMAN BLADDER."

*I*t will come as no surprise to anyone that filmdom's master of suspense—the man who gave the world *Psycho*—survived a somewhat twisted upbringing. The youngest of three children born into a strict lower-middle-class Catholic family in London's East End, Alfred Joseph Hitchcock forged a close, some would say creepy, bond with his parents. His mother, Emma, used to make him stand at the foot of her bed every night and report what had happened to him that day—a curious ritual he called "the evening confession." (The fact that it continued into early adulthood made it even curiouser.) Hitchcock's father, a cockney grocer, had a flair for unusual punishments. Once, when six-year-old Alfred misbehaved, William Hitchcock sent him to deliver a sealed letter to the local police station. The officer on duty opened it, read the message, and immediately locked Alfred in a jail cell, warning him: "This is what we do to naughty boys." For the rest of his life, Hitchcock was terrified of policemen. In fact, anyone in a uniform freaked him out. He even refused to drive a car for fear of being pulled over.

A solitary boy, Hitchcock found refuge in his personal obsessions. He became fixated on railway timetables, for example—at one point memorizing the schedules of most of England's train lines. He loved to visit the Scotland Yard Museum or to drop in on criminal trials at the Old Bailey. The fascination with small details, combined with an interest in crime and the criminal mind, were to be the hallmarks of his career as a filmmaker. After studying art and technical drawing and working as a draftsman for a London movie studio, Hitchcock made the leap into directing in 1925. He scored his first hit with 1927's *The Lodger*, a fog-enshrouded thriller about the crimes of Jack the Ripper that set the thematic template for his entire body of work.

By the end of the 1930s, Hitchcock had developed a reputation as England's finest filmmaker. Lured to Hollywood by producer David O. Selznick in 1939, he scored a best picture Oscar for 1940's *Rebecca* (the only one of his movies to win the award). Now certified and gold-plated as one of the world's top directors, Hitchcock set about adding classics to his growing corpus: *Spellbound* (1945), *Notorious* (1946), *Rear Window* (1954), *Vertigo* (1958), *North by Northwest* (1959), and, of course, *Psycho* (1960). Each was a box-office hit, and collectively they helped establish the Hitchcock "brand" and make him an international celebrity. An eponymous suspense anthology series he hosted for American TV from 1955 to 1965—not to mention "Hitch's" penchant for making cameo appearances in his own films—only enhanced his visibility.

It would be decades before the general public learned what a weirdo he was away from the camera. Hitchcock had a thing for icy blondes. He cast a succession of them in his films, tried to break down their defenses by telling them an endless stream of dirty jokes, and pried into their personal lives in a totally inappropriate fashion. When they resisted his control, or, in the case of Vera Miles, got married, he lost all interest, shutting them off or belittling them in front of others. His reputation within the industry as an old lech who liked to play perverse practical jokes on his actors may have preceded him, by all accounts his home life was fairly conventional. Despite all his psychosexual straying, he remained faithful to his wife, film editor Alma Reville, whom he married in 1926.

In his later years, Hitchcock spent less time making films and more time serving as a kind of roving ambassador of suspense. Instantly recognizable due to his stout frame and distinctive voice, he was regularly spoofed in film and on television. (An episode of *The Flintstones* reimagined him as a Stone Age wife murderer named "Alvin Brickrock"—one of many unauthorized uses of his likeness for which he was never compensated.) He appeared in commercials, was a guest on talk shows, and even supplied the voice of the shark at the *Jaws* ride at Universal Studios. Some measure of dignity was finally restored when Hitchcock was knighted in 1979, shortly after announcing his retirement. He died on April 29, 1980.

* * *

YOU CAN'T CALL ME AL

"Hitch" was the only nickname to which Hitchcock would answer. He especially hated it whenever anyone called him "Fred" or "Cocky."

SICK JOKE

Hitchcock was a notorious practical joker whose carefully planned pranks often betrayed his cruel streak. He once placed his daughter Patricia on a Ferris wheel, let her ride it to the top, then ordered the attendant to shut it off, stranding her in midair. On another occasion, he handcuffed stars Robert Donat and Madeleine Carroll together on the set of *The 39 Steps*—then pretended he'd lost the key. When Kim Novak showed up on the set of *Vertigo*, she entered her dressing room to find a freshly killed and plucked chicken hanging over her dressing table. Before she could let out a scream, Hitchcock appeared behind her, cackling maniacally.

GIFTS THAT KEEP ON GIVING

Hitchcock's repertoire of humiliating pranks included a special subcategory of insulting and creepy presents. He once sent vertically challenged actor Peter Lorre a small child's suit. And when a young Melanie Griffith visited her mother, Tippi Hedren, on the set of *The Birds*, Hitchcock gave her a truly disturbing Christmas gift: a miniature doll in Hedren's likeness, tucked inside a tiny wooden casket.

BLUE HUMOR

In what was perhaps his most sickening stunt, Hitchcock became famous for throwing "blue dye" dinner parties in his Hollywood home. Here the bill of fare included blue steak, blue peas, and blue mashed potatoes—all washed down by blue martinis. Apparently it tickled Hitchcock to see if changing the color of the food would turn people off. It did. Many of his guests became nauseous and few of them accepted his next invitation.

MERRY CHRISTMAS

Not all of Hitchcock's jests were quite so antisocial. Some were even kind of amusing. For years he sent out Christmas cards containing every letter of the alphabet except the one between K and M. It was his way of wishing people a happy "No-el."

CONTEMPLATING HIS NAVEL

As his adipose silhouette suggests, Hitchcock certainly had a belly, but no belly button. It had been sewn shut following his abdominal surgery. On the set of *Family Plot* the morbidly obese director once frightened actress Karen Black by lifting up his shirt and flashing her his curiously smooth gut.

FATHER FIGURE

Along with policemen (see above), Hitchcock had a lifelong aversion to priests. One day while driving through a village in Switzerland, he suddenly grew very agitated when he looked out the window and saw a priest talking to a small boy. "That is the most frightening sight I have ever seen!" Hitchcock shrieked, before urging the tyke: "Run, little boy, run! Run for your life!"

I AM (NOT) THE EGG MAN

Fear of cops and priests we can understand. But *eggs*? Hitchcock was repulsed by them, particulary that oozy yellow center. "I'm frightened of eggs,"

THE MASTER OF SUSPENSE SOMETIMES FRIGHTENED ACTRESSES BY LIFTING HIS SHIRT TO REVEAL A CURIOUSLY SMOOTH GUT—HIS BELLY BUTTON HAD BEEN SEALED AFTER STOMACH SURGERY.

he once declared. "Worse than frightened; they revolt me. That white round thing without any holes . . . have you ever seen anything more revolting than an egg yolk breaking and spilling its yellow liquid? Blood is jolly, red. But egg yolk is yellow, revolting. I've never tasted it."

ALL TIED UP

Like Howard Hawks, Hitchcock is one of those old-school directors that New Wave directors love to love. Francois Truffaut and Brian De Palma were two of his more reverent acolytes. Not so William Friedkin, director of *The Exorcist* and *The French Connection,* who despite working for Hitchcock in the 1960s on his *Alfred Hitchcock Presents* TV show never joined the Cult of Hitch. "I don't give a flying fuck about him," Friedkin candidly admitted. "I'm not a worshipper of his, nor have I ever set out to emulate him." The bad blood dates back to Friedkin's first day on the set of Hitchcock's anthology series, when Hitchcock upbraided the young director for his slovenly attire. "Mr. Friedkin, you're not wearing a tie," Hitchcock clucked. A few years later, the two men ran into each other again at a Directors Guild awards ceremony, where a tuxedoed Friedkin was picking up a prize for his work on *The French Connection*. "How'd ya like the tie, Hitch?" Friedkin taunted, snapping his bow tie in the great director's face. A befuddled Hitchcock, who had no memory of the incident in question, had no response.

MAYBE IT WAS THE CINEMATOGRAPHY?

In a 1999 interview with *Access Hollywood*, Hitchcock's daughter Patricia revealed that the great director's favorite film was 1977's *Smokey and the Bandit*, the Southern-fried trucks-and-cornpone comedy starring Burt Reynolds, Sally Field, and Jackie Gleason. Although that choice would puzzle most people, Reynolds was unsurprised. "I've had people who . . . were very intellectual, and my heroes, that have quietly said to me, 'I loved *Smokey and the Bandit*,'" he said. "And I said, 'It's all right, 'cause so did 150 million other people.' I'm thrilled that Mr. Hitchcock felt that way."

GOING TO THE DOGS

When he wasn't cheering on Bo "the Bandit" Darville, Hitchcock loved to check out anything with cute canines in it. After a long day on the set, he liked to unwind by eating dinner off a tray in front of the television set while watching reruns of *Lassie*. He was also known to be quite fond of the adorable dog movie *Benji*.

CHINA MAN

Hitchcock was murder on crockery. On the set of *North by Northwest*, he refused to allow his leading lady, Eva Marie Saint, to drink coffee from a Styrofoam cup. He insisted on having a production assistant bring it to her in a porcelain mug. Hitchcock himself loved to drink tea on the set, but whenever he finished a cup he would simply toss it and the accompanying saucer over his shoulder, letting them shatter on the floor.

BUBBLES ON THE BRAIN

Hitchcock loved expensive wines and food. When he worked in Hollywood, he used to have Dover sole shipped directly from England. Gastronomy consumed him, even more than film. Legendary film critic Pauline Kael once met

Hitchcock at a party—and found him to be a crushing bore. "He wanted to talk about movies but hadn't really gone to see anything," Kael later reported. In an odd tic, Hitchcock kept breaking off their cinema chat to drone on and on about his wine cellar and his collection of fine Champagnes.

IT REMINDS ME OF ME

According to friends, Hitchcock couldn't bear to look at his wife, Alma, while she was pregnant. Perhaps there was something about a large, distended belly that he found repellent?

WHAT A DRAG

Hitchcock's penchant for cross-dressing is legendary: He was known to dress up as a woman for the amusement of friends who came to visit him at his Hollywood home. At least one party, someone filmed him in full female drag. Reportedly, Hitchcock kept the footage in his office under lock and key, but it mysteriously disappeared when his office was cleaned after his death. In 2008, rumors began to circulate on Alfred Hitchcock online forums that the great director may have indulged his taste for transvestitism in one of his greatest films. The so-called secret drag cameo occurs around forty-four minutes into the 1959 classic *North by Northwest*, when a fat woman wearing a turquoise dress and a blue and white hat appears in a sequence set aboard a train. Could it be Hitchcock? There's no definitive proof, although the "woman" appears to have had all her lines cut somewhere between the screenplay and the finished film. Perhaps the baritone voice would have been a dead giveaway.

LUIS BUÑUEL

FEBRUARY 22, 1900–JULY 29, 1983

NATIONALITY:
SPANISH

ASTROLOGICAL SIGN:
PISCES

MAJOR FILMS:
AN ANDALUSIAN DOG (1929), *THE GOLDEN AGE* (1930),
VIRIDIANA (1961)

WORDS OF WISDOM:

*"NOTHING WOULD DISGUST ME MORE
MORALLY THAN WINNING AN OSCAR."*

The scourge of the bourgeoisie, Luis Buñuel lived to shock, scandalize, and disorient his audience. His work was sufficiently enigmatic that he could describe one of his most famous films simply as "an incitement to murder," and no one would deny that was an accurate encapsulation of its content. To say Buñuel was ahead of his time would be an understatement. Try to find another director who was shooting razor-sliced eyeball scenes in 1929.

To cook up so many grotesque and disturbing images over a fifty-year film career, one must have endured a screwed-up, grotesque, and disturbing childhood. Buñuel's was a heady stew of Old World religion, death, and carnality. One of his first memories was encountering the carcass of a dead donkey while on a walk with his father. He watched in rapt fascination while its fetid remains were picked at by vultures and ravenous dogs, and he literally had to be dragged away. From that moment on, Buñuel was transfixed by death—and by animals. He assembled a backyard menagerie that included at various points a large rat, a monkey, a parrot, a falcon, a snake, an African lizard, and a hatbox full of grey mice. Young Luis liked to lift the lid and watch the mice screw each other. Sex was another of his abiding obsessions.

The Catholic Church supplied the final piece of Buñuel's imaginative puzzle—at least until he renounced his faith and became an atheist at age sixteen. Buñuel attended Jesuit schools, where dogmatic religious instruction was the rule and the students never enjoyed a moment's privacy. In his memoir, for example, Buñuel describes the way a three-man team of priests would monitor a student's progress from study hall to the lavatory, from the moment he got up from his desk to the second he entered the bathroom door. This certainly explains his lifelong phobia about being watched—and perhaps his preference for the company of surrealists. At least they didn't cloak their bizarre behavior in robes of clerical eminence.

After graduating from the University of Madrid, Buñuel immigrated to Paris, where he started making films and began his fruitful collaboration with painter Salvador Dalí. Together, in 1929, they produced *An Andalusian Dog*, the sixteen-minute eyeball-slicing epic that would become one of the rune-texts of surrealist cinema. *The Golden Age* followed a year later and proved even more controversial. A wicked mix of religious and erotic images, it was condemned by the Church and provoked widespread riots upon its release.

Following a flurry of scandalous films that made him the bête noire of the Spanish right wing, Buñuel retreated from the limelight and did not make another movie for fifteen years. He fled to the United States to escape the Spanish Civil War and worked as a film archivist and Spanish-language dubber in Hollywood and New York. In 1946, he relocated to Mexico and resumed his career, directing another batch of surrealist allegories that openly mocked bourgeois value systems. *Viridiana*, an anticlerical polemic best known for its visual parody of Leonardo da Vinci's *Last Supper*, was blasted by the Vatican as "an insult to Christianity" and banned in Italy, which went the extra mile and sentenced Buñuel to a year in prison in absentia. In Belgium, copies of the film were seized and mutilated. Buñuel next settled in France, where he created a final string of masterpieces highlighted by the erotically charged *Belle de Jour*—starring Catherine Deneuve as a bored housewife who goes to work in a brothel—and the social satire *The Discreet Charm of the Bourgeoisie*, the 1973 Oscar winner for best foreign film.

Revered in his dotage as one of the innovators of avant-garde cinema, Buñuel clung to life until age 83. He never lost his sense of the absurd—or his distaste for the Catholic Church. Before his death, he cooked up one final joke for his atheist friends, which he never got the chance to play. He planned to invite them to gather around his deathbed and to watch their horrified faces as he summoned a priest to come in, take his confession, and grant him absolution for his sins—"after which I turn over on my side and expire." As it turned out, his actual last words—"Give me a cigar"—were somewhat less inspired.

*   *   *

FORGIVE ME, FATHER, FOR I HAVE HURLED

Before he renounced Catholicism, Buñuel was a regular churchgoer—though the porcelain god might have suited him better than the one approved by Rome. One day, while making his way to Mass, a group of Buñuel's classmates waylaid him into the neighborhood bar, which was not too conveniently located two doors down from the house of worship. There they convinced him to buy a bottle of cheap cognac known locally as *matarratas*, or "rat killer." Buñuel proceeded to get falling-down drunk, swigging mouthfuls straight from the bottle. With a little help from his friends, he eventually found his way to the Church, where the opportunity to kneel down and pray with his eyes closed brought some welcome relief to his churning stomach. When it came time for the congregation to rise, however, Buñuel could contain the demons no more. He staggered to his feet and threw up all over the church floor. "I was immediately escorted to the infirmary, and then just as quickly home," the director recalled. "There was talk of expulsion. My father was furious."

PARTY AT CHARLIE'S PLACE

A devotee of group sex, Buñuel once attended an orgy hosted by the like-minded satyr Charlie Chaplin. It didn't go well. Instead of hiring high-priced call girls, as was his usual practice, Chaplin made the mistake of bringing in three attractive "amateurs" from Pasadena. The young women spent most of their time arguing over which one got to have sex with Chaplin, then left without satisfying any of the four male guests, including Buñuel.

THE OBSESSIVE COMPULSIVE GOURMET

Buñuel was a man of intense likes and dislikes. He despised telephones, for example, and avoided talking on them as much as possible. (It may have had something to do with his being deaf in one ear.) He couldn't stand warm climates—an odd tic considering he lived most of his life in Spain and Mexico—and professed a hatred for "the desert, the beach, the Arab, the Indian, or the Japanese civilizations." He was also a stickler about punctuality. If guests showed up late to one of his dinner parties, Buñuel went into a frothing rage. One time he spent an entire afternoon slaving over a paella for visiting friends in New York. When his company arrived after the appointed time, Buñuel opened the door, threw the steaming tray of chicken and seafood to the floor, and screamed, "Here's the paella you wanted!"

SOMEBODY'S WATCHING ME

Buñuel lived in mortal fear of being watched while having sex. He had recurring dreams about people peeping into his windows while he made love to a woman. (In an even weirder twist, once he did manage to escape the

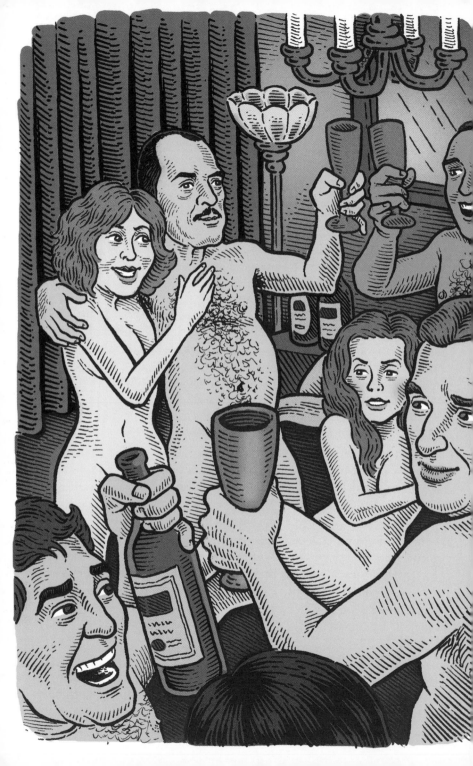

prying eyes, he would often discover that his dream partner's vagina was sewn shut.) As a result, when he and his wife were in bed together, Buñuel insisted on blocking all the doorways and keyholes with furniture. He also refused to have sex when other people were in the house, going so far as to concoct excuses to get his overnight guests to leave.

GUN CRAZY

Buñuel had a lifelong fascination with firearms. When he was fourteen years old, he stole a small Browning pistol from his father's armory and secretly carried it around, brandishing it at boys who tried to bully him. As an adult, Buñuel became adept at the fast draw, spinning on his heels in the manner of the Western movie heroes he so admired. He spent hours alone in his office working on his marksmanship, shooting live rounds at a metal box on a bookshelf opposite his desk. He got so good, in fact, that he was asked to serve as honorary captain on the 1968 Mexican Olympic shooting team. Contemporaneous accounts describe Buñuel as a manic tinkerer who could fill his own cartridges with experimental home-brewed gunpowder. At any given

A DEVOTEE OF GROUP SEX, LUIS BUÑUEL ONCE ATTENDED AN ORGY HOSTED BY THE LIKE-MINDED SATYR CHARLIE CHAPLIN. IT DID NOT GO WELL.

time, his personal arsenal included Winchester carbines, rare German Lugers, and antique dueling pistols.

LOOK INTO MY EYES

Buñuel was convinced he possessed the power to read and control women's minds. He often boasted of his ability to hypnotize a woman through the sheer force of his will, make her come over to his table in a restaurant, and rattle off the most intimate details of her private life.

THE BIG PAYBACK

Buñuel was a raging homophobe. As a youth growing up in Spain, he was not above a little weekend gay-bashing that, he later confessed, "in hindsight seems absurd and embarrassing." Buñuel's favorite prank involved entering a public men's room and batting his eyelashes at the chap at the adjacent urinal while his friends waited outside. "One evening, a man responded," he records in his memoir, "and the minute he emerged, we gave him a sound thrashing." Another time Buñuel bet one of his buddies that he could make twenty-five pesetas in five minutes. He walked up to a man he knew to be gay and started flirting with him. "We made plans to meet the following day for a drink, and when I hinted that I was very young and the school books were very expensive, he gave me twenty-five pesetas." The next day, Buñuel blew off the rendezvous. A week later, he ran into the man on a streetcar and gave him the finger. With such a lovely attitude, it's not surprising that the director made few friends in the gay community. All that bad karma may have finally caught up with him in 1977, when his film *That Obscure Object of Desire* opened in San Francisco. Within days of the premiere, the theater where the movie was being shown was firebombed. In the ensuing chaos, vandals absconded with four reels of film and slathered the walls with graffiti reading, "This time you've gone too far!" Buñuel suspected a gay plot. "There was some evidence to suggest that the attack was engineered by a group of homosexuals," he said, "and although those of this persuasion didn't much like the film, I've never been able to figure out why."

WALT DISNEY

DECEMBER 5, 1901–DECEMBER 15, 1966

NATIONALITY:
AMERICAN

ASTROLOGICAL SIGN:
SAGITTARIUS

MAJOR FILMS:
SNOW WHITE AND THE SEVEN DWARFS (1938), *FANTASIA* (1941)

WORDS OF WISDOM:

"I LOVE MICKEY MOUSE MORE THAN ANY WOMAN I'VE EVER KNOWN."

A black-hearted curmudgeon who distrusted liberals, loathed Jews, and mistreated everyone who had the bad fortune to end up in his employ, Walt Disney is an inspiration to tyrannical moguls everywhere. That other famous moviemaking misanthrope, Alfred Hitchcock, naturally saw him as a kindred spirit. "If [Disney] didn't like an actor," Hitchcock once exulted, "he could just tear him up!"

The "actors" in question were animated characters hand-drawn and transferred onto thin sheets of plastic, typically woodland animals inspired by Disney's rural Missouri boyhood. The fourth of five children born to Elias and Flora Disney, the future Hollywood magnate could trace his lineage back to Robert d'Isigny of Normandy, a French soldier who came to England with William the Conqueror and fought in the Battle of Hastings. From that lofty beginning, the family fortunes took a bit of a tumble, and by the time the Disneys relocated from Chicago to Marceline, Missouri, in 1906, they were just barely scraping by. Walt's father, Elias Disney, was a failed railwayman, farmer, and devout Christian who ruled over the family with an iron hand—which regularly found its way onto young Walt's backside. Elias Disney delivered daily beatings to each of his children, until one by one they left home to escape his abuse.

Walt hung on into early adulthood, cultivating a love of drawing that survived his father's despotic attempts to curtail it. At one point old Elias tore up all Walt's drawings, forcing him to play the violin for four hours a day instead. Desperate to escape the old wretch, Walt forged his dad's signature to enlist in the Red Cross during World War I. While overseas, he served in the same unit as Ray Kroc, future founder of the McDonald's chain, and passed the time painting amusing caricatures on the sides of the ambulances he was driving. When the war ended, he returned the United States and joined forces with his brother Roy to set up an animation studio in Hollywood. The Disney brand was born.

The success of the 1928 cartoon *Steamboat Willie*—the first to feature synchronized sound and the world's introduction to a mischievous rodent named Mickey (né Mortimer) Mouse—helped propel Disney to the upper echelon of American animators, alongside Popeye creator Max Fleischer and Woody Woodpecker progenitor Walter Lantz. Of the three, only Disney possessed the unique combination of drive, talent, and imperiousness to carve out his own multimedia empire, which he began to do over the course of the 1930s, '40s, and '50s. On film, Disney scored huge hits with feature-length animated adaptations of *Snow White*, *Pinocchio,* and *Bambi,* as well as the musical extravaganza *Fantasia.* In 1954, Disney conquered the new medium of television, where his *Wonderful World of Disney* and *Mickey Mouse Club* programs became long-running family staples. And in 1955, he opened Disneyland, a weird amalgam of amusement park and cult-of-personality shrine dedicated, in Disney's words, "to the ideals, the dreams, and the hard facts that have created America"—whatever that meant.

Away from the public eye, Disney was known as a gruff, bullying martinet whose loathing of organized labor poisoned his relations with everyone who worked for him. Not even his most talented animators were immune to his rages. Ub Iwerks, the Academy Award-winning draftsman who created Mickey Mouse, was routinely subjected to having the contents of his drawing board torn up and thrown away by an irate Disney—until he quit the studio in exasperation to escape Disney's wrath. But the public never saw this side of the animation pioneer, whose television image as America's kindly "Unca Walt" survived at least until biographers got hold of him after his death in 1966. By that time, the Disney entertainment empire spanned the continent and would soon expand around the globe, taking in annual revenues in excess of $35 billion. Shortly before he died, Disney reflected on what he considered his major accomplishment: "the fact that I was able to build an organization and hold it." It was a fitting epitaph for a man who set the standard for ruthlessness in Hollywood.

SCARED STRAIGHT

Among the many explanations for Disney's fascination with anthropomorphized animals, the Owl Killer Hypothesis may be the most compelling. According to a widely circulated anecdote, as a young boy Disney wanted an owl for a pet. One day he went into the woods to look for an owl's nest. He found the perfect specimen, but the owl refused to cooperate. It went berserk, prompting Disney to throw it on the forest floor and stomp it to death. He was so overcome with guilt over what he'd done that he dedicated his life to the promotion of wildlife through cartoons.

MY FAVORITE MASON

At age nineteen, Disney was initiated into the Order of DeMolay, a kind of junior auxiliary of the ancient secret society known as the Freemasons. The order's namesake, Jacques DeMolay, was the last leader of the league of fighting monks known as the Knights Templar. A suspected pedophile and warlock who reportedly worshiped a black cat named "Baphomet," DeMolay was arrested at the behest of King Philip of France in 1314. Charged with heresy, he confessed under torture and was burned at the stake. Screen legend John Wayne, voice of Bugs Bunny Mel Blanc, and baseball great Pete Rose were among the many notable Americans who have joined the Order of DeMolay over the years. Disney was awarded the DeMolay Legion of Honor in 1931.

KING BEE

"I never did believe I was worth anything as an artist," Disney once remarked. He wasn't kidding. The father of movie animation was a piss-poor draftsman who couldn't even draw his own iconic characters. As a teenager, he was turned down for a job as an artist at the *Kansas City Star*. (His lack of ability with pen and paper may have led to the oft-repeated rumor that Disney was dyslexic—a claim that has never been substantiated.) Later in life, when a small child asked him to do a sketch of Mickey Mouse, Disney demurred, confessing that he hadn't drawn anything in years. So what exactly was his role at his namesake animation studio? "Sometimes I think of myself as a little bee," Disney said. "I go from one area of the studio to another and gather pollen and sort of stimulate everybody."

MAKING A KILLING

Though he saw little in the way of actual combat during World War I, Disney did find a way to make a tidy profit from the carnage. He and a buddy would scour the front lines for German helmets, which they then sold to their American comrades as souvenirs of the fighting. When he found out that helmets with bullet holes in them could fetch a premium price, Disney dubbed them "Kraut Sniper Derbies" and quickly sold out his entire inventory. Ever the opportunist, Disney simply added fake bullet holes, caked-on mud, blood, and matted hair to undamaged helmets so that they looked suitably "battle worn" to fool his fellow doughboys.

THE WONDERFUL WORLD OF OCD

Disney was an obsessive-compulsive hand-washer who cleaned his palms and fingers several times an hour.

ONE STRIKE AND YOU'RE OUT!

Disney was a notoriously abusive boss who was universally loathed by the animators who worked for him. For years, he paid them less than animators at other studios and refused to give them any on-screen credit for their work. In 1941, they went on strike to protest the working conditions at the House of Mouse. The animators picketed outside the studio gates, holding up signs that read "Are We Mice or Men?" and "Disney: One Genius and 700 Dwarfs." An unabashed foe of unions, Disney dismissed the workers' action as a part of the "growing Communist conspiracy" in the United States and refused to negotiate with them. Eventually his brother Roy stepped in and reached a settlement.

MAN IS IN THE FOREST

Terrified that he would catch them shirking their duties, animators learned to fear Disney's arrival on the studio floor. Lucky for them, the boss was a chain-smoker whose hacking cough (which they called Walt's Warning Signal) could be heard minutes before his physical arrival. Disney drones even borrowed the famous line from *Bambi*—"Man is in the forest"—to alert each other that their despised overlord was approaching.

RED MENACE

How conservative were Disney's politics? He was one of the founding members of the Motion Picture Alliance for the Preservation of American Ideals, a right-wing organization dedicated to driving "Communists, radicals, and crackpots" out of Hollywood. John Wayne, Gary Cooper, and Clark Gable were among the other members. Disney himself could often be heard muttering about the "Goddamn Commies!" as he came out of meetings with union representatives during labor negotiations at his studio. Eventually he appeared before the House Un-American Activities Committee, where he gleefully named names of suspected Communists in Hollywood. Nor was his

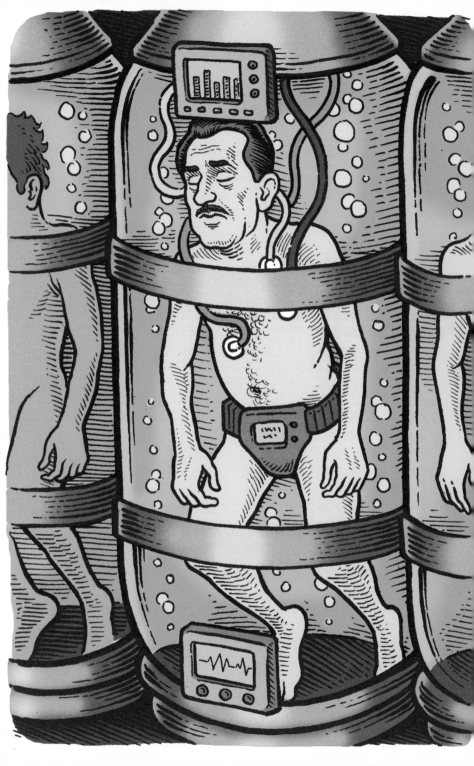

red-bashing confined to the entertainment industry. "Roosevelt called this the Century of the Common Man," he once railed about America's thirty-second president. "Balls! It's the century of the Communist cut-throat, the fag, and the whore! And FDR and his [National Labor Relations Board] made it so!"

THE AGONY PAVILION

Okay, so Disney was an archconservative who didn't treat his animators all that well, but was Unca Walt literally a sadist? For years, the respected experimental filmmaker Stan Brakhage charged in his lectures that Disney maintained a private collection of medieval torture devices—specifically, thumbscrews designed to torture children. "He thought this was a joke," said Brakhage, who claimed to have received eyewitness accounts of the ghoulish collection from people who had visited Disney's home. No wonder Brakhage remembers having to be carried kicking and screaming from the theater where he saw *Snow White and the Seven Dwarfs*—or that he once remarked that he would "rather take a chance on Hell than go to Disneyland."

WALT DISNEY'S "GRAVE" IS KEPT HIDDEN FROM THE PUBLIC, BUT RUMORS PERSIST THAT HE LIES IN CRYOGENIC STASIS BENEATH DISNEYLAND'S PIRATES OF THE CARIBBEAN ATTRACTION.

NO JEWS ALLOWED

Okay, so Disney may have been a right-wing union buster and a sadist, but he couldn't possibly have been a Nazi sympathizer . . . could he? The evidence of Disney's anti-Semitism is surprisingly strong, with multiple witnesses recounting conversations in which Disney ranted about Jewish influence in Hollywood. "Can you imagine that? Letting that fat Jew rescue me from bankruptcy!" Disney wailed about one studio chief, who helped him finance his films during the Depression. On another occasion, Disney chided a young animator for leaving his employ to go to work for "those Jews" at Columbia Pictures. Another animator, Art Babbitt, recalled seeing Disney at meetings of the pro-Nazi American Bund in the 1930s. Toward the end of that decade, Disney was the only executive in Hollywood willing to screen the work of German filmmaker Leni Riefenstahl, who was informally blacklisted due to her close association with Adolf Hitler. When Riefenstahl asked Disney for a job, he told her he admired her work but didn't dare hire her because of the damage it would do to his reputation.

IT'S A SMALL, DRUNK WORLD

On the morning of the New York premiere of *Pinocchio* in 1940, Disney hired eleven little people to dress up in Pinocchio costumes and caper about on the roof of the theater. Unbeknownst to Unca Walt, the hard-working extras were partially paid in free beer, in which they overindulged to such an extent that by three in the afternoon they were all stark naked, burping freely, and shooting craps in full view of the public. An enraged Disney called the police, who hauled the drunken revelers down off the marquee, bagged them in pillowcases, and took them into custody.

MR. FREEZE

Disney was a legendary animator, to be sure, but was he also an object of suspended animation? For decades, rumors have persisted that the dying Disney issued orders that his corpse be cryogenically frozen and revived later. Some even claim that his preserved remains are kept in stasis in a freezer on the grounds of Disneyland—allegedly underneath the Pirates of the Caribbean ride. Some biographers charge that Disney became "obsessed with death" after a fortune teller told him he would die at age thirty-five, and that he babbled on endlessly about the science of cryonics to whoever would listen. They also point to the supposedly unusual circumstances surrounding Disney's death and cremation, and the fact that his "grave" is kept hidden from the public. Reports have even surfaced that shortly after his death, Disney executives were shown a short farewell film in which he addressed each of them by name and concluded by saying cryptically, "I'll be seeing you." For their part, the Disney family has steadfastly denied all these claims. "There is absolutely no truth to the rumor that my father, Walt Disney, wished to be frozen," his daughter Diana declared six years after his death. "I doubt that my father had ever heard of cryonics." The official story—which is backed up by all available public documents—is that Disney's body was cremated and his ashes interred at Forest Lawn Cemetery in Los Angeles, California. In accordance with his wishes, there was no public funeral and the precise location of his grave is not publicized.

Louis B. Mayer and Other Legendary Producers

Where would the movies be without the moguls who make them happen? Meet four legendary machers whose deal-making prowess helped shape the history of film.

LOUIS B. MAYER (1884–1957)

Before there was C. B. (Cecil B. DeMille), there was L. B. The ambitious son of an illiterate peddler, Louis B. Mayer (born Lazar Mayer in present-day Belarus—he added the middle initial to make himself seem more "dignified") was one of the first of the legendary studio moguls of Hollywood's golden age. The pint-sized Canadian national sold scrap metal and ran a burlesque theater in the days before silent pictures took America by storm. In 1918, he formed his own production company, Louis B. Mayer Pictures Corporation, which later became Metro Goldwyn Mayer, the studio from which he ruled over Hollywood with an iron fist until the 1950s. A staunch conservative and early champion of "family values" in entertainment, Mayer was known to go to any lengths necessary to protect the wholesome image of his namesake studio. Over the years, this may have included covering up the real circumstances surrounding the mysterious deaths of comedian Ted Healy and director Paul Bern and dismissing MGM star William Haines for refusing to deny his homosexuality.

DAVID O. SELZNICK (1902–1965)

David O. Selznick also lacked a middle name. He adopted the "O" as an affectation, to give himself more panache, after the fashion of his famous father-in-law, Louis B. Mayer (at the time of his ascension to power in Hollywood, wags joked that "the son-in-law also rises"). Selznick is remembered first and foremost as the mogul behind *Gone with the Wind* and for his obsessive attention to detail. According to legend, Selznick confined screenwriter Ben Hecht in his office for five days, feeding him nothing but peanuts and bananas, until the script for *Gone with the Wind* was complete. A classic control freak, Selznick was famous for writing incredibly long-winded memos. He once sent to a publicist on one of his films a Western Union telegram that was literally more than thirty feet long. The interminably detailed memorandum concluded with the sentence: "I have just received a phone call that pretty much clears up this matter. Therefore you can disregard this wire." According to the editor of a book-length compilation of Selznick's private correspondence, for nearly fifty years the studio chief dictated his every waking thought to his secretaries. The resulting collection of memos filled more than two thousand file boxes.

ROBERT EVANS (1930–)

With his enormous tinted eyeglasses, garish leisure suits, and promiscuous use of show-biz argot, Robert Evans was once the very model of a modern major movie mogul. In his heyday during the 1960s and '70s, the one-time actor-turned-Paramount honcho seemed to have the Midas touch, guiding a string of smash hits like *Rosemary's Baby* and *Love Story* to the screen while maintaining a playboy lifestyle fueled by booze and cocaine out of his luxurious Beverly Hills mansion, known as Woodland. Until his movies started bombing in the 1980s (he was the genius behind Robert Altman's ghastly version of *Popeye*), Evans may have been the luckiest man in Hollywood. He inherited most of his money (from his family's women's clothing business), survived three near-fatal strokes, and turned down an invitation to a party at Sharon Tate's house the night she was killed by the Manson family. As if to prove that everybody's luck must run out some time, the semiretired Evans must now share a hedge with Slash—the debauched former Guns 'n' Roses guitarist who moved in next door to him in 1996.

HARVEY WEINSTEIN (1952–)

Morbidly obese, with a piggish personality to match his body type, Miramax cofounder Harvey Weinstein is for many people the incarnation of the negative stereotype of a Hollywood producer—even though he has long preferred to cut his deals from his lower Manhattan redoubt. A former concert promoter, he brought the aggressive, nut-cutting ethos of a rock show impresario to the world of independent cinema in the 1980s. Together with his slightly less unpleasant brother Bob, he produced a string of art-house hits in the 1990s that helped redefine the boundaries of mainstream cinema. He also made a lot of enemies. Among the particulars in this lugubrious mountebank's lifetime bag of sins: mounting ethically dodgy marketing campaigns to secure Academy Awards for favored stars like Gwyneth Paltrow and Kate Winslet and middling films like *The English Patient* and *Shakespeare in Love*; putting a newspaper editor in a headlock and throwing him out of a party as payback for an unflattering profile; and badgering a cancer-ridden Sydney Pollack on his deathbed to finish work on *The Reader* so that it could be released in time for Oscar season. Weinstein has often rhapsodized about how he was inspired to enter the movie game by a chance encounter with Truffaut's *The 400 Blows* when he was fourteen years old. The reason that Weinstein was in the theater at all is somewhat less inspirational: He thought it was a porno film.

LENI RIEFENSTAHL

AUGUST 22, 1902–SEPTEMBER 8, 2003

NATIONALITY:
GERMAN

ASTROLOGICAL SIGN:
LEO

MAJOR FILMS:
TRIUMPH OF THE WILL (1935), *OLYMPIA* (1938)

WORDS OF WISDOM:

"I FILMED THE TRUTH AS IT WAS THEN. NOTHING MORE."

T he fetching German filmmaker whom gossip columnist Walter Winchell once called "as pretty as a swastika" was the sexy, smiling face of National Socialism for more than a decade. She was a filmmaker of prodigious talents, giant appetites, and overweening ambitions—a combination of attributes that, in another time and a different historical context, might have made her a compelling, rather than a contemptible, figure.

Helene Berta Amalie Riefenstahl was born in 1902 in a working-class suburb of Berlin. She picked up her love of show business from her mother, who guided her toward a career in dance. An encounter with the pioneering German adventure film director Arnold Fanck tilted her toward acting instead, and by her early twenties she was appearing in several of his mountain-set films. Under Fanck's tutelage, Riefenstahl learned to climb, ski, and work a camera. In 1932, she cast herself as a beautiful mountain girl in her directorial debut, *The Blue Light*. The film's exaltation of the "perfect" Aryan physique attracted the attention of Adolf Hitler, who upon meeting her for the first time enlisted her in the Nazi propaganda cause with one simple declarative: "You will make our films." He quickly set her to work documenting the 1934 Nazi Party Congress, in the masterpiece of propaganda known as *Triumph of the Will*. Still revered by cinematographers and skinheads everywhere, the technically dazzling film was followed three years later by *Olympia*, a similarly chilling celebration of the master race shot on location at the 1936 Berlin Olympics. To trumpet its release, Riefenstahl embarked on a promotional tour of America. "Hitler's honey," the press called her.

Riefenstahl's personal life and commitment to the Nazi cause have been the subject of great controversy. Although it's doubtful she and Hitler ever consummated their long-rumored relationship (Riefenstahl preferred rugged mountain-man types), she certainly worshipped the ground Der Führer walked on—and she trod that ground all the way to the top ranks of the Nazi hierarchy. Many of the Third Reich's leading figures became her lovers; eventually they all

became ex-lovers. Riefenstahl changed her men as often as they changed their jackboots. (Reportedly, the only man who ever dumped *her* drove her into a spiral of self-mutilation by cutting.) As far as politics were concerned, to her dying day Riefenstahl denied any knowledge of the genocide being perpetrated by her Nazi boy toys. But she was a lifelong unabashed anti-Semite. She blamed the Jews for the poor reviews of her first feature and later used Roma (so-called Gypsies) on their way to the death camp at Auschwitz as unpaid extras in her film *Lowlands*.

After World War II ended, Riefenstahl was detained for three years by the victorious Allies for suspicion of pro-Nazi activities. In 1949, a war crimes court ruled that she was a Nazi party member and she was fined 28,000 marks. For a long time, her name was mud in cinematic circles. No one would hire her, so Riefenstahl contented herself with taking photographs of African tribesmen and, later, underwater scenes. Over time, however, her reputation within the film community was partially rehabilitated, with some critics calling her one of the world's greatest living directors and biographers working overtime to absolve her of responsibility for the crimes committed by her

"HITLER'S HONEY" MAY NOT HAVE KNOCKED JACKBOOTS WITH THE FÜHRER, BUT MANY OF THE THIRD REICH'S LEADING FIGURES BECAME LENI RIEFENSTAHL'S BOY TOYS.

Nazi patrons. Celebrities like Mick and Bianca Jagger rushed to have their portraits taken by her and bask in the delightful decadence of it all. To the end, Riefenstahl remained a deeply polarizing figure. She died just two weeks after celebrating her 101st birthday, on September 8, 2003. A big-screen biopic of the controversial filmmaker, rumored at various points to star Jodie Foster, Madonna, or Sharon Stone, has yet to see the light of day.

A WOMAN SCORNED

In 1931, Riefenstahl costarred opposite Austrian ski champion Hannes Schneider in *White Ecstasy* (also known as *The Ski Chase*), a film that helped popularize skiing worldwide. Shot on location in St. Anton, a snow-capped village in western Austria, *White Ecstasy* turned out to be a life-changing experience for all parties concerned. At one point, Schneider wiped out on the slopes, broke his thigh in four places, and nearly died. Rumors circulated that he was romantically involved with Riefenstahl, but the two had a falling out, and Schneider came to despise his costar. The slaloming superstar took special delight when a St. Bernard named Friedl bit Riefenstahl in the seat of her all-white ski suit during filming. Whatever mirth he derived from Riefenstahl's mishap was to prove costly, however. Seven years later, when Nazi troops marched into Vienna, Schneider was arrested and sent to prison. (He was later allowed to immigrate to the United States after a huge public outcry.) For the rest of his life, Schneider blamed an embittered Riefenstahl for ordering his incarceration.

WHATEVER HAPPENED TO NAZI GALLANTRY?

Whatever her feelings about Hitler, Riefenstahl had little use for another member of the Nazi high command. She called Josef Goebbels "the cripple" behind his back and was repelled by his clumsy sexual advances. The trollish propaganda chief would show up at Riefenstahl's apartment unannounced and fall to his knees, grabbing her ankles in a spasm of unbridled lust. On other occasions, he simply lunged for her breasts.

HUBBARD'S BUBBLES

In what would have been the ultimate chocolate-meets-peanut-butter pairing, Riefenstahl came close to collaborating with Scientology founder L. Ron Hubbard on a musical remake of her 1932 film *The Blue Light*. The year was 1960. Hubbard was toiling in obscurity as a pulp science-fiction writer, and Riefenstahl was looking for a collaborator willing to overlook her unsavory Nazi past. Introduced to her as a show-business up-and-comer who "is also head of a large international organization which is spread over the entire planet and has over a million members," Hubbard was soon buttering up Riefenstahl with telegrams describing the beautiful cinematic music they would make together. "We can win several Oscars with the wonderful story of *Blue Light*," he gushed. "Let's work together—it will be a great, record-breaking film!" Sadly, Hubbard was whisked away to South Africa on important Scientological business and the *Blue Light* project fizzled out. He later tried to enlist Riefenstahl in his lifelong dream of opening his own movie studio, but, Riefenstahl recorded in her diary, "this overblown project from Hubbard also burst like a soap bubble."

FISH STORY

Say what you want about her Fascist leanings, but don't say Riefenstahl didn't have guts. In 1973, at seventy-one years old, she lied about her age in order to secure a deep-sea-diving permit. She had taken up ocean photography in her old age and wanted to get some footage of aquatic life in the Pacific Ocean. But the tenacious Teuton got more than she bargained for when a shark showed up and repeatedly head-butted her camera. "I was anxious," Riefenstahl later quipped.

LIGHTS! CAMERA! LENI!

Riefenstahl was still courting danger in 2000, at age ninety-seven. That year, her helicopter crashed during a visit to war-torn Sudan. After being pulled from the wreckage, Riefenstahl was flown by rescue plane to a German hospital, where she spent several weeks recovering from two broken ribs and a punctured lung. Ever the opportunist, Riefenstahl lamented that the crash hadn't been caught on film. She even asked her personal documentarian, Ray Müller, whether he could reproduce the accident in a studio using blue-screen techniques.

LONG LAY-OFF

Talk about taking some time off between projects. After helming *Lowlands* in 1954, Riefenstahl did not direct another film for forty-eight years, until *Underwater Impressions* in 2002. Upon completing the latter film at age ninety-nine, she became the oldest person ever to direct a documentary.

NAZIS IN SPACE

As many eagle-eyed cinephiles have pointed out, several scenes in George Lucas's *Star Wars*—including the closing sequence in which Luke Skywalker and the rest of the protagonists receive medals for destroying the Death Star—are lifted shot-for-shot from Riefenstahl's *Triumph of the Will*. Plagiarism? Homage, more likely. Like many a young filmmaker, Lucas had seen *Triumph of the Will* in film school and come away impressed by its technical mastery—not its ideological underpinning.

ELIA KAZAN

SEPTEMBER 7, 1909–SEPTEMBER 28, 2003

NATIONALITY:
AMERICAN

ASTROLOGICAL SIGN:
VIRGO

MAJOR FILMS:
GENTLEMAN'S AGREEMENT (1947), *A STREETCAR NAMED DESIRE*
(1951), *ON THE WATERFRONT* (1954)

WORDS OF WISDOM:

*"ANYBODY WHO INFORMS ON
OTHER PEOPLE IS DOING SOMETHING
DISTURBING AND EVEN DISGUSTING."*

Even when I was a boy I wanted to live three or four lives," Elia Kazan once said. In a way, he did—leaving his mark not only as an innovative director of stage and screen but also as the consummate snitch—the *ur* rat against whom all other finks are measured. If they gave out Academy Awards for squealing, Kazan would be an eight-time Oscar winner.

Before he got the chance to alienate all his friends and enrage an entire artistic community, Elia Kazan was just your average immigrant outcast. Born Elia Kazanjioglou in the Turkish province of Anatolia, he was the son of an industrious Greek rug merchant and his bride who hoped to find a fecund market for their carpets in America. The family immigrated to New York when Kazan was four, settling first in a Greek section of Harlem and later in suburban New Rochelle. There, the swarthy Kazan clan stuck out like a sore thumb. Young Elia was severely bowlegged, and his father insisted on wearing a fez to work. Even the caption under Elia's high-school yearbook called attention to his exotic background and luxurious, feminine mane of hair.

Kazan's mother was determined that he assimilate into American culture, so she arranged to have him attend Williams College, one of the most staid, old-money schools in the country. There, Kazan won few friends, though his overall handiness did earn him a nickname—Gadge, short for Gadget—that he detested but was stuck with for the rest of his life. In fact, Kazan detested everything about Williams, which he later dismissed as "a pompous, reactionary gentleman's school." Once again, his awkwardness made him stand out, and he cited the class resentment he developed in college as one of the major reasons for his joining the Communist Party. "I had this antagonism to privilege, to good looks, to Americans, to WASPS," he said. "I always imagined society was hostile to me . . . till I was almost fifty."

After graduation, Kazan attended another bastion of elitism, the Yale University Drama School, and then joined the left-wing Group Theater in New

York City. The "progressive" theatrical company specialized in staging performances of "socially relevant" plays such as Clifford Odets's *Waiting for Lefty* when it wasn't aggressively agitating on behalf of Josef Stalin. Under the influence of his Group Theater comrades, Kazan formally joined the Communist Party in 1934. But he chafed under the control of party bosses and quit after eighteen months, although he remained a committed left-liberal in outlook. More on that later.

During the 1940s, Kazan found success as a Broadway stage director, hobnobbing with such leading lights of the theater as Tennessee Williams and Arthur Miller—not to mention Miller's soon-to-be second wife, Marilyn Monroe. Miller fell in love with Marilyn almost immediately, but it was Kazan who slept with her first. After sex, the two of them would moon over a photograph of Miller that Marilyn kept at her bedside. (It was an unconventional ménage, to put it mildly.) Broadway fame led to Hollywood opportunities, and the ambitious Kazan quickly cashed in. *Gentleman's Agreement*, the 1949 Oscar winner for Best Picture Oscar winner, catapulted him into the first rank of Hollywood directors, while Kazan's big-screen adaptation of Tennessee Williams's *A Streetcar Named Desire* in 1951 helped make Marlon Brando's career. Awash in money, starlets, and fame, the bowlegged boy from New Rochelle saw the world as one big oyster.

That didn't last long. In the early 1950s, Kazan's Communist past began to catch up with him. He was called before the House Un-American Activities Committee (HUAC) to testify about Communist influence in Hollywood. At first Kazan refused, but eventually he relented (some say under pressure from Twentieth Century Fox, which threatened not to renew his contract). In the end, he supplied the committee with the names of eight people he knew to be Communists, defending his actions on the grounds that the committee members already knew who they were anyway. (As it happened, they didn't.) Careers were destroyed or put on hold for decades by the ensuing blacklist.

After his testimony, Kazan became persona non grata in Hollywood—his name forevermore synonymous with "backstabbing rat bastard." People avoided him at parties. Comic Zero Mostel—himself a blacklist victim—dubbed him "Looselips." Some of the vitriol directed at Kazan was righteous and principled; some of it was self-serving and phony. "I had become an easy mark for every self-righteous prick in New York and Hollywood," the director lamented. One of those "self-righteous pricks" was Arthur Miller, his erstwhile friend, who wrote a scathing letter to the *New York Post* denouncing

Kazan's actions and later penned an entire play—*The Crucible*—condemning him in absentia. Another was Marlon Brando, who vowed never to work with Kazan again—and then comically retracted his pledge in the very next sentence. "That was terrible thing that Gadge did," Brando told a friend, "but he's good for me. Maybe I'll work with him a couple of more times, at least once." (The two went on to make *On the Waterfront* together in 1954. Apparently, finding out that Frank Sinatra was about to get the lead role was enough to make Brando swallow his reservations.)

Kazan continued to make movies after being excommunicated by Hollywood, although with the exception of *On the Waterfront* (itself a thinly veiled defense of his testimony before the committee), he never again reached the heights of fame and influence he achieved in his heyday. He refused to apologize for his actions in Congress and didn't seem all that interested in seeking forgiveness from his friends. In a strange way, the ostracism seemed to liberate him. "What keeps you looking so young?" someone once asked him. "My enemies," Kazan replied.

In 1999, Kazan received a Lifetime Achievement Award from the Academy of Motion Picture Arts and Sciences. The public display of appreciation for a man so widely reviled among his peers did not pass without controversy. An estimated five hundred protesters gathered outside the Dorothy Chandler Pavilion before the Oscar ceremony, holding placards that read: "Elia Kazan: Nominated for Benedict Arnold Award," "Don't Whitewash the Blacklist," and "Kazan—the Linda Tripp of the '50s." Fittingly, Kazan's thank-you speech was anodyne and perfunctory. He slipped off into the night and was rarely seen or heard from again until his death four years later, at age ninety-four.

ADULT EDUCATION

Kazan was married three times, but wedding rings meant little to a man who had a reputation as one of the biggest womanizers in Hollywood. The director's sex addiction stemmed, in large part, from his youthful insecurity. He left Williams College a virgin—and decades later he was still bitching about wild frat parties he waited on while enrolled there, gawking at nubile coeds who wouldn't give him the time of day. To exact his revenge, once he became famous, Kazan started screwing everything that wasn't nailed down—

marital vows be damned. "I was faithful to her in every way except sexually," he wrote of his first wife, Molly. Kazan never showed the slightest bit of apprehension about his extracurricular activities. "I was brought up to believe, when I was a boy, that adultery was a sin," he said. "As soon as I became an adult, my education said, that's ridiculous, it depends on the situation, what's behind it." Kazan's "situational" approach to fidelity allowed for numerous romps with his leading ladies, including Constance Dowling and Vivian Leigh, as well as the aforementioned dalliance with Marilyn Monroe. In each conquest, Kazan saw another chance to enrich his mind and stave off intimations of mortality. "The affairs I've had were sources of knowledge; they were my education," he wrote. "For many years, in this area and only in this area, I've used the lie, and I'm not proud of that. But I must add this: My 'womanizing' saved my life. It kept the juices pumping and saved me from drying up, turning to dust, and blowing away."

AFTER SEX, ELIA KAZAN AND MARILYN MONROE WOULD MOON OVER A PICTURE OF ARTHUR MILLER—MONROE'S SOON-TO-BE HUSBAND.

YOU'RE SO VAIN

On the set of *Splendor in the Grass* in 1961, Warren Beatty spent so much time gazing at his own reflection that Kazan ordered the crew to cover all the mirrors in the makeup area. At the wrap party for the cast and crew, he gave Beatty a hand mirror as a farewell present.

I'M OUTTA HERE

Elia Kazan was famous among his contemporaries for his complete lack of social graces. His sartorial sense was appalling. Actress Vivien Leigh once called him "the kind of man who sends a suit out to be cleaned and rumpled." Always awkward in groups, the director was known to get up and leave a gathering without apology or explanation if he decided he was bored with the company.

CASTING CALL

Kazan was director Francis Ford Coppola's first choice to play the part of gangster Hyman Roth in *The Godfather Part II*. The juicy role ended up going to another famous New York City acting teacher, Lee Strasberg—whose wife, ironically enough, Kazan had outed as a Communist during his testimony before the House Un-American Activities Committee in 1952. Strasberg earned an Academy Award nomination for his performance in the film—the first he had ever made.

POISON PENN

Old grudges die hard. When Kazan received his lifetime achievement Oscar in 1999, many of the Hollywood luminaries in attendance—including Nick Nolte, Ed Harris, and Annette Bening—refused to clap for him, still steamed over the HUAC controversies of nearly fifty years earlier. One of those most justifiably outraged at the Kazan tribute was Sean Penn, whose actor/director father Leo Penn had been one of the victims of the blacklist in the 1950s. Leo Penn never forgave Kazan for his perfidy. In 1976, when Kazan was filming *The Last Tycoon* near the Penn home in Malibu, the two men had occasion to cross paths. "My dad is a very warm, polite person," Sean Penn later recalled, "Kazan said hello to him, and Dad just walked by."

AKIRA KUROSAWA

MARCH 23, 1910–SEPTEMBER 6, 1998

NATIONALITY:
JAPANESE

ASTROLOGICAL SIGN:
ARIES

MAJOR FILMS:
RASHOMON (1950), *THE SEVEN SAMURAI* (1954), *RAN* (1985)

WORDS OF WISDOM:

"IN A MAD WORLD, ONLY THE MAD ARE SANE."

Notorious for a martial discipline bordering on insanity, Akira Kurosawa came by his perfectionism honestly. He was literally descended from a samurai. His father's ancestry could be traced back to Abe Sadato, an eleventh-century Shogun warrior known for his fighting prowess. Apparently the apple didn't fall far from the tree, even over the course of nine hundred years: Kurosawa's father was a pitiless taskmaster who made his son study *kendo* swordsmanship for a half hour a day beginning at age nine. Although Kurosawa never became a master swordsman, the rigorous practice sessions instilled confidence and helped—somewhat—to mitigate his major childhood problem: crippling physical awkwardness.

A slow learner and a weakling prone to crying jags, young Kurosawa stood out from the other kids thanks to his bizarre clothing selection—he liked wearing kimonos and big floppy hats—and catatonic affect. He walked around most of the time in an unexplained fugue state—"a wide-eyed daze," to use his own expression—that made some of his teachers think he was retarded. He rarely took part in school activities and spent most of his leisure time going to the movies. With his father and his older brother Heigo, he saw dozens of the earliest silent films from America, including works by Charlie Chaplin and Buster Keaton.

After briefly considering a career as a painter (given up after failing the art-school entrance exam), Kurosawa decided to follow Heigo into the movie business. Heigo had found steady work as a *benshi*—a narrator who supplies live voice-overs during silent films. With the advent of talkies and the arrival of the Great Depression, however, the work dried up. Heigo , who already had experienced emotional problems, committed suicide in 1933. Kurosawa was twenty-three years old at the time. His brother's death would haunt him for the rest of his life.

In 1935, Kurosawa took an assistant director's job with PCL Studios, later known as Toho and the producers of the improbably long-lived Godzilla series. He spent the better part of two decades there, honing his craft through the lean years of World War II. In 1943 he completed his first feature, *Sugata Sanshiro*, and scored a critical breakthrough in 1950 with *Rashomon*. The story of a murder filtered through four different perspectives became a pop cultural touchstone, providing the template for episodes of numerous American television sitcoms, from *Happy Days* to *Mama's Family*. It also won the Academy Award for best foreign-language film. The international acclaim accorded to *Rashomon* propelled Kurosawa into the first rank of world filmmakers, paving the way for many masterpieces to come.

Those included 1954's *The Seven Samurai*, later remade in the United States as *The Magnificent Seven*; 1957's *Throne of Blood*, an adaptation of Shakespeare's *Macbeth* set in medieval Japan (and poet T. S. Eliot's favorite film); and 1961's *Yojimbo*, which supplied the inspiration for Sergio Leone's seminal spaghetti Western *A Fistful of Dollars*. Kurosawa's star dimmed somewhat in the late 1960s, in part due to his increasingly erratic behavior, both on and off the set. Poor critical response to the 1970 bomb *Dodesukaden*—a heinous mishmash about a mentally handicapped boy who lives on a rubbish dump—sent Kurosawa into a depressive tailspin. In December of 1971, he attempted suicide by slashing his wrist and throat with a razor. Although he recovered, he found it nearly impossible to secure financing for his films until two American admirers, Francis Ford Coppola and George Lucas, helped bankroll the 1980 shogun epic *Kagemusha*. The success of that film afforded Kurosawa the freedom to direct one more career-capping masterpiece, the opulent *King Lear* adaptation *Ran*, in 1985. He died of a stroke in 1998 at age eighty-eight.

MR. GUMDROP

Kurosawa's grade-school days were anything but idyllic. He was, in his own words, "a crybaby" whose candy-sized tears earned him the derisive nickname "Mr. Gumdrop." With his "haircut like a sheltered little sissy's, a belted double-breasted coat over short pants, red socks, and low, buckled shoes," Kurosawa was the object of nearly constant mockery—from both students *and* teachers. "I immediately became a laughingstock," he said of his arrival at one new school. The other children, Kurosawa later recorded, "pulled my long hair, poked at my knapsack, rubbed snot on my clothes, and made me cry a lot."

HOPELESS ROMANTIC

Talk about a strange time to pop the question. In 1945, World War II was drawing to a close and the Japanese people were seriously contemplating mass suicide. Kurosawa chose that inopportune moment to ask his girlfriend, actress Yoko Yaguchi, to marry him. His proposal speech is worth quoting in full: "It looks as if we are going to lose the war, and if it comes to the point of the Honorable Death of the Hundred Million, we all have to die anyway. It's probably not a bad idea to find out what married life is like before that happens." Amazingly, the pitch worked. They stayed married for thirty-nine years and never had to kill themselves (although Kurosawa did try).

BEAT THE MEAT

Kurosawa was a true cinematic pioneer—and a boon to the Japanese meat industry. The two were occasionally interrelated. One day on the set of *Yojimbo*, Kurosawa approached his sound mixer, Ichiro Minawa, in the studio cafeteria. "Don't you think there would be some kind of sound when somebody is cut with a sword?" the director asked, referring to the multiple scenes of slaughter in the samurai epic. Minawa soon began assembling sound effects to meet Kurosawa's wishes, using slabs of pork and beef he procured from a local butcher and stabbed with a sword. The leftover meat was then fed to the crew at break time. Unfortunately, Kurosawa found that those particular cuts lacked the bone-crunching ferocity he was looking for. Finally, Minawa tried stuffing a whole chicken with chopsticks and hacking at *that* with a sword. Presto! A new sound effect—still used in samurai movies today—was born.

TORA! TORA! TERROR!

In 1968, a crazed Kurosawa screwed up the opportunity of a lifetime. He was hired by Twentieth Century Fox to direct the "Japanese half" of its epic World War II feature *Tora! Tora! Tora!* An ambitious retelling of the events leading up to the attack on Pearl Harbor, the film promised to make Kurosawa an international star and earn him some serious Hollywood coin. He cut a deal with the studio for 10 percent of the movie's net profits. From the moment he arrived on the set, however, the mercurial director seemed weirdly deter-

mined to sabotage the entire production. Some of his behavior even veered
into madness. In short order, Kurosawa

> Cast fifteen prominent Japanese businessmen, who had no acting ex-
> perience, in key roles—including the head of a huge chemical con-
> glomerate as Admiral Yamamoto. (Kurosawa hoped that by buttering up
> wealthy CEOs he could get them to bankroll his next film.)

> Demanded that shooting for all interior scenes take place on an insane
> 4 P.M. to midnight schedule.

> Insisted that the entire crew wear custom-made *Tora! Tora! Tora!* jackets
> and regulation Navy caps and salute his actors whenever they walked by.

> Cancelled an entire day's worth of shooting because he didn't like the
> particular shade of white paint used on the interior of a battleship. He
> ordered the whole crew to spend the afternoon repainting it.

> Had another battleship constructed out of plywood to his precise spec-
> ifications—though he seemed blithely unaware, despite repeated warn-
> ings, that it was facing the wrong direction.

As the shoot dragged on, the production fell far behind schedule, and
the cast and crew began to complain about Kurosawa's increasingly tyrannical behavior. At one point, he flew into a rage and physically assaulted the
clapperboard operator, beating the man over the head with a rolled-up piece
of paper. When the assistant director tried to intervene, Kurosawa began
pummeling him as well. He then ordered the battered A.D. to beat the entire crew over the head. When the man refused, Kurosawa fired him on the
spot. The studio cancelled shooting the next day, "to allow Mr. Kurosawa
time to regain composure and for the crew to cool their anger."
     Fat chance. Fearful that he was about to be fired—and convinced he
was receiving death threats—Kurosawa grew ever more paranoid. He demanded that the studio send a guard to escort him everytime he went to the
bathroom, provide him with a helmet he could wear on the set at all times,
and install bulletproof glass in his limo. Whenever he rode in the car, he
would crouch down on the floor to avoid the unseen assassins he believed

were stalking him. Things got so weird that Twentieth Century Fox hired a brain specialist to visit Kurosawa on the set to determine if he might be clinically insane. Massive doses of tranquilizers were prescribed, but they did little to curb the director's appetite for destruction. When Kurosawa summoned production coordinator Stanley Goldsmith to his hotel room in Kyoto at 2 A.M. a few days before Christmas to call for the wholesale dismissal of his mutinous crew, the studio chiefs had finally had enough. They fired him the next day, putting out the word in a Christmas Eve press release that Kurosawa was stepping down "due to fatigue." Two less unhinged Japanese directors, Toshio Masuda and Kinji Fukasaku, were hired to replace him. Kurosawa had spent twenty-three days on the picture and delivered only eight minutes of usable footage. His career in Hollywood was over.

> **AKIRA KUROSAWA DIRECTED SEVERAL CINEMATIC MASTERPIECES BUT COULD NEVER CONVINCE ANYONE TO FINANCE HIS ULTIMATE DREAM PROJECT— A GODZILLA MOVIE.**

MOTHRA VS. THE SEVEN SAMURAI, ANYONE?

Forget Shakespeare. From his earliest days in the film business, Kurosawa really longed to make a Godzilla movie. In the 1940s he had worked for Toho Studios, producers of the giant lizard series, and counted Godzilla director Ishiro Honda among his closest friends. Despite numerous entreaties by Kurosawa over the years, however, the studio wouldn't let him go near its low-budget monster franchise, for fear it would cost too much.

ORSON WELLES

MAY 6, 1915–OCTOBER 10, 1985

NATIONALITY:
AMERICAN

ASTROLOGICAL SIGN:
TAURUS

MAJOR FILMS:
CITIZEN KANE (1941), *TOUCH OF EVIL* (1958)

WORDS OF WISDOM:

"I STARTED AT THE TOP AND WORKED DOWN."

Blessed with talent to match his appetite, Orson Welles had achieved more by the age of thirty than most directors achieve in their entire lifetimes. The fact that he never again scaled the heights attained by *Citizen Kane*—and spent a long twilight decline cavorting with Muppets and weathering fat jokes from Burt Reynolds—should not diminish his standing as one of cinema history's handful of indisputable grand masters.

He was born George Orson Welles in Kenosha, Wisconsin. ("Hell, we had to call you Orson," his father, Richard Head Welles, informed him. "Every damned pullman porter in the country is named George.") Dad was a tinkerer who invented the U.S. Army mess kit. Mom was a concert pianist. Their youngest son was a born showman and the prototypical child prodigy. According to newspaper reports, Welles could carry on adult conversations at age two. He first appeared onstage at age three, was painting and performing magic at age eight, and wowed the town at age ten in a production of *Androcles and the Lion*—wherein he played both Androcles *and* the lion. He even dressed as a rabbit for a promotion at a Chicago department store.

After his parents split up, Welles was left to the tender mercies of a succession of relatives and guardians. He attended boarding school at the progressive Todd School for Boys in Illinois, where he honed his stage presence and his magic act. He then spent several years traveling throughout Europe, paying his way by selling his paintings to tourists. In 1934, he met producer John Houseman, the thespian eminence (and future Smith-Barney pitchman) who would become his principal mentor and tormentor for the next two decades. (Welles once threw a flaming sterno at Houseman's head during one of their periodic arguments.)

Houseman hooked Welles up with the New York theater scene, which proved a congenial setting for some of their crackpot stage ideas—including an all-black "voodoo" version of *Macbeth*. Together the two men founded the Mercury Theater, whose 1938 radio dramatization of H. G. Wells's *War of the Worlds* sparked a nationwide alien-invasion panic and thrust the twenty-three-year-old Welles into the national spotlight. He never left it. In 1941, despite having only a couple of unreleased short films under his belt, Welles directed his first feature, *Citizen Kane*. Today it is widely recognized as one of the best and most influential films ever made, but at the time it was a virtual career-killer. Denounced in the press because of its unflattering fictionalized portrayal of newspaper magnate William Randolph Hearst and shunned by many theater owners, the film bombed at the box office and took years to be recognized by critics. Welles himself was excoriated for his colossal ego and for attempting to do too much at too young an age.

If dues needed to be paid, Welles would pay plenty of them over the course of his remaining forty-five years in Hollywood. Never again entrusted with complete creative control over his projects, he cranked out flawed masterpieces (*The Magnificent Ambersons*—stripped from his grasp and re-edited by the studio), fascinating B-movies that transcended the limitations of genre (*Touch of Evil*), and a handful, of curious misfires that are appreciated today only by hardcore cinephiles and other filmmakers (*Mr. Arkadin*, *Chimes at Midnight*). Increasingly, he turned to acting, not directing, as a means of supporting his epicurean lifestyle.

In his later years, Welles became a self-parody—a morbidly obese voice-over performer known for showing up drunk to talk-show appearances and playing the role of America's genius laureate. He waved a cigar, reminisced about his love life, and occasionally did magic tricks for the likes of Johnny Carson and Mike Douglas. When he deigned to perform, it was usually opposite novelty acts like Pia Zadora or Miss Piggy. Outside the public eye, Welles became increasingly cranky. Impotent, isolated, and almost too fat to move, he shambled around his rented Laurel Canyon hideaway in a tent-sized muumuu, barking at his personal assistant. One time he ordered his valet to go get him some scissors. "Why?" the young man asked. "So I can stab you with them," Welles replied. On October 10, 1985, a decrepit Welles dropped by one final chat show—Merv Griffin's daily schmooze-a-thon—to sling a few final show-business anecdotes. He went home, had a massive heart attack, and died two hours later.

*   *   *

THE WEIGHT

"My doctor told me to stop having intimate dinners for four," Welles once remarked, "unless there are three other people." Like his most famous creation, Charles Foster Kane—who responded to the question, "Are you still eating?" with the rejoinder, "I'm still hungry"—Welles was a man of gargantuan appetites. You know you're too fat when you have to go on a diet to play Falstaff.

At his heaviest, Welles weighed close to 400 pounds. Critic Pauline Kael once described him as being "encased in makeup and his own fat." A typical dinner for Welles consisted of two steaks—cooked rare—and a pint of scotch. For casual dining, he preferred Pink's, the famous Los Angeles hotdog emporium. According to Merv Griffin, Welles once ate eighteen chili dogs there in a single sitting. As he got older, Welles's tremendous carriage combined with his flat feet to cause him serious mobility problems. His ankles constantly creaked under the weight of the excess tonnage. Rumors abounded that he had once gotten trapped in his own car and had to have it cut open to escape.

Though he gamely played the part of the jolly fat man on television, Welles was extremely sensitive about his weight. Burt Reynolds once wounded him by joking about his size during a talk-show appearance. The elephantine auteur kept an endless supply of billowy black silk shirts at the ready, the better to hide his enormous girth. Toward the end of his life, he consulted with a plastic surgeon about the possibility of having his lard surgically removed. When told the operation might kill him, he changed his mind. Another procedure that repelled and fascinated Welles was liposuction, or "that awful vacuum cleaner," as he called it. "Just turn on the Hoover and away goes the fat!" he crowed.

LET ME IN

Food wasn't Welles's only vice. The mammoth moviemaker was also a world-class womanizer with a fetish for a particular kind of lingerie. He insisted that all his lovers wear the lacy slips and embroidered silk nighties that he preferred. Garter belts, on the other hand, were strictly *verboten*. "From my happy time, the first cloud that fell over the horizon was the garter belt," he lamented. He disliked any kind of ladies' undergarment that could impede the advance of Little Orson. Panty hose were a particular bugaboo. "Just making an approach, you had to begin saying, 'Do you want to screw?'" he complained. "There was no other possible approach!" Determined to ensure

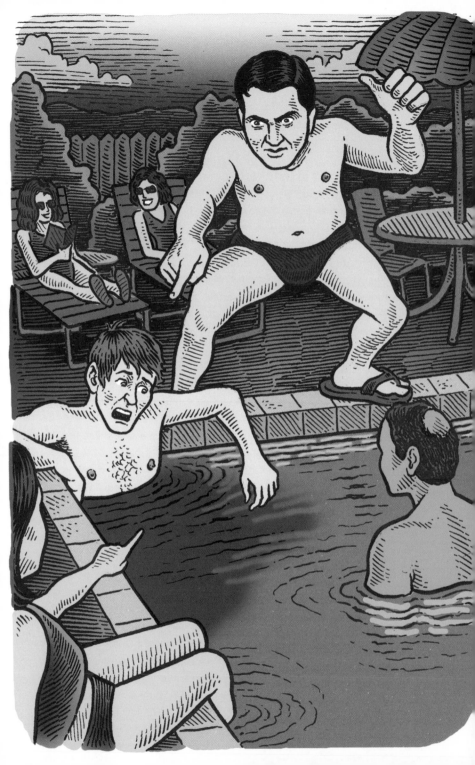

ease of access, Welles made sure to shop for women's underwear himself, preferably at the chi-chi Joel Parks boutique in Beverly Hills.

SHOT OF LOVE

Welles's penchant for sleeping with other men's wives occasionally got him into trouble. One time it almost killed him. While shooting a film on location in Brazil in 1942, he was shot at through the window while lying in bed, by what he presumed to be a jealous husband. The bullets barely missed him and lodged in his headboard. Clad in only a silk kimono, Welles had to crawl on his belly to escape further fire. He fled to a nearby hotel and telephoned a local government official he knew, hoping to arrange for police protection, but instead was told to visit a local bordello to calm his nerves. Welles took the advice and, *still* wearing nothing but the kimono, checked into the nearest high-class whorehouse for a night of sexual healing. He later called his romp in the sack "the greatest of my entire life. Nothing like being shot at to improve your performance!"

TO EXPOSE A PARTY GUEST'S POOR ETIQUETTE, ORSON WELLES SPIKED HIS SWIMMING POOL WITH A CHEMICAL THAT TURNED RED WHEN EXPOSED TO URINE. MORTIFIED, HE SAW THAT ALL HIS GUESTS HAD WEAK BLADDERS.

BLAME IT ON KANE

Did Welles commit one of the most gruesome murders in Hollywood history? That's the contention of author Mary Pacios, childhood friend of Elizabeth Short, the so-called Black Dahlia, an aspiring actress who was brutally butchered and literally cut in half by an unknown assailant in January 1947. In a 1999 book about the killing, Pacios charged that Welles did the deed while in the throes of a mental disorder known as diphasic personality, which left him prone to violent outbursts. She also claimed he had a fetish for bisecting women, and cited as evidence Welles's magic act (in which he sawed a female assistant in half) and some cut footage from his film *The Lady from Shanghai* during which a chopped-up female mannequin appears. Others have also chimed in on the speculation, suggesting that Welles left for an extended stay in Europe shortly after the murder. His own family denounced the allegations as a "sick joke." Welles isn't the only unlikely suspect in the Black Dahlia killing. *Los Angeles Times* publisher Norman Chandler and beloved folk icon Woody Guthrie have also been implicated by aficionados of the case.

YELLOW PERIL

An incorrigible prankster, Welles delighted in playing elaborate practical jokes on his party guests. One time he devised a cunning plan to humiliate a reveler he suspected of urinating in his swimming pool. Welles found a chemist who had developed a clear liquid that would color in the presence of urine. He dumped some into his pool before a party and watched in horror as raspberry-colored clouds began forming around each person who waded into the water. Almost *everyone* was peeing in his pool—especially the men and older women with weak kidneys. A mortified Welles then cleared the pool by telling his guests there were rattlesnakes in the water.

THE ONES THAT GOT AWAY

Welles desperately wanted the part of Vito Corleone in *The Godfather*. "I would have sold my soul to have done it," he once said. But Francis Ford Coppola never offered him the role. Coppola *did* consider him for the part of Colonel Kurtz in *Apocalypse Now*, but ultimately chose his old standby, Marlon Brando. Welles turned down an offer from George Lucas to supply the voice of Darth Vader in *Star Wars*. And although producer Aaron Spelling seriously considered him for the role of Mr. Roarke, the suave proprietor of television's *Fantasy Island*, that part went instead to Ricardo Montalban.

ALL'S (NOT) WELL THAT ENDS WELLES

Having been passed over for so many good parts, in the last decade of his life Welles was reduced to providing ponderous voice-overs for commercials and cartoons. As the spokesman for Paul Masson wines, he famously promised oenophiles that the vintner would "sell no wine before its time"—and occasionally oversampled the product to the point of total stupefaction, if the virally circulated video clips are to be believed. Another disastrous ad gig—likewise immortalized on the Internet—required Welles to rhapsodize at length about the virtues of frozen peas in a series of television spots for the British frozen-food company Findus. Aggrieved at the low quality of the copy he was asked to intone, Welles reportedly stormed off the set in frustration.

The great director's final film appearance was even more of an embarrassment, though at that point he was so out of it he didn't seem to notice. Shortly before his death, Welles supplied the voice of Unicron, a planet-eating robot, in the 1986 animated fiasco *Transformers: The Movie*. It was a huge step down even from the cartoon drek Welles had taken part in previously, such as 1975's *Bugs Bunny Superstar*. When people asked him about the movie, the ailing Welles didn't even pretend to know who his character was or what the film was about. "I play a big toy who attacks a bunch of smaller toys," was all he would say. Still, he took to his role with gusto. A story consultant on the film recalls Welles waddling onto the set and exulting, "I'm playing an entire planet!"

Leonard Nimoy, Judd Nelson, and Scatman Crothers also lent their pipes to the effort, which tanked at the box office and foreclosed the possibility of a Transformers live-action feature for another twenty-one years. Even Welles completists will come away disappointed. The great director's once-booming voice was so weak by the time he made *Transformers* that the crew had to alter it with synthesizers to salvage his performance.

INGMAR BERGMAN

JULY 4, 1918–JULY 30, 2007

NATIONALITY:
SWEDISH

ASTROLOGICAL SIGN:
CANCER

MAJOR FILMS:
THE SEVENTH SEAL (1957), *CRIES AND WHISPERS* (1972),
FANNY AND ALEXANDER (1982)

WORDS OF WISDOM:
"I HOPE I NEVER GET OLD SO I GET RELIGIOUS."

I have always had the ability to attach my demons to my chariot," Ingmar Bergman once wrote. "And they have been forced to make themselves useful."

The man certainly had his share of demons. At the very least, he tended to fixate on the morbid and unpleasant aspects of his life. Even though he grew up in relatively comfortable surroundings as the son of a Stockholm minister, Bergman's first memory is of the time he threw up all over his gruel plate. He slept in the bed with his mother until he was four, at which point the birth of his sister (a "fat monstrous creature," in Bergman's words) threw his ordered world into chaos. He and his brother Dag plotted to strangle the baby as she slept in her bassinette. But Bergman proved a poor assassin and merely succeeded in waking up the infant. Not to be deterred, he later tried to murder Dag by setting his bed on fire.

Where did all the hostility come from? The answer lies in Bergman's tortured relationship with his parents. A chronic bed wetter, Bergman was made to wear a red skirt all day as punishment for soiling his bed clothes. When he violated one of the family's petty house rules, the rest of the clan responded by refusing to talk to him or acknowledge his existence for days. More serious misbehavior was met with beatings. His father would apply the thrashing with a carpet beater, forcing little Ingmar to drop his pants and bend over a cushion while one of the other Bergmans held him down by the neck. After the punishment was administered, Bergman was made to kiss his father's hand in order to receive absolution from his "sins." When Ma and Pa Bergman were feeling especially sadistic, they simply locked Ingmar in a cupboard where, he was told, a ravenous monster lurked who ate the toes of small children. Is it any wonder the boy sought escape in the form of puppet theater and improvised "magic lantern" shows?

Bergman used his play acting as a means of overcoming the stress and anxiety of his nightmarish home life. At the age of ten, he projected his first film loop onto the whitewashed wall of his clothes closet. He became an accomplished storyteller. At school one day, he informed the entire class that his parents had sold him to the circus to be trained as an acrobat. When the teacher discovered he was lying, she put him up against the wall and pub-

licly humiliated him. Clearly, Bergman needed an outlet that required no adult supervision.

When he was nineteen years old, Bergman finally had it out with his father once and for all. Drawn into the latest in a series of increasingly angry confrontations, he challenged the old man physically for the first time. "If you hit me, I'll hit you," Bergman said. He did—and Bergman did. (The two didn't speak for many years and reconciled only after the death of Bergman's mother in 1966.) In 1938, Bergman enrolled at Stockholm University, where he became involved with student theater. He soon moved on to rewriting film scripts and directed his first feature, *Crisis*, in 1946. After toiling in obscurity for nearly a decade, Bergman finally achieved international acclaim with 1955's *Smiles of a Summer Night*, a whimsical romantic trifle that was nominated for the Golden Palm at the Cannes Film Festival. *The Seventh Seal* and *Wild Strawberries* quickly cemented Bergman's reputation as one of the leading lights of international "art" cinema.

INGMAR BERGMAN'S FILMS FEATURE PLENTY OF GHOSTS, SO IT'S NO SURPRISE THAT HE DECLARED HIS HOME IN SWEDEN TO BE HAUNTED BY TWO SPIRITS—A JUDGE AND A COBBLER.

By the 1960s, an interest in Bergman had become a universal signifier for pseudointellectual snobs the world over. As Bergman's films grew more opaque and the filmmaker himself became increasingly preoccupied with working out his own psychosexual kinks, his cachet as a visionary genius only expanded. *Persona*, *Cries and Whispers,* and *Scenes from a Marriage* were among his bleakest and most recondite films, and they were duly lauded by critics and a burgeoning cult of filmmaker acolytes—Woody Allen chief among them. Only a 1976 arrest for tax evasion put a damper on Bergman's prodigious film-a-year output. After a period of self-exile abroad, he returned to his native Sweden in 1982 in time to make one last masterpiece, the semi-autobiographical *Fanny and Alexander*, a critical and commercial success. There followed a long twilight during which Bergman mostly worked on Swedish television productions. He died of complications of hip replacement surgery on the Baltic Sea island of Fårö in 2007.

* * *

TEACHING TOOL

Bergman was notorious for his volcanic temper, on and off the set. In his early years as a director, he threw chairs to get a point across to his cast and crew. He called these fits of rage "pedagogic outbursts" and was still indulging in them years later, though less frequently. Bergman's unusual method of communication seemed to work for Swedish actress Ingrid Thulin. "When you talk to me I never understand what you say," she told him one day. "But when you don't talk to me I understand completely what you mean!"

TOILET HUMOR

Liv Ullmann, Bergman's longtime muse, often bore the brunt of his rampages. When once she made the mistake of questioning something the great director had done, Bergman began chasing her across the house in a blind, frothing rage. Fearing for her life, Ullmann locked herself in the bathroom, but Bergman responded by kicking a hole in the door. As he did so, his slippers flew off and landed on Ullmann. The sight of Norway's greatest actress cowering next to a toilet bowl with fuzzy footwear on her head so tickled Bergman that he lost all his anger and doubled down in paroxysms of laughter. "We made it up immediately," Ullmann reports.

SCENES FROM A MARRIAGE

Technically Bergman and Ullmann were never married—and judging from her account of their domestic life, it's easy to see why. "Living with Ingmar Bergman is not like living with Bob Hope," Ullmann once admitted, in what may have been the understatement of the century. Over breakfast, Bergman was known to recount the previous evening's nightmares to Ullmann and then outline his plans to have her act them out in his next movie. Even after the couple split, Bergman was still sending scripts to her, begging her to participate. "Do your own nightmares!" she finally wrote back, returning his latest screenplay unopened.

BERGMAN GOES POTTY

When not terrorizing Liv Ullman, Bergman was creepily dependent on her for emotional and psychological support. At times she played a role more suited to a mother than a lover. An exceedingly nervous flier and a compulsive hand washer, Bergman once nearly flipped out on Ullmann while on a vacation to Italy. During a layover in Copenhagen, he announced his need to wash his hands, which entailed a trip down the elevator to the airport men's room. Normally this would have required extensive reassurance and hand-holding on Ullmann's part, but on this occasion Bergman insisted on going alone. After about ten minutes, he emerged from the elevator with a childlike grin on his face. "He had done it!" Ullmann remembered years later. "I still think of that little smile, which seemed to say, 'Do you know what I've done all by myself?'" Bergman was in his late forties at the time.

DEAR OLD DAD

Given his myriad of hang-ups and idiosyncracies, Bergman was not exactly the world's most doting father. In fact, he was "nonexistent," to use Liv Ullmann's assessment of his parenting style. Nevertheless, his children idolized him and always looked forward to his infrequent visits and sporadic bouts of attention. One time Bergman's seven-year-old daughter Linn was hanging out in her mother Liv Ullmann's dressing room. Bergman showed up, after not having seen the child in four years. He picked her up and swung her around in his arms for thirty seconds, then coldly announced that he had work to do and left the room. It may have been warm, precious moments like this that earned Bergman his family nickname: the Big Gorilla.

TRUTH TELLER

As a young man, Bergman was such a horndog he even inspired a song. "I don't mind being wild and free / As long as Ingmar Bergman fancies me," went the lyrics to one popular Swedish ditty. Bergman himself has admitted to being a pathological liar who routinely led on his girlfriends. At a certain point, he resolved to stop lying and tell the truth at all times. This caused its own problems. In his late thirties, Bergman got seriously involved with a woman but decided to make it clear there were limits to his commitment.

"I'm not going to marry you," he informed her. "I don't love you that way. I want to fuck you."

THOSE LAZY, HAZY, CRAZY DAYS OF NATIONAL SOCIALISM

It's been glossed over by his devotees in the world of "cinema studies," but Bergman was once an enthusiastic and active Nazi. He first fell for Der

Führer in 1938, when he saw Hitler speak at a rally during a sojourn in Germany as an exchange student. Finding the Fascist dictator "unbelievably charismatic" and Nazism itself "fun and youthful," Bergman started keeping a framed photo of Hitler above his bed for inspiration. "For many years, I was on Hitler's side," Bergman later admitted, "delighted by his successes and saddened by his defeats." Back in Sweden, Bergman and his pals even joined in the cause, going out on a wilding spree during which they painted a swastika on the walls of a house owned by a Jewish family. To be sure, virulent Jew hatred was something of a family tradition for Bergman. His brother Dag was one of the founders of the Swedish Nazi Party and his father, Erik, often voted for extreme right-wing politicians.

GHOST WHISPERER

The spirit world figures prominently in a number of Bergman's films, so it's no surprise to learn that the director himself believed in ghosts. In fact, he contended that two separate poltergeists—a judge and a cobbler—took up residence on his property in Sweden. Bergman claimed to have heard their voices. He was convinced that he had once encountered the ghost of his dead mother standing behind him as he stared out to sea. Bergman also foresaw the day when he too would become a ghost and haunt the living. On a visit to the Royal Dramatic Theatre in Stockholm with his friend Lars Löfgren, Bergman stopped in the middle of a conversation to commune with the assembled spirits. "They're all here," Bergman croaked portentously, eliciting a puzzled reply from Löfgren. The souls of the theater's former inhabitants, Bergman believed, were still hanging around, taking care of unfinished business. "One day, we will be with them," he intoned solemnly and then moved on.

HE LOVED HER ONLY FOR HER BODY

If Bergman's films seem dark and disturbing and his characters preoccupied with death, there may be a simple biographical explanation. When he was ten years old, Bergman was once locked inside a morgue by a mischievous hospital caretaker. Left alone in a room full of corpses, Bergman suffered a severe panic attack and was snapped out of it only by the loud posthumous farting of one of the cadavers. Titillated by the sight of a fresh female corpse, Bergman then began fondling the woman's body, touching her breasts and gazing in fascination at her genitals. After a few minutes, he became convinced that the dead woman was looking at him and hurled himself at the door until it opened and he could escape.

KICKIN' IT FREESTYLE

His films may have been morbid and gloomy, but Bergman did have his lighter side. One of his favorite pastimes was watching BMX bike racing on television.

DEATH WISH OF A SUMMER NIGHT

Bergman had an unlikely connection to coriaceous action star Charles Bronson. The two men shared the same agent and publicist. They met once, during Bergman's first visit to Los Angeles in the late 1970s. Bronson was filming one of his trademark shoot 'em ups at the time, and Bergman visited him at the studio at their agent's behest. After exchanging pleasantries, Bergman became entranced by the squibs that were placed on Bronson's body to simulate blood-spattering gunshot wounds. "Fascinating," Bergman marveled. "I never knew how they did that!" "You mean you don't use machine guns in your movies?" Bronson replied.

ANIMAL MAGNETISM

Like a lot of highbrow filmmakers, Bergman had surprisingly populist tastes in entertainment. In his later years, he could often be found holed up in the private screening room at his home on the Swedish island of Fårö, watching Marx Brothers movies, Quentin Tarantino's *Pulp Fiction*, or one of his personal favorites, *Jurassic Park*. "Those Americans know how to put on the pants!" he once gushed during a viewing of Stephen Spielberg's rampaging dinosaur epic. U.S. television shows also fascinated the moody genius. Bergman was a huge fan of *The Muppet Show*, especially Animal, the manic drummer in the show's house band, Dr. Teeth and the Electric Mayhem. *Sex and the City* also tickled the Swedish auteur's fancy. He almost never missed an episode of the raunchy HBO sex comedy. "The women are beautiful, and they talk dirty," he told his daughter Linn by way of an explanation. "Do you talk that way with your girlfriends?"

Ed Wood Jr. and Other Masters of Schlock

S ometimes you have to do what you can with a limited budget—or limited talent. These four filmmakers made the most with the least, which in some cases turned out to be very little, indeed.

EDWARD D. WOOD JR. (1924–1978)

Major Films: *Bride of the Monster* (1955), *Plan 9 from Outer Space* (1959)

Widely recognized as the Orson Welles of schlock cinema, the cross-dressing, Angora-sweater-loving Wood specialized in low-budget exploitation films and Z-grade science fiction. His *Plan 9 from Outer Space* tops almost every list of the worst films of all time. A one-time carnival freak, Wood claimed to have fought in the World War II Battle of Tarawa wearing a bra and panties under his uniform. His cult status was cemented by the 1994 Tim Burton biopic *Ed Wood*.

WILLIAM BEAUDINE (1892–1970)

Major Films: *Billy the Kid vs. Dracula* (1966), *Jesse James Meets Frankenstein's Daughter* (1966)

Known as "One Shot," for his habit of shooting scenes in only one take, Beaudine had a long and distinguished career in Hollywood before he started cranking out schlock like *Billy the Kid vs. Dracula* in the 1960s. He worked as an assistant under both D. W. Griffith and Mack Sennett during the silent era and directed the highly regarded W. C. Fields comedy *The Old-Fashioned Way* in 1934. A longtime friend of Walt Disney's, he was also one of the creative forces behind television's *Mickey Mouse Club*. When he died in 1970 he was one of the longest-working professionals in Hollywood.

ROGER CORMAN (1926–)

Major Films: *Attack of the Crab Monsters* (1957), *Little Shop of Horrors* (1960)

Ed Wood may get the love, but Roger Corman was the real master of the B-movie, as his many fans and cinematic protégés know. Filmmakers who apprenticed under Corman include Francis Ford Coppola, Ron Howard, Jonathan Demme, and Martin Scorsese. He also helped launch Jack Nicholson's career by giving him the part of a crazed dental patient in the killer-plant shocker *Little Shop of Horrors*. Corman's specialty was shooting films fast, for little or no money—a trait he claimed to have picked up from his training as an engineer. It was said that Corman could close a deal for a film on a pay phone, shoot it in the phone booth, and pay for it with the money he found in the coin slot. The dirty little secret of his career: Most of his films are actually pretty good.

UWE BOLL (1965–)

Major Films: *House of the Dead* (2003), *BloodRayne* (2005)

The golden age of schlock film may be over, but this much-derided German auteur seems not to have gotten the memo. Boll's peculiar specialty is movies adapted from video games, which he self-finances by exploiting a loophole in German tax law. His violent, nihilistic films typically tank at the box office, irritate game players, and agonize critics—whose snarky pans so vex Boll that he once challenged his detractors to take him on in a series of public boxing matches. In 2008, aggrieved moviegoers launched an online petition campaign to force Boll to retire from filmmaking. He responded by releasing a video in which he dismissed his critics as "retards" and declared himself "the only genius in the whole fucking [movie] business."

FEDERICO FELLINI

JANUARY 20, 1920–OCTOBER 31, 1993

NATIONALITY:
ITALIAN

ASTROLOGICAL SIGN:
AQUARIUS

MAJOR FILMS:
LA STRADA (1954), *LA DOLCE VITA* (1960), *8 1/2* (1963)

WORDS OF WISDOM:

*"I MAKE A FILM BECAUSE I SIGN A
CONTRACT, THEY GIVE ME AN ADVANCE,
I DON'T WANT TO GIVE IT BACK, AND SO
I HAVE TO MAKE THE FILM."*

When I speak for myself," Federico Fellini once observed, "I feel that I have spoken for everyone." It was a characteristically self-aggrandizing statement from one of cinema history's most self-indulgent filmmakers. Yet it perfectly captures the aesthetic of a man who used his personal fetishes, fascinations, and predilections the way a painter uses paint, turning private obsessions into some of the most arresting images moviegoers have ever seen.

Italy's greatest filmmaker was born in the resort city of Rimini, the son of a traveling salesman with an eye for the ladies and a devoutly religious mother. He was educated in Catholic schools but never really accepted Church teachings, preferring the company of clowns and circus performers to dour Italian priests. One of Fellini's earliest objects of fascination was "La Saraghina," a morbidly obese prostitute who bartered her body to local fishermen in exchange for their unsold sardines. This "horrible and splendid dragon," as Fellini called her, was exemplary of the weird, luxuriant, frankly sexual figures who would haunt his dreams and repeatedly turn up in his films.

In the Fascist period, under Benito Mussolini, Fellini and his brother Riccardo were compelled to join the Avanguardista, a kind of brownshirt Boy Scouts—though Fellini himself never subscribed to Fascist ideology. In fact, he deliberately "forgot" to wear certain elements of his uniform in a small act of anti-authoritarian rebellion. As a young man, Fellini worked for various Italian newspapers as a crime reporter and later as a columnist and caricature artist. He avoided the draft during World War II and adopted a pose of political apathy. Shortly before the war ended he married the woman he considered his soul mate, Giulietta Masina, who would stay with him for the rest of his life—through his endless on-screen explorations of his own sexual obsessions—and appear in several of his films. One of the first films they made together, 1954's *La Strada*, provided Fellini with his big international breakthrough.

Worldwide celebrity followed with 1960's *La Dolce Vita*—an extravagant exploration of postwar decadence that introduced the term *paparazzi* to the world—and 1962's autobiographical *8 1/2* (so called because it was Fellini's "8 1/2-th" directorial effort, after seven full-length and three short features). In fact, almost all Fellini's films were autobiographical to some extent. Even the quasipornographic fantasia *Satyricon*, set in ancient Rome, derives more from Fellini's personal fascination with albino hermaphrodites and other erotic grotesques than from Petronius's fragmentary original text. Fellini's other major influence was Carl Jung, whose theories about archetypes and the collective unconscious supplied intellectual ballast for the director's psychosexual dreamscapes.

In his later years, Fellini largely abandoned filmmaking, breaking his silence only to whip out the occasional graphic novel or craft some insouciant television commercials for Campari vermouth and Barilla pasta. (The Barilla ad played off the word *rigatoni* as slang for fellatio and concluded with the guarantee, "Barilla always make you feel al dente.") Fellini died of complications from multiple strokes in a Rome hospital in October 1993. Fittingly, a paparazzo was able to sneak into his hospital to take a few final morbid snapshots of the dying director. To the eternal credit of the Italian press, almost no one chose to publish them.

MY PENUS CAN SEE THE FUTURE

Although he rejected Catholicism and his films are a celebration of all things carnal, Fellini was obsessed with the spirit world and never missed an opportunity to "tap the table" in the company of his favorite psychic medium, the delightfully named Penus. The elderly mystic tooled around Rome in the late 1960s in a chauffeur-driven limo, accompanied by a young male assistant. Fellini once attended a séance conducted by Penus in which the old man repeatedly and cryptically said, "Ask me if the lions are here." "Are the lions here?" a rapt Fellini queried. "No," Penus replied. End of séance.

Before he got hold of his Penus, Fellini tugged at the robes of a succession of crackpot holy men, including a German-born astrologer, an Italian faith healer, and a magician known only as "Uncle Nardu" who claimed he could change himself into a horse at will. In the mid-1960s, the director became a devotee of the celebrated Italian clairvoyant Gustavo Adolfo

Rol, who, it was alleged, could read closed books, move objects with his mind, and predict the future. One time, Fellini insisted, he personally saw Rol kill a hornet in a park using only his telekinetic abilities. "At forty meters, simply with a gesture, he blasted the hornet!" Fellini marveled. "It gave me goose flesh."

Fellini also relied on his psychic friends to tell him how his movies would perform at the box office. Once, when word got out that one of his mediums had informed him that his "next two films would die," actors stopped returning his phone calls, fearful that working with him would place the kiss of death on their careers. As it turned out, both films *did* bomb—cementing Fellini's faith in the spirit realm forever.

QUIET ON THE SET

Fellini always insisted on closed sets for all his movies, but not in hopes of keeping the plots secret. No, let's just say the man liked his privacy. "Critics say my films are cinematic masturbation," he explained. "My films are acts of *real* masturbation. Therefore I like as few people on the set as possible when I do this."

MY MAN STAN

In many ways, Fellini's life *was* a comic book, so it's no surprise he drew inspiration from that medium. In the mid-1960s, the Italian auteur became a huge fan of Marvel Comics—particularly their superhero stalwarts the Amazing Spider-Man and the Incredible Hulk. Fellini first sampled Marvel's wares while visiting New York City in November 1965. He was holed up with a virus in the Hotel Pierre when someone gave him some comics to read on his sickbed. Fellini became so enthralled with the superhero exploits that he immediately called the Marvel offices and arranged a visit with the company's editor in chief, Stan Lee. During an appearance at ComicCon in 2007, Lee recalled how his receptionist informed him, "Stan, there's a Fred Felony to see you." Fellini then swooped in the door with a four-man entourage, all wearing black raincoats and in descending order by height. Through a translator, the two creative geniuses had a long chat, during which Fellini peppered Lee with comics-related questions. The pair also worked out an "exchange program" whereby "Smilin' Stan" would stay at Fellini's villa the next time he was in Rome and Fellini would accompany Lee to a Broadway show the next time he came to New York. "He's my buddy now," Lee said afterward.

GONE TRIPPIN'

Given the hallucinatory nature of his creative vision, LSD is probably one drug Fellini didn't really need to take. Yet take it he did, in 1965, under the supervision of his analyst and a full medical team, who recorded his every physiological response after carefully injecting him with the drug. Fellini's trip lasted for almost eight hours, during which he paced around the room talking constantly. His hallucinations, he revealed later, included "a vision of heaven and hell, in keeping with my Catholic upbringing." Best of all, the entire controlled experiment was audiotaped for posterity. To his consternation, Fellini experienced no mind-altering epiphany and had no desire to go back and review the stenographic record of his trip. "I was a little bit disappointed with the experience," he said afterward.

FLASH TRASH

Fellini was a serial exaggerator, prone to embellishing his own creative exploits for the history books. One fish story that has persisted throughout the decades contends that the young Fellini drew the Italian-language version of

OBSESSED WITH THE SPIRIT WORLD, FEDERICO FELLINI NEVER MISSED AN OPPORTUNITY TO "TAP THE TABLE" IN THE COMPANY OF HIS FAVORITE PSYCHIC MEDIUM, THE DELIGHTFULLY NAMED PENUS.

the Flash Gordon comic strip during the late 1930s. Nothing could be further from the truth. In interviews, Fellini claimed that he secured the gig after Fascist dictator Benito Mussolini banned all American comic strips in 1938. But Il Duce issued no such order. Fellini *was* a fan of Alex Raymond's swashbuckling space adventurer, but his assertion that it was *he* who came up with the famous storyline in which Flash Gordon is seduced by the high priestess of the planet Phoebus and transported to the planet of the hawkmen is pure jive. That plot was Raymond's own, and later became the basis for the 1936 Flash Gordon movie and its 1980 remake. Fellini *did* try his hand at concocting his own Flash Gordon comic strips after the American strip was discontinued, but his work was never published. When an Italian journalist confronted him with proof that his Flash Gordon boast was a lie,

Fellini sheepishly copped to it. "It might be," he conceded. What *is* true is that Fellini was producer Dino De Laurentiis's original choice to direct the over-the-top big-budget *Flash Gordon* feature in 1980. But a deal was never consummated.

QUOTE MACHINE

Fellini was one of the world's most quotable directors, a veritable font of bons mots on all manner of topics. Here are a few of his most memorable quips:

On Dieting

"I went on a diet for three months and all I took off was my hat."

On Losing His Hair

"The only advantage about going bald is that you get rid of dandruff by removing its hiding place."

On Fidelity

"It's easier to be faithful to a restaurant than it is to a woman."

On Genius

"Nietzsche claimed that his genius was in his nostrils, and I think that is a very excellent place for it to be."

ROME, IF YOU WANT TO

If you're a fan of the B-52s, you owe a debt of gratitude to Fellini. The director was a major influence on the Athens, Georgia, party band, whose hits include "Love Shack" and "Rock Lobster." In fact, band members Kate Pierson and Cindy Wilson credit Fellini for inspiring their trademark bouffant hairdos. "He's responsible for our look, particularly in the videos," says guitarist Keith Strickland.

ROBERT ALTMAN

FEBRUARY 20, 1925–NOVEMBER 20, 2006

NATIONALITY:
AMERICAN

ASTROLOGICAL SIGN:
PISCES

MAJOR FILMS:
M*A*S*H (1970), *NASHVILLE* (1975)

WORDS OF WISDOM:

"TO PLAY IT SAFE IS NOT TO PLAY."

A hard-drinking, pot-smoking, left-leaning radical with a jones for gambling and low-rent prostitutes, Robert Altman may be the consummate Hollywood maverick. He spent a good portion of his life curled up in a fetal ball at the bottom of a Cutty Sark bottle, and another chunk whacked out of his mind on weed. Yet he still managed to leave an indelible mark on the cinema of the 1970s with a series of fiercely original, personal, and eccentric films.

A child of privilege, Altman was the oldest son of one of the most prominent insurance salesmen in Kansas City. His mother could trace her lineage back to the *Mayflower*. His father, Bernard Clement "B. C." Altman, set a standard for whiskey drinking, skirt chasing, and poker playing that Robert would later do his best to match. As an adolescent, Altman was already something of a hell raiser—so much so that his parents had him shipped off to military school when he was sixteen years old. The discipline didn't take, although the prospect of dropping bombs on the Japanese was enough to entice Altman into doing a tour in the Army Air Corps during World War II. He spent most of his downtime playing cards, pinching nurses, and dreaming up a crazy idea of maybe one day becoming a movie director.

Dissatisfied with his other job prospects, after the war Altman headed to Hollywood to see about making good on that scheme. He found occasional work as an actor, appearing as an extra in the 1947 Danny Kaye classic *The Secret Life of Walter Mitty*, but could never make enough to bankroll his increasingly profligate lifestyle. After a couple years, he found himself back in Kansas City, directing dreary industrial films and desperately trying to maintain his movie-star image. Every day at lunch he would disappear to a local bordello for a quick $2 blowjob. "Altman had this idea that that was a very Hollywood thing to do," said a friend, "to get your cock sucked on your lunch hour."

Eventually, he found steady work in television—first for *Alfred Hitchcock Presents* and later for popular genre shows like *Bonanza*, *Maverick*, and

Combat. These were days when Altman drank heavily, enjoying every minute of his first brush with success—when he wasn't passed out on the set, that is. Colleagues from that period recall Altman as a particularly belligerent, nasty drunk, whose skirt-chasing antics occasionally got him in trouble with jealous husbands. He never lost his yen for gambling and racked up huge debts with impromptu trips to Las Vegas. Professionally, Altman felt hemmed in by the constraints of network television and only started to mellow out when he traded in the booze for marijuana in the mid-1960s. Before anyone knew it, he was a certified hippie—partial to turtlenecks, ankhs, and love beads. Now all he needed was a movie career to match his zonked-out, self-created image.

That opportunity finally came in 1969, when Altman was offered the script for M*A*S*H, an anti-war comedy based on Richard Hooker's novel about a group of libertine surgeons in a mobile army field hospital during the Korean War. Fifteen other directors—including Stanley Kubrick and Sidney Lumet—had already turned down the project, but Altman was intrigued. He agreed to direct the picture for a flat fee of $75,000 with no percentage of the gross. Released in 1970, the movie went on to earn $36.7 million and make stars out of Elliott Gould and Donald Sutherland. Altman got hosed on the dough, but he did snag an Oscar nomination as best director and the chance to keep making movies on his own terms, which is all he ever wanted to do anyway. The success of M*A*S*H begat McCabe & Mrs. Miller in 1971, The Long Goodbye in 1973, and Altman's masterpiece, Nashville, in 1975— a string of bold, idiosyncratic films that slyly subverted genres and empowered actors through the then-radical reliance on improvisation and overlapping dialogue.

After a halcyon run in the 1970s, Altman was bound to hit the skids— and he did in a big way with the colossal 1980 bomb Popeye, one of the worst musicals ever made. A long fallow period ensued, during which changing audience tastes made the kind of informal, experimental pictures Altman preferred to make increasingly uncertain commercial ventures. Beginning in the 1990s, Altman enjoyed something of a late-life renaissance, highlighted by the Hollywood satire The Player in 1992 and then the multiple Oscar-nominated Gosford Park in 2001. Although he churned out his share of duds as well (the 1994 stinker Prêt-à-Porter was a real lowlight), within the Hollywood community he had banked enough positive vibes (and shared enough of his legendarily prodigious stash of weed) to score a coveted Lifetime Achievement Oscar in 2006. He died of leukemia later that year.

* * *

TATTOO YOU

Think how different movie history would be had Altman succeeded in his first career choice: personalized dog tattoo artist. After leaving the Army at the end of World War II, the future Academy Award honoree was looking for something to do with the rest of his life. He was also in the market for a dog. One day the two goals overlapped. The man who sold Altman his bull terrier had an idea for tagging dogs on their hindquarters with a distinctive identifying number. He called it "identicode" and he needed someone to join him in the venture as his resident tattoo artist. Altman loved the idea and left the man's pet shop as the newly anointed vice president of the company. Altman's job entailed shaving the pooches, applying antiseptic fluid, and tattooing the identicode on the inside of their groins. He suffered a few dog

> ROBERT ALTMAN WAS DEDICATED TO HIS HIPPIE LIFESTYLE, ESPECIALLY WHEN IT CAME TO SMOKING POT, WHICH HE BELIEVED TO BE A HEART-HEALTHY ALTERNATIVE TO ALCOHOL.

bites, but that seemed a small price to pay. "We thought we were off to be millionaires!" Altman exulted. Unfortunately, the business never took off, although Altman did get the chance to tattoo President Harry Truman's dog in Washington as part of a publicity stunt promoting the procedure. "I also tattooed a waiter," Altman told an interviewer many years later. "He was bringing drinks up to a hotel and he said, 'What are you guys doing.' We told him we tattooed and he said, 'I always wanted to have that!' So, we were a little drunk, I remember this guy took his shoe off and I tattooed on the bottom of his foot his army serial number and his name. His name was D. W. Stiles. I don't remember his number."

GONE TO POT

From his earliest days in Hollywood, Altman was a world-class pothead, unapologetically blazing up in any social situation, no matter what the company. One interviewer describes meeting him for drinks in a restaurant in the middle of winter, "the snowy air and the aroma of marijuana" wafting in through the door as Altman entered the establishment. Altman was known to light up a joint *during* an interview, and he once bragged that he had smoked pot while sitting across from British Prime Minister Tony Blair at a party. In his 1970s heyday, Altman held nightly screenings of the day's rushes for his cast that inevitably devolved into impromptu pot parties. Almost everyone joined in the fun—with one notable exception. When he first started filming *M*A*S*H*, Donald Sutherland was so strait-laced he claimed not to be able to identify the aroma of cannabis that hung over the set like a skunky cloud. "I literally didn't know what the smell was." Sutherland recalled. "I thought it was smoke effects for the movie!"

Altman always said that he started toking up in the 1960s, in the belief that marijuana was a healthy alternative to alcohol, which he contended was bad for his heart. He must have clung to that belief to the bitter end, because in 2005, Altman received a heart transplant and emerged from the operation a more committed stoner than ever. "I even have a prescription for marijuana pills," he boasted to the *New York Post*. For years, Altman served on the board of NORML, the National Organization for the Reform of Marijuana Laws, and spoke out openly in favor of pot legalization. "Marijuana should be legalized," he declared. "It's ridiculous that it isn't. If at the end of the day I feel like smoking a joint, I do it. It changes the perception of what I've been through all day."

"SAVED BY BIMBOS"

After early screenings appalled studio executives, *M*A*S*H* was almost consigned to the drive-in circuit—a fate worse than death for a prestige picture. Luckily for Altman, fate intervened in the form of Twentieth Century Fox chief Darryl F. Zanuck's libido. "Zanuck came back from a year in Europe, he had these two European girls with him," Altman told *Maxim* magazine, "and they just went crazy over the film. The studio people said, 'Of course, we're taking out all these bloody operating scenes. We can't show that to the public,' and these girls said, 'Ooh, no, zat ees what makes eet so brilliant!' And, incredibly enough, he listened to them! Saved by bimbos. I'm forever grateful."

KEEPING IT IN THE FAMILY

Altman's fourteen-year-old son Mike wrote the lyrics to the *M*A*S*H* theme song "Suicide Is Painless"—later used over the opening credits of the long-running TV series. According to Altman, his son earned more than $1 million in royalties over the years—more than ten times what dad made for directing the movie.

TEXAS TWO-STEP

Reliably left-wing in his politics, Altman was among a handful of American celebrities—Alec Baldwin and Eddie Vedder among them—who threatened to leave the country if Republican George W. Bush was elected to the presidency in 2000. "If George Bush gets elected president, I will move back to France," Altman bragged to reporters at the 2000 Cannes Film Festival. "He's not a very smart man. He's been put up by his father and a bunch of cronies." After Bush won the presidency later that year, Altman denied ever making the pledge—despite the fact that the entire exchange was captured on film. He then lamely claimed he had meant to say that he would relocate to Paris, Texas, "because the state would be better off if [Bush] is out of it."

THE WATCHMAN

In 1995, Altman joined fellow filmmakers Akira Kurosawa and Pedro Almodóvar in designing commemorative Swatch watches in honor of the 100th anniversary of the motion picture. Altman's timepiece—called "the sleekest of the three" by *The New York Times*, featured a mirrored watchface and tiny black hands that read "time to reflect."

SAM PECKINPAH

FEBRUARY 21, 1925–DECEMBER 28, 1984

NATIONALITY:
AMERICAN

ASTROLOGICAL SIGN:
PISCES

MAJOR FILMS:
THE WILD BUNCH (1969), *STRAW DOGS* (1971)

WORDS OF WISDOM:

"YOU'RE GIVEN A STORY TO DO AND YOU DO IT THE BEST WAY YOU KNOW HOW, THAT'S ALL. SO WHAT'S ALL THIS SHIT ABOUT INTEGRITY?"

Bloody Sam" Peckinpah cut a swath of violence and misogyny through American film in the 1960s and '70s. His reputation as a cinematic bloodletter so preceded him that a 1972 Monty Python sketch imagined the havoc he would wreak on the twee stage musical *Salad Days*. The grisly skit climaxed with a cast member impaled on a piano keyboard, gore spurting everywhere. But Peckinpah's veneer of ultraviolence was undergirded by a personal code he assembled from old Westerns, his California ranch upbringing, and the teachings of behavorial scientist Robert Ardrey, whose "killer ape" theory was a major influence on his films.

David Samuel "Sam" Peckinpah grew up in Fresno, California, the second son in an upstanding family with a long history in that part of the country. (In later years, Peckinpah liked to boast that he had Indian blood, although in fact he did not.) His mother was a teetotaler and a Christian Scientist and his father was a judge. Peckinpah enjoyed a typically rambunctious ranch childhood, with his earliest memory of being "strapped into a saddle when I was two for a ride into the high country."

As a teenager, that rebellious spirit became more problematic. An indifferent student, Peckinpah preferred shooting off guns with his friends to attending class and was constantly getting into fights. When he was seventeen years old, his parents shipped him off to military school, although the discipline didn't really take. Peckinpah served in the Marines during World War II—without seeing any combat—and didn't really find an outlet for his pent-up creative energies until after the war, when he enrolled at Fresno State College and started taking theater classes.

In 1952, Peckinpah took a job as a stagehand at a Los Angeles TV station, but was personally fired by Liberace for not wearing a suit. (The flamboyant pianist apparently believed that mopping floors required business attire.) He then apprenticed for several years under director Don Siegel, serving as a dialogue director on Siegel's 1956 sci-fi classic *Invasion of the Body Snatchers*. Peckinpah also had a bit part in the movie as a meter reader who becomes one of the alien "pod people." (For decades, Peckinpah claimed in interviews that he did extensive rewrites on the script for *Body Snatchers*— although there is little evidence to suggest he did so. After the real screenwriter pointed out in an angry letter that Peckinpah had contributed perhaps one line total to the finished film, Peckinpah stopped bragging in public.)

In 1961, Peckinpah directed his first film, the Western *The Deadly Companions*. From his earliest days in Hollywood, he was already developing a reputation as a temperamental genius who was hell to work with and had a fondness for firearms, drink, and casual sex. He cycled through three wives— divorcing one three separate times. "I live plenty," Peckinpah once said. "I like good drink, good food, comfortable clothes, and fancy women." As his star rose he got plenty of all those things—not to mention drugs in increasingly large quantities. An inveterate pill popper and coke fiend, Peckinpah was known to drop his pants on the street in broad daylight in order to give himself a vitamin B12 injection.

The chemical stimulation fueled his creative output—for a while anyway. Peckinpah's 1969 film *The Wild Bunch* redefined the Hollywood Western. Its graphic, balletic portrayal of violence was a major milestone in the breaking down of the old production codes regulating what could and couldn't be shown on screen. *Straw Dogs* outraged feminists with its depiction of a woman seeming to enjoy her own rape, whereas *Pat Garrett and Billy the Kid* and *Bring Me the Head of Alfredo Garcia* divided critics and won Peckinpah a substantial cult following. In interviews, Peckinpah began to spout off about the cathartic power of violence and male dominance—a reflection of both his personal proclivities and his reading of Ardrey, the controversial author of *The Territorial Imperative,* whose work he'd been introduced to by actor Strother Martin.

Peckinpah's final decade was squandered in an alcohol- and cocaine-induced haze. His last few films—*The Killer Elite*, *Cross of Iron*, *Convoy*, and *The Osterman Weekend*—seemed slipshod and confused compared to his earlier work, as if the director were stoned as he made them. A lot of the time, he was. In 1984, Peckinpah hit rock bottom with his final project: directing two music videos for the late John Lennon's untalented son Julian. Peckinpah was paid $100,000 for the assignment, which he took only after Robert Altman backed out. He was desperate for money and it showed. The generic-looking clips for "Valotte" and "Too Late for Goodbyes" helped launch the young Lennon's short-lived career, but they did little to resuscitate Peckinpah's. Shortly before he died of complications from a blood clot in his lung in December of 1984, Peckinpah lamented to his wife that "my last movie was only two minutes long."

* * *

PRODUCE THIS!

Peckinpah loathed producers, considering them mere "administrators" too interested in defending their own prerogatives than giving the director free creative rein. "I'm always at war with these cats," he declared. One cat who scratched back was Martin Ransohoff, the producer of 1965's *The Cincinnati Kid*. Ransohoff fired Peckinpah after only four days of shooting, claiming the director was trying to insert a nude scene into the picture in violation of the production code. "He had a tremendous hatred of real talent," Peckinpah said of Ransohoff. Eventually the two men came to blows. Peckinpah got the best of it—at least according to his version of events. "I stripped him as naked as one of his badly told lies," he claimed. But the victory proved costly. It would be four long years before Peckinpah worked again in Hollywood.

SERPICO RIDES AGAIN!

Two years before Sidney Lumet signed on to direct Al Pacino as *Serpico*, Peckinpah was first in line to helm the project. At the time, *Serpico* was being pitched as a buddy film starring then red-hot stars Paul Newman and Robert Redford as Sergeant David Durk and Detective Frank Serpico, respectively. Novelist John Gregory Dunne was all set to write the screenplay. However, Peckinpah balked at the casting of Redford, whom he disliked (he reportedly boasted that if he had directed *Butch Cassidy and the Sundance Kid* it would have been a much better movie), whereas Dunne feared the story of the two men who blew the whistle on police corruption in New York City was too thin to be turned into a feature-length film. "What the hell is this picture all about?" an exasperated Dunne asked Peckinpah during a meeting at Paul Newman's house in Malibu to discuss the project. "Write me a Western," Peckinpah replied. Dunne reminded him that this was a story about two cops in present-day New York City. "Every story is a Western,"

Peckinpah insisted. "You put the hare in front of the hound and let the hound chase the hare!" Ultimately, the Peckinpah-directed Serpico project never got off the ground. Lumet's grittier, more contemporary take on the story was nominated for two Academy Awards in 1973.

PARANOIA, SELF-DESTROYER

At the nadir of his cocaine period in the mid-1970s, Peckinpah literally went insane. He would call friends around the country at all hours of the day and night spinning weird paranoid fantasies. At one point, he became convinced that actor Steve McQueen was plotting to murder him. At other times, he suspected conspiracies involving the IRS or the Mexican government. On the set of *Convoy* in 1976, one friend found him holed up in his trailer half-naked with a live goat and a .38 revolver, giving himself B12 injections. The director's jones for blow knew no bounds. In 1978, he entertained the idea of doing a film about the sleazy subculture of druglords—principally so he could arrange a trip to Colombia to score some coke. He ended up being placed under house arrest by the Bogota authorities. Convinced that his

AN INVETERATE PILL POPPER AND COKE FIEND, SAM PECKINPAH WAS KNOWN TO DROP HIS PANTS ON THE STREET IN BROAD DAYLIGHT TO GIVE HIMSELF A VITAMIN B12 INJECTION.

phone was tapped and that he was being monitored by aliens, Peckinpah started sleeping with a loaded shotgun in his bed—with the muzzle pointed at his head. He finally hit rock bottom in May of 1979, when he suffered a massive heart attack. Hopes that this health crisis would prompt him to clean up his act proved premature, however. "It scared him for about two weeks," his agent said. Peckinpah enjoyed five more years of hard partying before a blood clot in his lung finally killed him in 1984.

THE SCRIBBLER

Peckinpah insisted on writing his screenplays in longhand, although his terrible penmanship made them nearly illegible. Over the course of his nearly forty-year show-business career, he employed only two secretaries—the only two women in America who could transcribe his god-awful handwriting.

TAINTED LOVE

Peckinpah had a love–hate relationship with the influential film critic Pauline Kael, who shared his tendencies for alcohol and spirited conversation. Kael usually admired Peckinpah's work but objected to what she perceived as his endorsement of rape in *Straw Dogs*. When an interviewer for *Playboy* magazine raised Kael's concerns with Peckinpah, the director's reply was cutting—and cryptic. "I like Kael," he said. "She's a feisty little gal and I enjoy drinking with her—which I've done on occasion—but here she's cracking walnuts in her ass." Peckinpah then went on to lecture Kael on the difference between sodomy and anal rape, before concluding, "I guess Miss Kael and her friends have anal complexes."

LADIES MAN

"I ignore women's lib," Peckinpah once declared—which should come as no surprise to anyone who's seen one of his movies. Women are invariably depicted in the most unflattering, reductive way imaginable—a reflection of the director's less-than-enlightened views about gender. "There are two kinds of women," Peckinpah once said. "There are women and then there's pussy. . . . Most of us marry pussy at one time or another." Although he claimed to prefer "marriages made in heaven" he was less than sanguine about the prospects for such a union. "A smart, unscrupulous cunt can always use her looks to get some poor slob to marry her," he railed. Peckinpah himself preferred anonymous sex with groupies. "One of the advantages of being a celebrity is that a lot of attractive pussy that wasn't available to you before suddenly becomes available," he enthused. As for lesbians, Peckinpah had no use for them, bemoaning "those bull dykes and the crazies in their tennis sneakers and burlap sacks." "Not that I'm knocking lesbianism," he hastened to add. "I consider myself one of the foremost male lesbians in the world."

SIZE MATTERS

Although he boasted about his ability to procure "attractive pussy" by the boatload, Peckinpah's taste in women reportedly ran more to side-show oddities and the morbidly obese. One friend remembers watching him perform cunnilingus on a 400-pound woman for four hours. In fact, Peckinpah felt safer having sex with physically unattractive specimens. "He could have screwed any starlet with a casting-couch promise, but he didn't," a friend recalled. "He'd just as soon get a whore off the street in Mexico."

ANIMAL LOVER

PETA would not have been fond of Peckinpah. An avid gun owner, the director loved to hunt game—not for sport, but for food. He preferred to personally skin and eat his quarry whenever possible. He also had a pet boa constrictor that he kept in his office. One day, a friend walked in to find Peckinpah gazing into its cage, into which he had placed one decidedly terrified white mouse. "Who do you think will win?" Peckinpah asked. "You will, Sam," replied the friend.

MODERATE FASCIST DEMOCRAT?

Given Peckinpah's idiosyncratic views on women—and his passion for firearms—it's fair to wonder where exactly he fell on the political spectrum. Some saw him as an extreme right-winger, a conclusion he seemed to endorse when he told *Time* magazine: "I'm not a fascist, but I am something of a totalitarian." Others claim he was really a closet liberal, pointing to his avowed antipathy for Republican presidents. "He hated Nixon—and Reagan," said Peckinpah's daughter Sharon. "He thought they were hopeless." During the height of the Watergate scandal, Peckinpah sent a Republican friend a gag gift: a wooden carving of two elephants screwing.

THE ONE THAT GOT AWAY

Peckinpah was offered the chance to direct producer Dino De Laurentiis's big-budget 1976 remake of *King Kong*, but turned it down. Journeyman John Guillerman took the reins instead.

STANLEY KUBRICK

JULY 26, 1928–MARCH 7, 1999

NATIONALITY:
AMERICAN

ASTROLOGICAL SIGN:
LEO

MAJOR FILMS:
DR. STRANGELOVE, OR: HOW I LEARNED TO STOP WORRYING AND LOVE THE BOMB (1964), *2001: A SPACE ODYSSEY* (1968)

WORDS OF WISDOM:

"THE DESTRUCTION OF THIS PLANET WOULD HAVE NO SIGNIFICANCE ON A COSMIC SCALE."

With their stunning production design and fluid camera work, Stanley Kubrick's films are instantly identifiable. But the reclusive director himself? Not so much. Kubrick once went ten years without giving an interview. Occasionally a journalist or film student would show up on his doorstep, hoping to score an elusive Q&A. "He's not home," Kubrick would intone, and shut the door in the visitor's face. Since few people knew what he looked like, the line actually worked.

He came by his introversion honestly. The son of a prominent New York City doctor and a Romanian-born mother, Kubrick lived a fairly solitary childhood on the Grand Concourse in the Bronx. He developed a passion for chess at an early age, played drums in his school band, and spent nearly all the rest of his downtime sitting alone in New York's Depression-era movie palaces, studying films. He received a camera for his thirteenth birthday, the beginning of a lifelong fascination with visual composition and photography.

When he was sixteen years old, Kubrick took a photo of a beleaguered New York City newspaper vendor the day after President Franklin Delano Roosevelt died. *Look* magazine paid $25 for the shot and hired Kubrick as a staff photographer. Over the next four years, he photographed everything from bubble-gum-blowing contests to celebrity portraits. He shot Montgomery Clift, Frank Sinatra, and Rocky Graziano, among others. In 1950, he plowed the proceeds from one of his *Look* photo essays into the production of his first short film, a sixteen-minute boxing documentary called *Day of the Fight*. Two more documentaries followed before he made his first feature, *Fear and Desire*, in 1953.

The noir thriller *The Killing* (1956) earned Kubrick his first rave notices, including a gushing review in *Time* magazine that likened him to Orson Welles. Its success attracted the attention of actor Kirk Douglas, who asked Kubrick to direct him in the anti-war drama *Paths of Glory* in 1957. Even at this early age, Kubrick was showing signs of being a consummate control freak. He micromanaged every aspect of his films and filled volu-minous notebooks detailing every nook and cranny of a production, from sets to costumes to music. The only film on which he didn't have total con-trol was 1960's *Spartacus*, and the experience so infuriated him that he left Hollywood for good. He moved to England, went into seclusion, and culti-vated an affected, eccentric lifestyle. Every few years, with increasing in-frequency, he would pop out another brilliant, maddening, critically polarizing film.

Lolita in 1962 was followed by *Dr. Strangelove or: How I Learned to Stop Worrying and Love the Bomb* in 1964 and then, arguably, Kubrick's masterpiece, *2001: A Space Odyssey*, in 1968. This last film, an orphic sci-fi mind trip set to classical music and featuring state-of-the-art special ef-fects, divided reviewers and moviegoers alike. Some found it transcendent; others merely baffling. Reportedly, Rock Hudson stomped out of the screen-ing in exasperation, screaming, "Will somebody tell me what the fuck this is about?" Kubrick himself offered little in the way of guidance, saying only: "If the film stirs the emotions and penetrates the subconscious of the viewer, if it stimulates, however inchoately, his mythological and religious yearnings and impulses, then it has succeeded." Of course, the various mind-altering substances most moviegoers were consuming in order to get through the turgid two-and-a-half-hour space epic might just as easily account for what-ever subconscious stirring was taking place, but that was par for the course in 1968. Whatever you thought of *2001*, there was no denying it was a huge cultural event, and it garnered four Academy Award nominations, including one for Kubrick as best director.

Kubrick's output declined precipitously in the 1970s and so, arguably, did the quality of his films. Unwilling to fly, he shot everything on sound-stages near his London estate—even films, like *The Shining* and *Eyes Wide Shut*, that clearly take place in America. As a result, these later films have an otherworldly, dreamlike quality that reflect the crazed interior world into which Kubrick himself was sinking. Stories of his mercurial tempera-ment and odd behavior, particularly his mistreatment of actors, were al-ready beginning to circulate publicly when he died suddenly of a heart attack in 1999. He was buried in the grounds behind his house, beside his favorite tree.

* * *

FEAR AND LOATHING

Like a lot of young directors, Kubrick had to come up with innovative ways to fund his projects. His third film, *Fear and Desire*, was financed almost entirely using money Kubrick won by hustling chess matches in New York's Washington Square Park. Maybe he should have pocketed the cash. Calling the finished film a "bumbling, amateur exercise," Kubrick spent several decades suppressing any attempt to show the only existing print in public.

THE KING OF PONG

Chess wasn't Kubrick's only game. He also loved table tennis and made sure to include ping-pong scenes in a number of his movies. He had a world-class ping-pong table installed on the grounds of his estate in England. Visitors were often enticed into playing against him. Kubrick especially liked playing against actors, in the belief that beating them at ping-pong allowed him to achieve dominance over them and thus more easily control them on the set.

VOICE ACTIVATED

Kubrick never learned to type. He dictated all his scripts into a tape recorder.

SPECIAL RELATIONSHIP

Kubrick shared a unique bond with *A Clockwork Orange* star Malcolm McDowell. The director's second choice for the role of Alex DeLarge (Mick Jagger was the first), McDowell won him over by revealing his special talent: an ability to belch on command. The two men became fast friends during filming, often engaging in spirited ping-pong matches between takes. Mc-Dowell thought they had a good thing going, but sadly it was not to last. For Kubrick, McDowell was apparently just a "work friend." After they wrapped up the production, he never spoke to him again.

IN SPACE, NO ONE CAN HEAR YOU SUE

Kubrick was notoriously protective of his copyrights. He once refused to allow the Beatles to use a landscape shot from *Dr. Strangelove* in one of their movies, for fear it would demean his work. In 1975, seven years after the release of *2001*, he threatened to sue the makers of the TV science-fiction

series *Space 1999*. "It would appear that *Space 1999* may very well become a long-running and important television series," Kubrick wrote to one of his assistants. "There seems nothing left now but to seek the highest possible damages. . . . The deliberate choice of a date only two years away from 2001 is not accidental and harms us."

MAN ON THE MOON

For years, rumors have been circulating in conspiracy circles about the role Kubrick supposedly played in faking the moon landings. According to legend, in early 1968 Kubrick was secretly approached by NASA officials who presented him with a lucrative offer to "direct" the first three moon missions. After some negotiation, Kubrick agreed and spent the next sixteen months on a specially built soundstage in Huntsville, Alabama, staging every aspect of the Apollo 11 and 12 moon landings. The resulting film of Neil Armstrong, Buzz Aldrin, et al. frolicking on the lunar surface was then shown on television and passed off as the real thing to a gullible American public. Kubrick himself orchestrated the telecast remotely from the Johnson Space Center in Houston, using the same front-projection process he had developed for the "Dawn of Man" sequences in *2001*. When it came time for Apollo 13, so the

A PING-PONG WIZARD, STANLEY KUBRICK LOVED BEATING HIS ACTORS AT TABLE TENNIS. HE BELIEVED IT MADE THEM MORE CONTROLLABLE ON THE SET.

story goes, Kubrick backed out, citing creative differences. (He reportedly wanted the mission to fail, but NASA officials rejected his screenplay.) Needless to say, no evidence has ever been offered in support of this theory, which, if true, would make Kubrick the greatest hoaxster in recorded history.

I SHOT THE SERIF

Kubrick was a man of many obsessions. One such idée fixe was typography. He maintained an enormous collection of font books, insisted on using sans-serif fonts for all his movie posters, and argued late into the night with his assistants about the virtues of various typefaces. (For all you graphic designers out there, his favorites were Futura Extra Bold, Helvetica, and Univers.)

PAPER TIGER

Stationery was another of Kubrick's passions. He fixated on paper, pads, and everything that went with them. He demanded that his staff write memos only on six-by-four-inch paper because, one of his assistants told *Rolling Stone*, "Stanley thinks that six by four is the best size for a memo." One time, when he learned that a particular brand of brown ink he preferred was about to be discontinued, Kubrick bought every remaining bottle—one hundred in all. A compulsive hoarder, Kubrick also had a jones for boxes. Vexed by the difficulty he experienced in removing lids, he once commissioned a box manufacturer to construct four hundred boxes to his personal specifications.

BE VERY AFRAID

Kubrick was almost comically phobic. Deathly afraid of germs, he banned anyone with a cold from his movie sets. He refused to let his chauffeur drive more than thirty miles per hour. And he suffered from an intense fear of flying borne out of his habit of listening to the air-traffic controllers at London's Heathrow Airport for hours on end. Not surprisingly, Kubrick was extremely picky about which medical professionals he would allow to treat his various real and imagined ailments. He refused to see a doctor he didn't know, and once had his personal dentist flown from the Bronx to London to treat him. Because the dentist did not have a license to practice in England, the procedure had to be performed on the grounds of the American embassy.

WILD AND CRAZY KUBRICK

One of Kubrick's favorite movies was *The Jerk*, the 1979 comedy starring Steve Martin as a white nitwit adopted by black sharecroppers. Kubrick was so tickled by Martin's performance that he seriously considered casting him in the lead role in *Eyes Wide Shut* and reconfiguring it as a sex comedy. The director actually met with the comedian several times to discuss the project, but the "wild and crazy" concept never came to fruition.

BIRD BRAIN

Kubrick's other pop-culture favorites were just as unpredictable. He loved *Freebie and the Bean*, a lowbrow cop comedy starring Alan Arkin and James Caan that was savaged by every critic in the country. Kubrick preposterously dubbed it "the best film of 1974." His television favorites included the sitcoms *Roseanne*, *The Simpsons*, and *Seinfeld*. He was a huge fan of Woody

Woodpecker cartoons and longed to put footage in every one of his movies. Unfortunately, Woody's creator, Walter Lantz, refused to grant permission.

ANIMAL INSTINCT

Though he wasn't crazy about people, Kubrick did have a soft spot for animals. At one point, he owned sixteen cats, any number of which could be seen lolling around his editing room while he worked. He also had a dog, whom he so adored he took several months off from filming to care for it as it was dying. And according to actor Matthew Modine, Kubrick was so upset when a family of rabbits was accidentally killed on the set of *Full Metal Jacket* that he canceled filming for the rest of the day.

OUT OF THIS WORLD

During the production of *2001*, Kubrick grew paranoid about NASA's ongoing Mars probes. Terrified that the missions to the Red Planet would turn up signs of extraterrestrial life and preempt his entire storyline, he asked Lloyds of London if he could purchase insurance against losses caused by the discovery of aliens. The reply: No.

THE NUMBER OF THE AUTEUR?

Kubrick died 66 days into the year 1999. For the record, that was 666 days before the official start of the year he made famous: 2001.

NAPOLEON COMPLEX

When he died, Kubrick left behind an extensive personal archive. One of the highlights was the famed "Napoleon Room," a massive library filled with books about one subject: Napoleon Bonaparte. Kubrick was obsessed with making a film based on the life of the French emperor and maintained a collection of 25,000 index cards, each one detailing the events of a particular day in Napoleon's life.

SERGIO LEONE

JANUARY 3, 1929–APRIL 30, 1989

NATIONALITY:
ITALIAN

ASTROLOGICAL SIGN:
CAPRICORN

MAJOR FILMS:
THE GOOD, THE BAD, AND THE UGLY (1966), *ONCE UPON A TIME IN THE WEST* (1968)

WORDS OF WISDOM:

"I CAN'T SEE AMERICA ANY OTHER WAY THAN WITH A EUROPEAN'S EYES. IT FASCINATES ME AND TERRIFIES ME AT THE SAME TIME."

T he Western is finished," American director Raoul Walsh told his young Italian counterpart Sergio Leone on the set of *Helen of Troy* in 1955. "The public does not want it anymore." Leone, then twenty-six years old, begged to differ, and after a decade spent apprenticing on cheaply made sword-and-sandal epics, he set about resuscitating the genre. Derisively labeled "spaghetti Westerns," Leone's films recast the Western hero in the steely image of Clint Eastwood, the American TV actor who became an international movie star under Leone's tutelage.

Leone was born in 1929 in Rome, Italy, where his parents both worked as actors in silent films. Educated by a Roman Catholic religious order and indoctrinated from an early age with the ideology of Mussolini's fascist government, he sought imaginative refuge in some of his favorite childhood pursuits: fencing, studying magic, and attending puppet shows. He also excelled at exhibitions of public urination. As a boy, Leone and his friends would gather around an anthill and pee on it in a contest to determine who could drown the greatest number of ants. Another game involved tinkling down a plank of wood to see whose stream would reach the bottom first. It passed the time, and it was preferable to marching and singing fascist anthems, which was all the other kids seemed to do.

After completing high school, Leone studied law for a short time, before following his parents into the world of Italian cinema. He worked as an unpaid assistant on Vittorio DeSica's 1948 classic *The Bicycle Thief*, with a cameo as a German priest. In the 1950s, he found steady work on American/Italian coproductions called *pepla*, which retold the heroic deeds of the Greeks and Romans. By the end of the decade, these "sword and sandal" films had become big business in the United States. The trend culminated in a best picture win in 1959 for *Ben-Hur*, on which Leone worked as a second unit director, helping orchestrate the famous chariot race sequence. During this period, Leone hobnobbed with visiting Hollywood directors such as

Robert Wise, William Wyler, Fred Zinnemann, and the aforementioned Raoul Walsh, whose reminiscences about the golden age Westerns would prove to be a formative influence.

At this point in his career, Leone was a hack—albeit a well-paid and respected one—occasionally called upon to finish work on other people's movies. He received his first solo directing credit on 1960's *The Colossus of Rhodes*, a film he later claimed he made only so he could pay for his honeymoon in Spain. In 1961, Leone finally found the template for the kind of movies he really wanted to create when Akira Kurosawa's samurai film *Yojimbo* was released in Rome. Recognizing the potential for a Western remake, Leone set about securing the financial backing. The result was 1964's *A Fistful of Dollars*, a revisionist take on one of the oldest cinematic genres that put Leone, Eastwood, and composer Ennio Morricone on the map for good.

More westerns followed: *For a Few Dollars More* in 1965, *The Good, the Bad, and the Ugly* in 1966 (both featuring Eastwood's laconic Man with No Name character), and *Once Upon a Time in the West* in 1968. All were heavy on style, low on budget, and delightfully idiosyncratic—thanks in large part to Morricone's unforgettable musical cues, which revolutionized film scoring. Later in his career, Leone moved away from westerns to focus on the development of more ambitious projects, like his gangland epic *Once Upon a Time in America*. (Reportedly, Leone turned down an offer to direct *The Godfather* because he felt that its subject matter was too similar.) Leone spent ten years working on *Once Upon a Time in America*, only to see it butchered by the studio and savaged by critics upon its release in 1984. When he died of a heart attack in 1989, Leone left a number of other pet projects unrealized—including an epic film about the World War II siege of Leningrad and his life's ambition, a big-budget remake of *Gone with the Wind*.

HOW TO GET AHEAD IN MOVIES

Anyone who doesn't think actors should take out decapitation insurance should talk to Vic Morrow's widow—or Eli Wallach, who was nearly beheaded on the set of *The Good, the Bad, and the Ugly*. Leone had set up a scene in which Wallach's "Ugly" character is lying handcuffed athwart a railroad track with a train bearing down upon him. Unfortunately, the threat was all too real. The train missed Wallach's head by six inches. Amazingly, Leone asked for a retake. Wallach wisely refused and declined to participate in any more stunts for the duration of the shoot.

SAFETY LAST

Losing his noggin wasn't the only mishap to befall Eli Wallach on the set of *Il Buono, Il Bruto, Il Cattivo* (to use the original Italian title). The entire shoot was chaotic, according to the actor. Leone barely spoke English, and Wallach—a Brooklyn-born Jew playing a Mexican bandit—spoke little Italian, so the two conversed almost entirely in French. Not that they talked often. Early on in the shoot, Clint Eastwood warned Wallach that Leone was insane and that he should stay out of the director's way as much as possible. He was right. Safety, as evidenced by the train incident, was not high on Leone's list of priorities. At one point, Wallach nearly poisoned himself after accidentally drinking from a bottle of acid that a member of Leone's crew had placed next to his soda container. When Wallach went to the director to complain, Leone just handed him a jug of milk to wash out his mouth and remarked that "accidents will happen." During the filming of the movie's climactic cemetery gunfight scene, Leone unleashed a vicious dog on an unsuspecting Wallach to "motivate" him to run around in a blind panic.

SAM, I AM

Leone's volcanic temper and cowboy affectations earned him a colorful nickname. Clint Eastwood called him Yosemite Sam, after the irascible Warner Brothers cartoon character.

MIGHT AS WELL JUMP

Leone was such a tyrant that he drove one of his actors to commit suicide. Al Muloch, a rugged character actor and Leone regular who played "Knuckles" in *Once Upon a Time in the West*, killed himself by jumping out of his hotel window while on location in Guadix, Spain. Leone reacted to the tragedy with typical disdain for human life. While Muloch's splattered body was being loaded into a car to be taken to the hospital, Leone ordered his production manager to remove the dying man's cowboy regalia first. "Get the costume! We need the costume!" he barked. Later, when he was editing the film, Leone repeatedly lamented the poor timing of Muloch's leap. "Why couldn't he have died just a day later?" the director groused. "I had one more close-up to do!"

A FISTFUL OF YEN

Anyone who has seen Akira Kurosawa's 1961 samurai classic *Yojimbo* knows that Leone's *A Fistful of Dollars* is an almost scene-for-scene remake. But Leone seemed oblivious to the legal ramifications of his copycatting. He never publicly acknowledged his creative debt to Kurosawa and refrained from offering the Japanese master any royalties. In fact, during production on *Dollars*, Leone's production company explicitly put out word to everyone concerned to "refrain under any circumstances from mentioning the word *Yojimbo*." When Kurosawa learned what was going on, he sent Leone a letter praising the Italian's film and asking for his cut of the pie. "[*A Fistful of Dollars*] is a very fine film, but it is my film," Kurosawa wrote. "Since Japan is a signatory of the Berne Convention on international copyright, you must pay me." Leone, who was thrilled that a filmmaker of Kurosawa's stature would threaten to sue him, eventually agreed to cough up fifteen percent of *Fistful's* worldwide box-office receipts.

> DURING THE FILMING OF THE GOOD, THE BAD, AND THE UGLY, SERGIO LEONE UNLEASHED A VICIOUS DOG ON AN UNSUSPECTING ACTOR TO "MOTIVATE" HIM TO RUN AROUND IN A BLIND PANIC.

DIRECT, YOU SUCKER

In the annals of unlikely collaborations, the unholy alliance between Leone and Peter Bogdanovich must surely rank near the top. Amazingly, it was Bogdanovich, not Leone, who was originally slated to direct the 1971 spaghetti Western *A Fistful of Dynamite*. In United Artists' configuration, Bogdanovich—then an up-and-comer fresh off the cult hit *Targets*—would report directly to Leone, who was slated to serve as producer. The two men eventually parted company due to creative differences. At that point, Bogdanovich's version of the dispute differs from Leone's in virtually every detail. According to Bogdanovich, Leone routinely showed up late for story conferences and spent most of their time together acting out scenes from the screenplay in a clownish manner. Leone especially enjoyed re-creating his favorite scene, in which a Mexican bandit lights his own fart with a match. At one point Leone even threatened to cast himself in the movie just so he could do this on screen. The two men also sparred over the film's title. Leone wanted to call the picture *Duck, You Sucker*, insisting that this was a common American expression. When Bogdanovich informed him that no one in America actually used the phrase "Duck, you sucker," Leone nearly blew a gasket. (The film was eventually released in America under that title and later changed to *A Fistful of Dynamite*.) But the final straw for Bogdanovich was Leone's insistence that Bogdanovich shoot the film exactly as he was acting it out in their story meetings, fart for fart and close-up for close-up. When Bogdanovich informed Leone that he preferred long shots to close-ups, Leone lost all faith in him as a director and had him removed from the project.

Leone's version of the story is quite a bit different. According to the Italian director, Bogdanovich—who had never before been to Rome—spent his first two weeks on the project whoring *Targets* around town at special screenings for influential Italian tastemakers. When he finally showed up for story conferences, he shot down all of Leone's creative suggestions and repeatedly called out for his "mother"—a creepy reference to his wife, designer Polly Platt, who served as Bogdanovich's muse. To facilitate work on a much-needed script treatment, Leone agreed to give her a part in the film and set up the couple in a plush villa. Two weeks later, Bogdanovich finally delivered his rewrite, which so appalled Leone that he lobbied United Artists to have him removed from the project. The studio agreed with Leone that Bogdanovich was a bad fit and asked him to send the temperamental American back on the first plane to New York—in tourist class.

Don Siegel and Other Masters of Genre Films

Some great filmmakers transcend genres. Others express their vision through them. Here are four directors who managed to create high-quality work while still coloring within the lines.

DON SIEGEL (1912–1991)
Major Films: *Invasion of the Body Snatchers* (1956), *Dirty Harry* (1971)
"I'm a whore," Don Siegel once declared. "I work for money. It's the American way." But this unapologetic hack was also a superb craftsman whose action-packed films influenced a generation of more artistically ambitious moviemakers. The son of a mandolin virtuoso, Siegel enjoyed an upper-crust upbringing that belied his tough-guy Hollywood persona. He spent most of his youth in England and attended Jesus College at Cambridge and the Royal Academy of Dramatic Arts. After working his way up in the movie business from assistant film librarian to director, he made his initial splash with the 1956 sci-fi classic *Invasion of the Body Snatchers*. Action films were his real forte, however, and he left his most lasting mark with a series of violent-crime and Western pictures starring his protégé, Clint Eastwood.

SAM FULLER (1912–1997)
Major Films: *Pickup on South Street* (1953), *The Big Red One* (1980)
A jack-of-all-genres, Sam Fuller was equally at ease directing war movies, film noir, and socially relevant melodramas. He was so versatile, in fact, that a documentary on his career bore the catch-all title *Crooks, Psychos, and Soldiers*. But Fuller did more than just chronicle the exploits of such subjects from afar. He had lived among them—first as a journalist on the gangland beat in New York City, then as a U.S. Army infantryman in World War II. He saw action at Omaha Beach on D-Day, was present at the liberation of the Nazi death camps, and received the Silver Star, Bronze Star, and Purple

Heart for his service. Although few of his low-budget, hard-boiled films could be considered classics, Fuller did influence the new wave of American and European directors in the 1970s. Late in life, he embraced his status as a cult director, although he claimed his real ambition was to "join the cult of the 100 to 200 million grossers and still make an artistic picture."

WES CRAVEN (1939–)

Major Films: *The Last House on the Left* (1972), *A Nightmare on Elm Street* (1984)

The slasher movie finally found its Cecil B. DeMille when Wes Craven unleashed *The Last House on the Left* on an unsuspecting world in 1972. Craven's grisly, nihilistic take on the genre anticipated themes still dominant today. He then went on to direct several more seminal shockers, including the minor classic and Reagan-era pop cultural touchstone *A Nightmare on Elm Street* in 1984. Away from the set, Craven is known as a cultured, urbane gentleman who enjoys birdwatching and once taught humanities at a small arts college in upstate New York. The only horror that ever touched his life—if Joe Eszterhas's book *American Rhapsody* is to be believed—came when his second wife left him after he had an affair with actress Sharon Stone.

GEORGE A. ROMERO (1940–)

Major Films: *Night of the Living Dead* (1968), *Dawn of the Dead* (1978)

There's something to be said for playing to your strengths. George A. Romero is really good at making one specific kind of horror movie—the zombie flick—and he practically defined the parameters of that subgenre with his 1968 masterpiece *Night of the Living Dead*. A longtime resident of Pittsburgh, Romero started making movies with an 8-mm camera when he was fourteen years old. One of his first paid gigs involved shooting a segment on oral hygiene for an episode of the locally produced children's show *Mr. Rogers Neighborhood*. "Probably the scariest movie I've ever done was *Mr. Rogers Gets a Tonsillectomy*," he later joked. In 1967, Romero and his friends pooled their meager resources to finance the making of *Night of the Living Dead*. The gore-spattered zombie fest cost around $70,000 and earned $500,000 in its first year. Against all odds, *Living Dead* and its sequels revived a genre that had been moribund since the 1940s, and Romero charmed critics through his use of brain-eating mayhem as a vehicle for social comment about violent revolution, consumerism, and the social-networking craze.

JEAN-LUC GODARD

DECEMBER 3, 1930–

NATIONALITY:
FRENCH

ASTROLOGICAL SIGN:
SAGITTARIUS

MAJOR FILMS:
BREATHLESS (1960), *CONTEMPT* (1963)

WORDS OF WISDOM:
"ALL YOU NEED TO MAKE A MOVIE IS A GIRL AND A GUN."

Like a cult rock band known more for its influence than its achievement, Jean-Luc Godard has left an outsized footprint on the history of cinema. If it's true that anyone who ever bought a Velvet Underground album went on to form a band, then anyone who saw a Godard film in the 1960s went on to become a filmmaker. Directors from Martin Scorsese to Quentin Tarantino claim him as a formative influence.

For Godard the road from birth to beatification was relatively unencumbered. He was a child of privilege, the scion of a prosperous Parisian family. His parents were affluent literary snobs who deeded to him their passion for German Romantic poetry and impenetrable French novels. Young Jean-Luc spent his childhood reading, skiing, and shuttling back and forth between his family's various estates. He even escaped the horrors of World War II by sitting out the Nazi occupation at his parents' place in Switzerland.

After the war, Godard returned to Paris, where he joined the community of hardcore cinephiles centered on the Cinémathèque Française. He hooked up with other movie buffs like François Truffaut, Claude Chabrol, and Eric Rohmer and engaged in all-night bull sessions devoted to their shared interest in art-house films and American "B" pictures of the thirties and forties. At times, Godard sampled as many as five different movies in an afternoon, watching only enough to get a sense of the style and conventions of each genre. He recorded his observations in the form of criticism for such publications as *Les Cahiers du cinéma*, an oracle for Francophone film snobs ever since.

Then, as now, it was nearly impossible to earn a living as a film critic, and Godard—who no longer had the financial support of his family—was reduced to stealing from relatives and employers to pay his rent. When he got caught, his father bailed him out of jail and had him briefly consigned to a mental institution. That event precipitated a final break with his wealthy family. Now totally on his own, Godard took a series of odd jobs—working on a dam in Switzerland and as the press agent for the Paris office of Twentieth Century Fox—and vowed to save up enough to finance his first feature. With some help from French producer Georges de Beauregard, he did. Released in 1960, *Breathless* is still considered Godard's masterpiece. Shot without a script and studded with stylized jump cuts, the tale of lovers on the lam helped usher in the new wave school of filmmaking.

After *Breathless*, Godard largely eschewed the pursuit of commercial success. Between 1960 and 1967, he made fourteen features; none made any significant money. Each was more recondite and self-consciously "artsy" than the last. Film students, French intellectuals, and the more academically oriented critics hailed him as a visionary. Others were left cold by his growing didacticism and contempt for narrative. Within the revolutionary demimonde of the late 1960s, Godard was a rock star. When he embarked on a speaking tour of U.S. colleges in 1968, one student described him as being "as irreplaceable, for us, as Bob Dylan."

Godard's celebrity status didn't survive the decade he helped define. Fed up with capitalism, he retired from commercial filmmaking in 1968. He cofounded a Marxist cinema collective and disappeared into a haze of strident Maoism. For nearly five years, by his own admission, he completely checked out of popular culture. "I didn't read, I didn't go to movies, I didn't listen to music," he said. "In those years I wasn't alive." When he finally decided to rouse himself from his creative slumber, he started making television documentaries and videos commissioned by wealthy benefactors. Only in the late 1970s did he return to filmmaking. His later films have been every bit as maddening as his earlier work, though few have made a mark outside the post-graduate film-school bubble. In 1985, *Hail Mary* generated some controversy with its depiction of Jesus's mother as a horny, basketball-playing gas station attendant. The Vatican condemned the film, and its release was met with protests. Generally speaking, however, the audience for a new Godard film could conceivably be fit inside a reasonably sized Paris elevator on any given day.

PUTTING THE GOD IN GODARD

For an avowed atheist, Godard sure had a lot of churchy ancestors. On his mother's side, he is directly descended from the Monods, one of the most prominent Protestant families in French history. His ancestors include nineteenth-century pastor and theologian Adolphe Monod; Frédéric Monod, the founder of the Union of the Evangelical Churches of France; not to mention numerous Nobel prize winners, scientists, politicians, and financiers.

JUST SAY *NON*

His name is synonymous with 1960s revolution, but in his personal life Godard was quite abstemious. He never took drugs, for example, claiming they would have too strong an effect on him.

SPEED READER

As a young man, Godard developed a novel way of expanding his literary horizons. He would drop by other people's apartments, head over to their bookshelves, and read the first and last pages of forty books in one sitting.

'TIL DEATH DO WE PART

At the height of his fame in the early 1960s, Godard endured a tempestuous four-year marriage to one of his leading ladies, Anna Karina. For a time, they were the "It" couple of Paris, tooling around town in their enormous Ford Thunderbird. But beneath the glamorous façade was a gurgling cesspool of dysfunction. Godard was known to disappear unexpectedly for weeks at a time—sometimes even leaving the country. Once he informed Karina he was going out for a pack of cigarettes. She didn't see him again for almost a month. And when they were together, they fought like roosters in a cockfighting ring. Screenwriter Paul Gégauff described a visit to the couple's home, where he found them squared off on opposite sides of a freezing cold room, buck naked, their clothes heaped in tatters at their feet, and shredded with a razor blade. There was broken glass all around. "I'd offer you a glass of something," Godard told Gégauff, "only there aren't any glasses left." He then asked their guest to go out and buy them a couple of raincoats so they could leave their apartment. "Godard and his wife," remarked another friend, "have achieved perfect harmony in destroying each other." The bickering pair agreed to split in 1965, though even that became a source of some disagreement.

"She left me because of my many faults," Godard explained. "I left her because I couldn't talk movies with her." Karina offered a somewhat different assessment. "As soon as we were happy, he tried to get at us by another means, another path. He provoked a new ordeal. One could have thought that it bored him, happiness."

A SHAKESPEAREAN TRAVESTY

Not satisfied with one match made in hell—his marriage to Anna Karina—Godard tried arranging another, an ill-starred collaboration with author Norman Mailer. The trouble began at the 1985 Cannes Film Festival, where Godard—fresh off the success of *Hail Mary*—pitched an idea for a modern-day adaptation of Shakespeare's *King Lear* to producer Menaham Golan. The schlockmeister behind such classics as *The Happy Hooker Goes to Hollywood* and *Breakin' 2: Electric Boogaloo*, Golan was thrilled at the prospect of working with such an eminent auteur and agreed on the spot, drawing up a contract on the back of a cocktail napkin. His only condition was that the screenplay must be written by Mailer—then on the skids and looking to break into the movie business. After some initial resistance—he wasn't sure he could get along with the notoriously temperamental Godard—Mailer agreed to sign on to the project.

Just like the play's titular character, this *Lear* was doomed from the start. Mailer turned in a script that was laughable even by his own hyperbolic standards. He somehow convinced himself that the only way to re-imagine Lear in modern dress was to make him a Mafia godfather—"Don Learo," he called him. Godard accepted the screenplay without even bothering to read it. (No surprise there; he had never read Shakespeare's version, either.) The director then compounded the problem by asking Mailer to play the lead. (His first choice, Orson Welles, had mercifully died before production began.) Even worse, during rehearsals, Godard discouraged Mailer from trying to play King Lear—the character he was supposed to be portraying. "You will be Norman Mailer in this," he told the bewildered novelist. Summoning his cast to his mansion in Switzerland, Godard staged anarchic read-throughs that he presided over in his pajamas. With cameras rolling, he began feeding Mailer lines that weren't in the script, encouraging him to improvise as himself. After watching the resulting footage, Mailer pronounced it "dreadful" and promptly quit the project. Godard then tried to get Rod Steiger, Lee Marvin, and—most curiously of all—Richard Nixon to replace Mailer in the part, but had to settle for elderly *Batman* villain Burgess Meredith instead. *Pretty in Pink* pixie Molly Ringwald was brought in to play Lear's daughter Cordelia. Godard cast himself as a mad, dreadlocked professor and asked Woody Allen to do a cameo as an inept film editor called "Mr. Alien." Allen agreed to take part in exchange for $10,000 and the promise that his name not be used to promote the film—a smart deal, as it turned out. Allen later confessed to

film critic Roger Ebert that being directed by Godard was like taking orders from Rufus T. Firefly—the lunatic head of state played by Groucho Marx in *Duck Soup*. Indeed, Godard was quite the merry prankster around the set. According to Ringwald, he spent most of his downtime playing practical jokes on Meredith—short-sheeting his bed and dousing the dignified old trouper in fake blood. (Meredith, who was in the early stages of dementia at the time, had no idea what to make of this.)

To no one's surprise, Godard's *King Lear* bombed at the box office and baffled critics. *The Washington Post*'s Hal Hinson derided it as a "not terribly funny practical joke," and Vincent Canby of the *New York Times* damned it with faint praise, complimenting the cast for being "remarkably good under terrible circumstances." Godard himself admitted, "I don't understand half of what is said in the film," prompting producer Golan to accuse him of having "spit in his own soup." Years later, Norman Mailer described the experience of working with Godard as "probably the most disagreeable single experience" of his career.

> JEAN-LUC GODARD AND WIFE ANNA KARINA HAD A TEMPESTUOUS ROMANCE. THEY WERE ONCE FOUND SQUARING OFF BUCK NAKED, THEIR CLOTHES HEAPED ON THE FLOOR AND SHREDDED BY A RAZOR BLADE.

HÉLAS, GOODBYE

Like a prophet without honor in his own country, Godard has been a ripe target for the French press, which routinely derides his films for being impenetrable and inaccessible. When one of Godard's rare commercial efforts *Hélas pour moi* (*Woe Is Me*) opened in 1993, the Paris newspaper *Le Figaro* ran a scathing review underneath the snarky headline, "Hélas pour Nous" ("Woe Is Us").

SCHINDLER'S DISSED

Don't invite Godard and Steven Spielberg to the same *vin et fromage* reception. When the New York Film Critics' Circle offered to honor Godard in 1995, he turned down the invitation, citing his loathing of American film—and Spielberg in particular—in his RSVP letter. Spielberg's best picture winner

Schindler's List deeply offended Godard, who considered any effort to render the horrors of the Holocaust on film to be a moral obscenity. In fact, Godard judged himself to have failed in his duty "to prevent Mr. Spielberg from reconstructing Auschwitz" and therefore undeserving of the Critics' Circle honor. Spielberg, he railed, aspired "to dominate the world by the fact of wanting to please before finding truth or knowledge. . . . In that, there is something very totalitarian."

PARDON MY FRENCH

Godard had a mean streak a mile wide. Informed of the Manson family's brutal murder of Sharon Tate, wife of Roman Polanski (who had just outbid him on the rights to adapt a book) Godard crowed: "Good—he just stole those rights from me." When the Apollo 13 moon mission was rocked by an oxygen tank explosion in 1971, Godard repeatedly expressed his hope that all the astronauts die in space. And when he learned in 1984 that his former friend and longtime rival François Truffaut was dying of a brain tumor, Godard was practically giddy. "That's what happens if you read so many bad books," he clucked.

KUNG PHOOEY

Nobody expects Godard's movies to connect with a mass audience. They're much too avant-garde for that. But even some fellow filmmakers find his work a little tough to digest. Ingmar Bergman once called Godard's work "mind-numbingly boring."

"I've never gotten anything out of his movies," declared the Swedish auteur. "They have felt constructed, faux intellectual, and completely dead. Cinematographically uninteresting and infinitely boring. Godard is a fucking bore." Werner Herzog was less profane, but even more cutting. "Someone like Jean-Luc Godard is for me intellectual counterfeit money when compared to a good kung-fu film," he sniffed.

FRANÇOIS TRUFFAUT

FEBRUARY 6, 1932–OCTOBER 21, 1984

NATIONALITY:
FRENCH

ASTROLOGICAL SIGN:
AQUARIUS

MAJOR FILMS:
THE 400 BLOWS (1959), *JULES AND JIM* (1962)

WORDS OF WISDOM:
"FILM LOVERS ARE SICK PEOPLE."

He may not have been the brightest star in the firmament of world cinema, but no great director loved film—or appreciated its rich history—quite as much as François Truffaut. Decades before Quentin Tarantino made the fanboy/filmmaker cool again, Truffaut went from a Hitchcock-obsessed ragamuffin slipping into the movie palaces of occupied Paris to an international auteur beloved by cinephiles everywhere. To mass audiences, he'll always have a place of honor as that French scientist guy from *Close Encounters of the Third Kind*.

The bastard son of a Parisian wanton, Truffaut never knew his biological father. His mother and his new stepfather, architectural draftsman Roland Truffaut, essentially abandoned him to the care of his maternal grandmother until he was ten years old. By the time the three of them were reunited, the Germans had occupied Paris. The Truffauts all lived together in cramped quarters in Pigalle, the city's red-light district. It was there that little François first acquired his lifelong fascination with prostitutes, who would become key players several of his films.

Home life wasn't happy for the young Truffaut. In fact, it was miserable. He didn't share his parents' obsessive enthusiasm for mountain climbing and was often left behind with relatives while they went off on weekend climbing excursions. "I can still remember them returning, wearing shorts and carrying knapsacks on their backs," Truffaut remarked years later. Although the neighbors regarded the Truffauts as harmless kooks, François took a less charitable view. "My parents are no more than human beings to me," he wrote. "It is mere chance that they happen to be my father and mother, which is why they mean no more to me than strangers."

Alone all the time and desperate for an outlet, he found one at the local movie theater. He would sneak in without paying and plant himself in the front row to immerse himself more fully in the cinematic experience. Sitting so close to the screen sometimes made him sick, but for Truffaut that only heightened the sensation. He made good on a vow to watch three movies every day. By the time he turned thirteen, he had seen more than four thousand films. He maintained a diary of all the movies he watched, with notes on his favorite directors. American films fascinated him the most, and he became a passionate fan of Alfred Hitchcock, Howard Hawks, and other pioneers of Hollywood's Golden Age.

The hours of solitary study soon gave way to the desire to organize. When Truffaut was a teenager, he stole his stepfather's typewriter, sold it, and used the proceeds to bankroll his new *ciné-club*, a floating bull session for fellow movie lovers. Enraged by the theft, Roland Truffaut committed the boy to a juvenile detention center as punishment. Incarcerated for six months, Truffaut tried to continue his cinema studies in the hoosegow. He asked his parents to bring him jars of jam—and all his files on Charlie Chaplin and Orson Welles. Officials at the House of D didn't know what to make of the movie-mad teen. At first they diagnosed him with "psychomotor instability with perverse tendencies." Later they determined that his instability was the consequence of his traumatic family environment. A sympathetic counselor managed to wrangle Truffaut an introduction to the eminent French film critic André Bazin, an association that would later pay big dividends for him.

First, however, Truffaut had to conquer his personal demons. "I don't gaze at the sky for long, for when I look back down again the world seems horrid to me," he observed around this time. In 1950, at age eighteen, he attempted suicide by slashing his arm twenty-five times with a razor. Not long after, Truffaut enlisted in the French army and was shipped off to Saigon. But he was comically ill-suited for a soldier's life. He realized his mistake and tried to desert, was caught, and thrown into a military jail. Discharged on grounds of "unstable character," he returned to Paris and tried to commit suicide a second time.

Only a job in the movies would save him. Truffaut used his connection to Bazin to secure a gig writing criticism for the influential film journal *des Cahiers du cinema*. Before long, he was pretty much running the joint, cutting a swath through the French film world of the 1950s with his insightful and acerbic reviews. He could have had a long and successful career as a film critic, but he longed to make his own feature. In 1959, he did, channeling all the loneliness and despair of his Parisian childhood into the semi-autobiographical masterpiece *The 400 Blows*. That film earned Truffaut the best

director nod at Cannes and helped usher in the wildly influential moviemaking movement known as the French new wave.

Truffaut went on to direct twenty-five films in all—five short of the personal goal he had set for himself at the outset of his career. *Jules and Jim* and the Academy Award–winning *Day for Night* garnered the most international acclaim, and the diminutive director's infectious enthusiasm for film and outspoken evangelism on behalf of auteurist cinema inspired a generation of moviemakers—including Steven Spielberg, who gave Truffaut his most famous acting role, as the French UFOlogist Claude LaCombe in *Close Encounters of the Third Kind*. In 1983, soon after completing his final film, Truffaut was diagnosed with brain cancer. He died on October 21, 1984.

* * *

LITTLE LOVE MACHINE
Truffaut was a pathological womanizer, known for having one of the most active casting couches in the history of cinema. Jeanne Moreau, Julie Christie, Fanny Ardant, and Jacqueline Bisset were just a few of the gorgeous leading ladies he took back to his boudoir over the years. For Truffaut, there were no rules to the mating game. He slept with glamorous actresses as well as

FRANÇOIS TRUFFAUT SPENT TIME IN MILITARY JAIL AFTER DESERTING THE FRENCH ARMY BUT WAS SOON DISCHARGED ON THE GROUNDS OF "UNSTABLE CHARACTER."

budget-priced prostitutes. He carried on affairs with both Catherine Deneuve *and* her older sister Françoise Dorléac. Nor was age any barrier to his amorous ambitions. He bedded both the nineteen-year-old Claude Jade, costar of *Stolen Kisses*, and the seventeen-year-old Marie-France Pisier, star of *Love at Twenty*. Much of this tomcatting went on under the nose of his wife, Madeleine Morgenstern, who finally pulled the plug on their six-year-old marriage in 1965.

Truffaut's Gallic good looks and reputation as a genius only go so far in explaining his luck with the ladies. The 5'6'' Casanova was known to be extremely shy and had a habit of biting his nails in the company of women, which they evidently found irresistibly charming. It also helped that Truffaut hated the company of his own gender. "I wouldn't consider having dinner with a man," he once said. "I have this in common with Hitler and Sartre. I can't stand male companionship in the evening. For me, the evening means private life, in a private place."

WHEN AUTEURS COLLIDE

They are the twin titans of the French new wave, and they were once the fastest of friends, but Truffaut and Jean-Luc Godard turned on each other with a vengeance in the 1970s. The bad blood started flowing when Godard—who had rebranded himself as a Maoist revolutionary—derided Truffaut in print as "a businessman in the morning and a poet in the afternoon," that is, a total sellout. "He made one film that truly expressed him, *The 400 Blows*," the *Breathless* auteur continued. "Afterward, he merely told stories." For a time, Truffaut held his return fire, but after Godard savaged his 1973 film *Day for Night* and branded him a "liar," the aggrieved director shot back. In a letter to his former friend, he wrote: "I've always felt that true militants are like cleaning women, performing a thankless, daily, necessary task. But you, you're like Ursula Andress, you make a four-minute appearance, just enough time for the cameras to flash, and then you disappear again, trailing clouds of self-serving mystery." A few years later, Truffaut suggested a good title for Godard's next autobiographical film: *Once a Shit, Always a Shit*.

DEAR OLD DAD

In a plot worthy of the American film noir movies he loved so much, Truffaut once hired a private investigator to locate his biological father, who had abandoned his mother shortly before his birth in 1932. The man turned out to be a married Jewish dentist from a small town in the east of France (an interesting development, since one of Truffaut's close friends was the film critic and outspoken anti-Semite Lucien Rebatet, who had called for Jews to be expelled from the French motion picture industry during World War II). Having found his long-lost papa, Truffaut briefly stalked the man but never actually confronted him—out of respect for his stepfather, his wife later said.

THE CRITIC

Truffaut's early film criticism was so influential that it earned him the sobriquet "The Gravedigger of French Cinema." The bilious tastemaker was even banned from the 1958 Cannes Film Festival, for fear of the damage he might do with his poison pen. And although he gave up full-time criticism once he started making his own pictures, Truffaut never shied away from expressing his opinion. Nor was his venom reserved only for French films. Among the American directors he assailed over his years in the spotlight:

Robert Altman, whose direction on *M*A*S*H* Truffaut derided as "disastrous." Altman, he railed, "never once, throughout the entire picture, put the camera in the right place."

Norman Jewison, whose Academy Award–nominated work on *In the Heat of the Night* Truffaut found "absurd." "There was no need whatsoever for Norman Jewison to do all those zoom shots on the red taillights of that automobile," the Frenchman complained.

Mike Nichols, whose overuse of Simon and Garfunkel tunes ruined *The Graduate*, in Truffaut's opinion. "What bothered me the most . . . was the constant interruption of the drama with all that music," he kvetched.

Of Arthur Penn's *Bonnie and Clyde*, Truffaut was more complimentary (perhaps because he was one of Warren Beatty's first choices to direct the picture). But he still would have preferred another leading man, "because Beatty had no genuine innocence, no authenticity." And don't get Truffaut started on Stanley Kubrick's *2001: A Space Odyssey* which, the Gallic genius admitted, "I just didn't understand. There was too much machinery; all those yellow and red buttons. . . . I must admit that I have an anti-scientific mind. It bores me to look at rockets."

ROMAN POLANSKI

AUGUST 18, 1933–

NATIONALITY:
POLISH

ASTROLOGICAL SIGN:
LEO

MAJOR FILMS:
ROSEMARY'S BABY (1968), *CHINATOWN* (1974)

WORDS OF WISDOM:

"THE BEST FILMS ARE BECAUSE OF NOBODY BUT THE DIRECTOR."

He eluded the Nazis, managed to avoid being butchered by the Manson family, and has stayed just outside the reach of the long arm of the L.A. law since 1978. Roman Polanksi must be either the luckiest or the unluckiest man on the planet. Violence and scandal seem to follow him wherever he goes, but at least he manages to keep on going.

The child of a Polish father and a Russian mother, Polanski was actually born in France—a minor fact of biography that would turn out to be quite important later on. When he was four, his parents returned to Poland. They would have been better off staying in France. When the Nazis invaded Poland, Mr. and Mrs. Polanski were sent to separate concentration camps. Little Roman managed to survive the war—in part by posing as a German. The plush movie houses in which the occupying German officers luxuriated became his place of refuge as well. After the war, with the Communists now in charge in Poland, he enrolled in the imposingly named State Film College to pursue his dream of becoming a director. By the time he turned thirty, he had directed several short films and a debut feature, *Knife in the Water*, which became an international sensation. The film received an Oscar nomination for best foreign film and afforded Polanski the chance to leave Poland for the less repressive milieu of the West.

During the 1960s, Polanski took full advantage of his newfound freedom. He became a fixture on the "Swinging London" scene alongside Twiggy, the Beatles, Peter Max, and Mary Quant. With his elfin good looks and infectious charm, Polanski was something of a babe magnet—and he took advantage of his opportunities with the avidity you might expect from someone who had grown up amid such privation. "Roman was a kind of mascot for us," said the Fab Four's leader, John Lennon. "The kid who runs out in front of the team at the Cup Final." When he wasn't partying with the rock 'n' roll elite, Polanski made three well-received English-language films while living in London and capped off the decade with his first Hollywood feature, the Satanic horror classic *Rosemary's Baby*. He had a new wife, actress Sharon

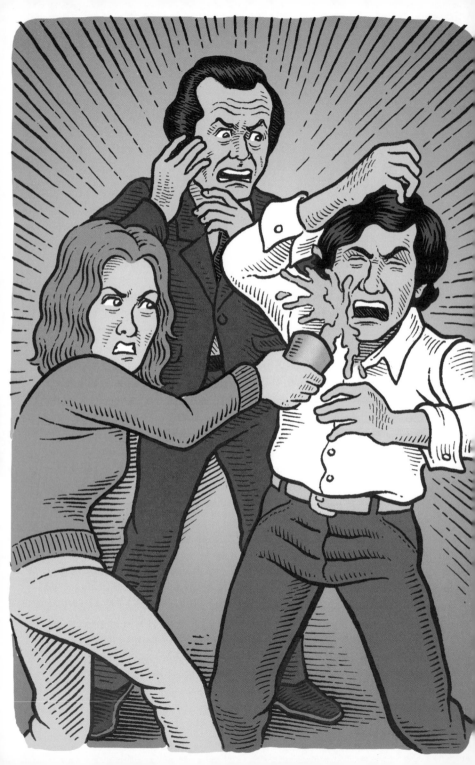

Tate, a baby on the way, and all the drugs he desired. What more could a little Pole want of life?

Polanski's Hollywood dream turned into a nightmare on August 9, 1969, when Tate and three of their friends were brutally murdered by members of Charles Manson's "family" at the couple's home in Los Angeles. The killing devastated Polanski—who was in London prepping a movie at the time—as did the accompanying media firestorm in which the blonde starlet's fate was blamed on his debauched lifestyle. Desperate to escape the spotlight, Polanski temporarily relocated to Europe and filmed a gory version of *Macbeth* that many cinephiles consider his personal response to the Manson tragedy. His final Hollywood film, 1974's *Chinatown*, was even darker—if not quite as bloody—and it seemed likely that the post-Manson Polanski would continue on in this vein, had the little matter of a 1977 child rape charge not put the kibosh on his career in America. After fleeing to France, which is not legally obligated to extradite its own citizens, Polanki continued to make movies. Some, like the outlandish swashbuckler epic *Pirates*, seemed to indicate he had lost his marbles, whereas other, more recent efforts, such as 2002's *The Pianist*

THINGS ONCE BECAME SO TENSE BETWEEN ROMAN POLANSKI AND FAYE DUNAWAY THAT THE LEADING LADY FLUNG A CUP OF URINE INTO THE FILMMAKER'S FACE.

(which earned him his first Best Director Oscar) suggest a filmmaker still capable of surprising, disquieting, and moving his audience.

'LUDE BEHAVIOR

Not since Charlie Chaplin's heyday has Hollywood gotten so worked up over a director having sex with a minor as it did in the summer of 1977, when Polanski went on trial for the statutory rape of a thirteen-year-old aspiring actress and model named Samantha Gailey. The facts of the case are sordid, even by Tinseltown standards. Polanski, who had a well-known weakness for underage girls, was commissioned by French *Vogue* to guest edit a special issue devoted to the subject of jailbait. (One imagines the director dropping to his knees and

thanking his maker for the good fortune to live in a world where such opportunities existed.) He found the perfect subject in Gailey, a sandy-haired teen
eager to break into show business and thrilled that someone as eminent as
Polanski would want to photograph her. After taking a few topless test shots in
the Hollywood hills, Polanski arranged for Gailey to accompany him on a full-
on unchaperoned photo shoot inside Jack Nicholson's mansion. (The antic
Oscar winner was conveniently away on a skiing trip at the time.) After plying
her with champagne and taking several shots of her nude in Nicholson's
whirlpool bath, Polanski decided to drop trou himself and join her in the tub.
A grossed-out Gailey feigned an asthma attack to get away from the pint-sized
Pole, but Polanski merely fed her half a Quaalude to calm her nerves and suggested they move into the bedroom. Once there, Polanski had intercourse with
the girl, performed oral sex, and repeatedly sodomized her despite being told
to stop. He then drove her home, warning her not to tell her mother or her
boyfriend what had happened.

The next night, Polanski was arrested—by Detective Philip Vannatter,
as it happens, who would go on to become the lead investigator in the O. J.
Simpson murder case seventeen years later. Charged with child rape, the unapologetic director faced the prospect of spending the rest of his life behind
bars, not to mention the ruination of his movie career. As the details of the
incident became public, an anti-Polanski media feeding frenzy ensued.
"Pole, on Perv Charge, Faces Fifty Years," blared one headline. Amazingly,
Polanski's legal team was able to plea bargain to a lesser charge and a ninety-
day stay in state prison. Polanski wound up spending only forty-two days behind bars. At the conclusion of his sentence, Polanski was supposed to be
set free, but he soon got wind that the judge in his case had changed his
mind. "I'll send him away forever," Judge Laurence Rittenband vowed. That
was all Polanski needed to hear. On January 31, 1978, the scandal-scarred
filmmaker drove his Mercedes to L.A. International Airport and boarded a
plane to London, never to return. Fearful that he would be extradited back
to the United States, he quickly relocated to Paris, where he has maintained
a residence ever since. For the next three decades, stateside authorities
seemed reluctant to pursue an extradition proceeding against Polanski, who
would have been subject to arrest the second he set foot outside France.
That all changed on September 26, 2009, when the doll-size fugitive from
justice was nabbed by Swiss police at Zurich Airport while en route to an international film festival to pick up a lifetime achievement award. Polanski's

ensuing detention in Switzerland reignited a raging debate over the 30-year-old case, with many in the film community—including Woody Allen and Martin Scorsese—lining up to sign a petition demanding his immediate release.

OY, FAYE!

Other than Adolf Hitler, Charles Manson, and possibly Judge Rittenband, no one caused Polanski quite as much heartburn as Faye Dunaway. The *Chinatown* leading lady was a "gigantic pain in the ass," to use the director's own words, demonstrating "certifiable proof of insanity" with her diva-like behavior. She was obsessed with her hair and makeup, Polanski contends, and went though so much lip balm that the crew gave her an oversized tube of the stuff as a going-away present. Even more distressing, according to several eyewitnesses, was Dunaway's personal hygiene. She urinated in her trash basket and refused to flush her own toilet, demanding that one of the teamsters on the set do it for her. Moody and temperamental, Dunaway would also periodically stop shooting to ask Polanski what her character's "motivation" was—actor speak for, "I have no idea what I'm doing." "Say the fucking words!" Polanski exploded after one such interruption. "Your salary is your motivation!"

For her part, Dunaway found Polanski boorish and dictatorial. She later charged that the director's treatment "bordered on sexual harassment." At one point, things got so tense that Dunaway flung a paper cup filled with urine into Polanski's face. "You cunt, that's piss!" Polanski shrieked. "Yes, you little putz," Dunaway replied. Toward the end of filming, she and the director weren't even speaking. Polanski relayed all his direction through her agent, Freddie Fields, while Dunaway in turn would instruct Fields to "ask Mr. Polanski what my character does now."

In the end, Polanski got the last laugh. In his 1984 memoir, *Roman by Polanski*, underneath a grisly photograph of Dunaway's death scene in *Chinatown*—in which her character is shot through the eye—he inserted the caption "Farewell to Faye Dunaway." They never worked together again.

CONDÉ NASTY

Whatever happened to the statute of limitations? In 2005, Polanksi successfully sued Condé Nast Publications and *Harper's* magazine editor Lewis Lapham for libel over an anecdote that appeared in a 2002 issue of *Vanity Fair* magazine, relating a dinner conversation from August 1969. Got all that?

The incident in question purportedly took place at the famed New York City celebrity hangout Elaine's, shortly after Sharon Tate's murder. According to Lapham, one night a randy Polanski sauntered over to his table and started aggressively hitting on a beautiful Norwegian model dining with him. "Fascinated by his performance, I watched as he slid a hand inside her thigh and began a long, honeyed spiel which ended with the promise: 'And I will make another Sharon Tate out of you,'" Lapham reported. The fact that this entire scene was playing out while Polanski was supposedly grieving for his dead wife lent an extra note of tastelessness to the affair. There was only one problem with Lapham's story: It was all a lie. Using testimony from actress Mia Farrow, the Norwegian model, and Polanski himself via videoconference, the director's legal team was able to prove conclusively that he was nowhere near Elaine's on the night in question. Polanski was awarded £50,000 damages, and *Vanity Fair* editor Graydon Carter was left sputtering about the unfairness of British libel laws.

CALIFORNIA DREAMIN'

Before the police rounded up Charles Manson and the members of his "family," Polanski drew up his own list of suspects in the murder of Sharon Tate. It included several jealous husbands whose wives Polanski had philandered with— including "Papa John" Phillips of the seminal sixties folk-rock group the Mamas and the Papas. Polanski had enjoyed a one-night stand with "Mama" Michelle Phillips and thought Papa John might have killed Tate in a jealous rage. To test out his theory, Polanski even had Phillips' car checked for blood and hair samples. He also threatened the folkie's life with a meat cleaver.

FEELING CAVITY'S PULL

Maybe the prospect of Polanski returning to Hollywood isn't such a good idea after all. His most recent foray into mainstream American moviemaking came in 2007, when he played a small role as a bumbling French police inspector in the lowbrow buddy comedy *Rush Hour 3*. Among other indignities, the part called for Polanski to perform a full-body cavity search on stars Chris Tucker and Jackie Chan. And for this he *wasn't* prosecuted?

WOODY ALLEN

DECEMBER 1, 1935–

NATIONALITY:
AMERICAN

ASTROLOGICAL SIGN:
SAGITTARIUS

MAJOR FILMS:
ANNIE HALL (1977), *MANHATTAN* (1979), *HANNAH AND HER SISTERS* (1986)

WORDS OF WISDOM:

*"I AM A LOW-CULTURE PERSON.
I PREFER WATCHING BASEBALL WITH
A BEER AND SOME MEATBALLS."*

Like his idol Ingmar Bergman, Woody Allen has always preferred to focus on the negative aspects of his life. "There was a dark cloud over my head in the cradle," he once cracked. Although he had his share of hardships growing up (as Allan Stewart Konigsberg in Midwood, Brooklyn), his early life wasn't nearly as dismal as he would later paint it. In grade school, for instance, he wasn't the scrawny, timid loser he has often portrayed himself as, but an outgoing jock best known for doing magic tricks, loafing in class, and sneaking out to the movies in the middle of the day. What little drama there was in the Konigsberg household was provided by Allan's bickering parents, Nettie and Martin. "They stayed together out of spite," Woody Allen would later recall. "Did everything short of exchange gunfire."

While still in high school, Allan turned his way with a joke into a paid gig providing gags to New York newspaper columnists. He flunked out of New York University in 1953, ending a brief inglorious academic career in which he rarely showed up to class, and instead pursued a job as a television writer, under the less Jewish-sounding name Woody Allen. Within a few years he was earning $1,500 a week as a staff writer on *Caesar's Hour*. He also embarked on the first of his three marriages, to neighborhood girl Harlene Rosen. She quickly became comic grist for his increasingly popular stand-up act and, in 1962, the beneficiary of his alimony payments. It was the beginning of a long string of rocky romantic relationships for the insecure but erotically voracious funnyman.

In the 1960s, Allen grew into one of America's biggest comedy celebrities. He churned out hit plays and droll *New Yorker* essays, appeared incessantly on *The Tonight Show*, and even made the cover of *Life* magazine. A second tempestuous marriage, to actress Louise Lasser, wheezed to a predictable conclusion in 1969, around the time Allen was first starting to make his mark in feature films. Between 1965 and 1975 he wrote, cowrote, or directed a string of anarchic comedies that won him a sizable box-office following. Later derided in one of his scripts as "the early, funny ones," slapstick-heavy films like *Bananas* and *Sleeper* soon gave way to more artistically ambitious fare centered on themes of contemporary romance and relationships. *Annie Hall* swept the Oscars in 1977, and 1979's *Manhattan* established him as the tribune of upper-middle-class neurotic intellectuals everywhere.

In the 1980s and '90s, Allen continued to churn out smart, sophisticated comedies (and the occasional turgid drama) at the rate of about one per year. Increasingly they served as star vehicles for his new romantic companion, Mia Farrow, with whom he adopted two children and produced one biological child throughout their twelve-year relationship. It all ended in 1992, when Farrow discovered nude Polaroids of her twenty-one-year-old adopted daughter, Soon-Yi Previn, on the mantelpiece in Allen's apartment. It turned out that Allen and Previn had been having a sexual relationship for months and continued to do so even after the affair became public. There ensued a lengthy and sordid court battle in which Farrow successfully sued for custody of their children. (According to Allen, she also threatened to kill him and sent him a Valentine's Day card pierced with knives and skewers.) When Farrow charged that Allen had molested the couple's seven-year-old daughter, Allen countersued. A judge later dismissed the molestation charges, but banned Allen from seeing his own children and, for good measure, branded him "the most opaque of narcissists."

The rotten publicity did little to slow Allen's movie career. (He later called Farrow's discovery of his nude photos of Soon-Yi "one of the great pieces of luck in my life.") After a brief surge in popularity in his late-seventies heyday, Allen had never been a big box-office draw anyway, and his small but loyal audience of urban sophisticates continued to come out to see his films. He married Soon-Yi in 1997 and continued to pursue his passions of making movies, playing jazz clarinet, and attending New York Knicks games, in approximately that order. Although critics have derided the middling quality of some of his later work (the concept for one such turkey, 2002's *Hollywood Ending*, was literally scribbled on the back of a matchbook), A-list actors still clamor to work with a man widely considered one of the few true geniuses working in contemporary cinema.

* * *

CASTING GROUCH

Allen is notorious for his brief, unconventional—and sometimes downright weird—casting calls, which can unsettle even the most experienced actors. When veteran writer, actor, and voice-over performer Stanley Ralph Ross tried out for the part of Sears Swiggles, an interior decorator in the 1973 film *Sleeper*, Allen insisted on conducting the audition from a separate room, forcing Ross to read his lines to him from the other side of a half-closed door. Ross got the part. Christopher Walken's interview for *Annie Hall* was less bizarre, but just as unnerving. "I was called into an office," Walken says. "Woody Allen sat there. I don't remember that he ever said anything. And then I was in his movie." Dianne Wiest recalls that her au-

AMONG WOODY ALLEN'S MANY NEUROSES IS A DEEP FEAR OF INSECTS. HE HAS BEEN KNOWN TO WEAR A BEEKEEPER'S MASK TO PREVENT BEING STUNG.

dition for *Hannah and Her Sisters* lasted all of thirty seconds. "He looked at me, said hello, asked someone to take a Polaroid, thanked me very much, and I was shown the door," Wiest remembers. "When I came out, the woman due after me was still doing the same thing as when I went in. She was shocked. . . . But that's how it is. My agent had warned me. Not hers. She was stunned." Goldie Hawn's interview for *Everyone Says I Love You* was held at Allen's private screening room, a location he prefers because it allows him to establish dominance over the performer. Typically, Allen likes to arrive first, so he can deny the actor the most comfortable seat, but in Hawn's case, she beat him to the couch. Allen responded by giving her the silent treatment. "I was just eating the air in the room, because he was saying nothing," said Hawn—a fairly common Allen technique, according to other actors who have auditioned for him. When Hawn attempted to regale the director with stories about her recent travels, Allen cut her off. "Could you leave the room, so I could talk?" he quipped. British actress Rebecca Hall "auditioned" over the course of several years and didn't even know it. At their first meeting, the painfully shy Hall complimented Allen on his green sweater. "Yes, it's for St. Patrick's Day," Allen replied. End of interview. A few years passed, during which Allen made several films in England—none of them starring Hall. Then in 2007 she returned to try to land a role in *Vicky Cristina Barcelona*. This time the meeting took place in the doorway of Allen's office. "He looked at me quizzically and said, 'Have we met before?' and I went, 'Yeah, I remember.' He said, 'Can you do an American accent?' I went 'Yeah, I can.' Then he went, 'OK, bye.'" Two weeks later, Hall got the part.

SEPTEMBER SONG

Allen's odd treatment of actors doesn't end with the casting call. On the set, he can be a pain in the neck to work with. In the words of Alan Alda: "Woody throws you into the Mixmaster and turns on the switch." On occasion, that Mixmaster chops you out of the movie entirely. In 1987, Allen elected to recast his gloomy melodrama *September*—twice—including once after the film was completed. Christopher Walken was originally cast as Peter, the struggling writer who spurns the affections of his Vermont neighbor in favor of her married best friend. Before shooting began, Allen dumped him, deciding he was "too sexy" for the part, and replaced him with playwright and actor Sam Shepard. When Allen watched the finished film, however, he had some new reservations. "I saw many mistakes and character things I could do better," he groused. "I didn't need certain speeches, and certain things needed to be said that weren't said." Rather than release what he considered a substandard product, Allen opted to reshoot the entire film with a new cast. Sam Waterston replaced Shepard, with other actors plugged into virtually all the key roles. (Some of the new casting choices were more inspired than others; rumpled schlub Jack Warden awkwardly stepped into the role of a brilliant physicist, originally played by Denholm Elliott, for example.) Critics reacted tepidly to the version that ended up playing to empty theaters in December of 1987—although Allen remained nonplussed. "The fact is, I'd like to shoot *September* a third time," he threatened.

FEAR MONGER

To call Woody Allen phobic would be an understatement. Among the director's many pet peeves and neurotic fears: boats, planes, sunlight, darkness, dogs, deer, the sound of crickets chirping, driving, bridges, and enclosed spaces. (Allen reportedly once took a hundred mile detour just to keep from having to pass through a tunnel.) Elevators freak him out. He has admitted to sometimes buying a newspaper prior to a brief elevator ride "because I didn't want to be alone with my thoughts in the elevator for thirty seconds." He so hates to ride in the contraptions that he forced stars Christina Ricci and Jason Biggs to climb three flights of stairs to appear at a news conference prior to a screening of his 2003 film *Anything Else*. Bright colors also unnerve Allen—one of the reasons he always wears drab earth tones in his films. When outdoors, Allen has been known to walk around in a beekeeper's mask to protect himself from insects. But germs are by far his main bugaboo. He is so paranoid about microbial invaders that he forbade then-girlfriend Mia Farrow from using dishes, demanding that she use disposable paper plates and cups instead. He refused to sleep at her house until she installed a separate shower and then declared that he couldn't use it because the drain was in the middle of the tub rather than off to the side, putting his precious feet closer to dirty water. Farrow's penchant for adopting infants only exacerbated Allen's germophobia. By his own admission, he would flee Farrow's apartment whenever she had to change a baby's diaper. And when Farrow broached the subject of switching from polyester to cotton bedsheets, Allen needed several weeks of therapy before agreeing to the change.

DAMNED SPOT

Not surprisingly, Allen is also a first-class hypochondriac. Toward the end of his relationship with Mia Farrow, he stopped having sex with her, citing at various times his fears of contracting Lyme disease, chronic fatigue syndrome, and AIDS. (For her part, Farrow claimed that Allen was merely impotent.) According to actress Penelope Cruz, Allen fled the set of *Vicky Cristina Barcelona* on the day of her on-screen sex scene with Scarlett Johansson to go see his dermatologist after discovering a spot on his hand.

GOING BANANAS

Then there are the Allen compulsions that are neither phobic nor hypochondriacal, but merely strange. For instance, he has the same thing for breakfast every morning: Cheerios, a banana, and prune juice—the banana sliced into precisely seven segments before being put into the cereal. For lunch, he demands tuna salad on white bread—no tomatoes, no lettuce, no substitutions. He harbors a hatred of animals so pronounced that he once flew into a frothing rage after an overzealous fan left a bunny rabbit with his doorman. In 2008, the New York Bird Club issued a public call for Allen to "atone" for his "racial slurs" against the city's pigeon population by making a personal appearance at the first-ever National Pigeon Day. Allen, who once called pigeons "rats with wings" in one of his scripts, declined the invitation.

REBEL REBBE

The Mia Farrow custody proceeding wasn't Allen's first—or last—visit to a courtroom. In fact, he's been quite litigious—especially when it comes to protecting his likeness from use by advertisers. In 1985, he successfully sued a national video retailer for using a Woody Allen lookalike in an ad. The next year, he won a $425,000 judgment against Men's World Outlet, a discount clothier that tried the same trick. You'd think such companies would have learned their lesson, but in 2008 the hipster casualwear purveyors at American Apparel tried a new tack: plastering billboards and online ads with an image of Allen dressed in Hasidic garb from a fantasy sequence in *Annie Hall*. "Woody Allen is our spiritual leader," a representative for the edgy schmatte seller explained to the Jewish newspaper *The Forward*. Allen was not amused. He sought $10 million in a lawsuit declaring the unauthorized Web and outdoor displays "especially egregious and damaging." In 2009 the two sides settled out of court for $5 million.

FRANCIS FORD COPPOLA

APRIL 7, 1939–

NATIONALITY:
AMERICAN

ASTROLOGICAL SIGN:
ARIES

MAJOR FILMS:
THE GODFATHER (1972), *THE GODFATHER: PART II* (1974), *APOCALYPSE NOW* (1979)

WORDS OF WISDOM:
"I PROBABLY HAVE GENIUS. BUT NO TALENT."

One of the seminal directors of the 1970s, Francis Ford Coppola seems in some ways a curious amalgam of his most famous characters. Like *The Godfather's* Don Vito Corleone, he was a benevolent patron within his community—a boy genius whose early success paved the way for a generation of film-school-bred American auteurs. Like Kurtz, the mad colonel at the center of *Apocalypse Now*, he was a self-indulgent, self-destructive figure—laid low by his own excesses and appetites.

Coppola was born in Detroit, Michigan, on April 7, 1939. His mother, Italia, used to act in movies. His father, Carmine, was a one-time concert flautist who had fallen on hard times and was reduced to playing the piccolo at a local race track. A miserable man who never lived up to his potential and "hated anybody who was successful," to use Francis's own words, Carmine longed to compose symphonies, though he usually had to settle for whatever local radio gigs came his way. Francis's middle name was bestowed in honor of automaker Henry Ford, whose namesake company sponsored one of the weekly shows on which Carmine Coppola performed.

Not long after Francis' birth, Carmine took a job playing for the NBC Orchestra in New York City. The family moved to Queens, where Francis and his sister Tallie (later known as actress Talia Shire) hoped to follow their parents into show business and redeem the promise of their aborted careers. Acting seemed an unlikely path for the ungainly Francis. As a child, Coppola was skinny and physically awkward, with a cleft chin, jug ears, and Coke-bottle glasses. He fared poorly at school and had health problems that killed any hope of a social life. At age nine, he contracted polio while on a Cub Scout trip and spent the better part of a year in bed, paralyzed on his left side. Nobody would come to see him. During his convalescence, he studied puppetry, watched television, and lost himself in the fantasy world of his own imagination. After recovering, he started to put some of those visions on film, using an 8-millimeter camera and a tape recorder.

At Long Island's Hofstra College (today known as Hofstra University), Coppola began to train more formally in film and theater. Becoming a director so consumed him that he once sold his own car to pay for a 16-millimeter camera. After graduation, he moved to California to continue his studies at the UCLA Film School. (One of his classmates was Jim Morrison, future lead singer of the Doors.) A professor's recommendation led Coppola into the employ of B-movie mogul Roger Corman, who put Coppola to work editing, writing, and generally helping out on his films. In 1963, that association culminated in Coppola's mainstream directorial debut, the low-budget horror feature *Dementia 13*.

If Coppola's next film, *You're a Big Boy Now*, certified him as a young director of promise, then the calamitous big-budget musical *Finian's Rainbow* nearly smothered that promise in its cradle. Hollywood kept calling, however, and in 1970 Coppola won an Oscar for his screenplay on *Patton*. He was then handed the creative reins of a prestige adaptation of novelist Mario Puzo's Mafia potboiler *The Godfather*, a film that would add a best picture to the thirty-three-year-old director's mantel and gold-plate his reputation as a leading light of the 1970s generation of American directors.

Coppola milked that reputation for the rest of the decade, turning out such masterpieces as *The Godfather Part Two* and *The Conversation* and helping launch the career of pal George Lucas by producing the mega-hit *American Graffiti*. Away from the set, he adopted an increasingly luxe lifestyle in which he sashayed about his sprawling Northern California compound wearing nothing but a caftan, collecting original works by Warhols and rare Enrico Caruso records, and occasionally pointed to a large building and said, "I'd like to buy that." He devoted an entire room in his mansion to electric trains and was so obsessed with toys that his friends dubbed him "FAO Coppola."

The good life came crashing down with the release of *Apocalypse Now* in 1979. Although it was undoubtedly an artistic triumph, the hallucinatory Vietnam War epic ran way over budget, nearly bankrupted the studio, and became Exhibit A in the case against giving auteurs too much control over their projects. The interminable Philippine shoot nearly drove Coppola irredeemably insane, and a string of self-financed bombs in the 1980s all but obliterated his life savings. A spectacularly ill-conceived third *Godfather* sequel, in which Coppola cast his untalented daughter Sofia in a key role, applied the final coat of formaldehyde to his artistic integrity in 1990. By the end of the decade, Coppola was a total burnout, reduced to taking on hack

work like *Jack* and John Grisham's *The Rainmaker* just to keep his burgeoning wine business afloat. As it turned out, Coppola's vineyards produced some mighty tasty wines, and in recent years the now seventysomething director has wisely chosen to channel his creative energies into stomping grapes, leaving others to assess his cinematic legacy.

✳   ✳   ✳

THE GODFATHER OF PORN

"The Wild, Wild West Has Never Been Wilder . . . Beautiful Babes . . . Bashful Cowboys!" That was the tagline plastered on posters for Coppola's 1962 soft-core porno film *Tonight for Sure*, a curious professional debut that the Oscar-winning director undoubtedly wishes had remained lost in the mists of time. The 69-minute nudie feature was actually an expanded version of a 12-minute short called *The Peeper*, which Coppola directed shortly after graduating from the UCLA film school. *The Peeper* chronicled the exploits of an ambitious Peeping Tom who strikes pervert gold when he discovers

> FRANCIS FORD COPPOLA HAS DIRECTED MANY CINEMATIC MASTERPIECES—BUT THE ONE YOU'VE PROBABLY NEVER SEEN IS HIS 3-D SOFT-PORN EPIC, *THE BELLBOY AND THE PLAYGIRLS*.

that a photographer is staging a naked photo shoot in the apartment next door. The hero employs a powerful telescope so that he can ogle the women's bare body parts with impunity. Coppola likened the short to a Tom and Jerry cartoon and was none too distressed when no one volunteered to distribute it. Then another group of filmmakers approached him with a proposition: integrate his Peeping Tom footage into *their* Western stag reel *Wide Open Spaces*, about a drunken cowboy who conks his head and starts seeing visions of naked women. Jazzed by the prospect of finally seeing his name on a feature film, Coppola agreed. The result was *Tonight for Sure*. In the finished picture, Coppola's voyeur and the lascivious cowboy compare notes about their experiences over drinks at a tawdry strip joint. The on-screen action was quite tame by contemporary standards. Coppola called the porno opus "an inane comedy, in which you saw a couple of boobs once in a while." Music for the dingy-looking venture was supplied by Coppola's father, Carmine (who wisely asked that he be billed as "Carmen"—presumably so that he could deny having participated).

Tonight for Sure might never have played outside of a Times Square grindhouse theater, but *someone* must have seen Coppola's soft-core debut, because he was soon offered a second porno project. This time the job entailed shooting new 3-D nudie footage and inserting it into an existing German film entitled *Mit Eva Fing die Sunde (Sin Began with Eve)*. The resulting film, now called *The Bellboy and the Playgirls*, followed a horny hotel bellhop as he used various ruses to sneak into a room full of lingerie models. The women were topless—all but one, a seventeen-year-old girl who claimed her father would kill her if he found out what she was doing. Coppola let her keep her bra on. "June is busting out all over!" screamed the posters for this one—a reference to the film's nominal "star," *Playboy* Playmate June Wilkinson. The tagline also boasted that Coppola's 3-D wizardry "puts a girl in your lap," although what else might end up in your lap is left to the imagination. Both *Tonight for Sure* and *The Bellboy and the Playgirls* were later released on video, to Coppola's considerable consternation.

APOCALYPSE ME

Colonel Kurtz wasn't the only person who lost his mind in the jungle. During production of *Apocalypse Now* in the Philippines, Coppola flipped his wig. The shoot was famously ill-starred. Typhoons, budget and scheduling snafus, and a heart attack suffered by leading man Martin Sheen were just some of the plagues that bedeviled Coppola's 1970s masterpiece. For a long time, the director seemed curiously oblivious to the disasters happening all around him. While his crew struggled with tropical disease and a desperate shortage of food, drinking water, and toilet facilities, Coppola decamped to a makeshift palace he had fashioned inside a dormant volcano. There he lived a life more suited to a Turkish pasha than a humble moviemaker from Queens. He imported the finest wines, gourmet food, stereo equipment, and Lalique crystal from San Francisco, and he had fresh pasta flown in every week from Italy. At one point he summoned one of the best chefs in Tokyo to prepare a side of Kobe beef for him—all while not paying many of the crew their daily meal stipends.

The high living didn't do much for Coppola's well-being—nor did his increasingly self-destructive behavior. The director smoked cigarettes and joints like they were going out of style. He brazenly cheated on his wife with his personal assistant. One day, in the middle of rehearsals, he suffered what appeared to be an epileptic seizure—falling to the floor and thrashing about while foaming at the mouth. Two days later he was back behind the camera as if nothing had happened. Friends began to fear he might be on the verge of suicide. Marlon Brando described Coppola during this period as "alternately depressed, nervous, and frantic."

After the shoot, the cause of the problem was finally discovered. Coppola was diagnosed with manic depression and prescribed lithium. But the drug made him nauseous, and he lived in fear that people in Hollywood would find out he was taking it. He made arrangements to have his prescriptions filled under the name "Kurtz." After four years, he quit taking it entirely and chalked up the entire episode to a "midlife crisis."

I'M BUSTED

Ostracized in Hollywood after the *Apocalypse Now* fiasco, Coppola went belly up financially by personally bankrolling the $25 million turd *One from the Heart* in 1982. By the time he made *The Outsiders*, the first of his S. E. Hinton adaptations, the following year, the once-flush filmmaker was flat broke. Actor Rob Lowe told *GQ* magazine that Coppola would literally be on the phone trying to keep the repo man from gaining access to his Napa Valley home while he was directing a scene. "I remember Francis directing me in a close-up while he was on the phone with his wife," Lowe said. "'Don't fucking open the door! Just tell them to go away. I'm sorry. . . . Action!' The next day, he said, 'Did you know I bought a sailboat?'"

MR. AMBASSADOR

In 1999, Coppola was named Honorary Ambassador to the United States from the Central American nation of Belize. The sun-worshipping director has owned property in Belize since 1981 and operates a successful chain of resort lodges there. The consular position does not require him to maintain Belizean citizenship and seems to have no official responsibilities, although he is entitled to refer to himself as "His Excellency Ambassador Francis Ford Coppola" in all Belize-related correspondence.

BRIAN DE PALMA

SEPTEMBER 11, 1940–

NATIONALITY:
AMERICAN

ASTROLOGICAL SIGN:
LEO

MAJOR FILMS:
CARRIE (1976), *DRESSED TO KILL* (1980), *SCARFACE* (1983)

WORDS OF WISDOM:

"I TRY TO GET AWAY WITH AS MUCH AS POSSIBLE UNTIL PEOPLE START LAUGHING AT IT."

His films have been called "perverse tales of voyeurism and violence," their plots likened to Hitchcock thrillers, brimming with psychosexual rage. All those descriptors could just as easily be applied to Brian De Palma's own early life, which provided the template—in some cases, literally—for many of his movies.

The youngest of three boys, De Palma grew up in the shadow of his older brothers, who were both brilliant and talented. His own mother called him "a mistake." His father was an orthopedic surgeon who was distant and disapproving and whom Brian rarely saw. Even as a toddler, De Palma was always looking for unique ways to garner attention. He used to bang his head repeatedly against the headboard of his crib until his old man would come into the room and sit with him. Known as "Dip," Dr. Anthony De Palma did provide something that would later prove invaluable when his youngest son started directing films: the opportunity to see free-flowing human blood and guts, close-up. "I've seen my father amputate legs and open people up," De Palma says. "So I was used to it at a young age."

When De Palma was five, his family settled in Philadelphia. He attended a private Quaker academy just outside the city and lived the quiet life of a tech nerd. "I was one of those science types who was always up in his room with all these parts," he has said. Much of his time was spent designing primitive computers and entering them into science fairs. In high school, De Palma won second prize in a National Science Fair for a project entitled "The Application of Cybernetics to the Solution Differential Equations." No matter how many ribbons he collected, however, he could never outdo his brother Bruce, the certified family genius, in his parents' eyes. Eventually he stopped trying.

The summer after graduating from high school, De Palma found another way to win his mother's approval: by helping her catch his father cheating with one of his nurses. The tech-savvy teenager spent several months spying on the randy surgeon with a reel-to-reel tape recorder, tapping the old man's phone in hopes of capturing an incriminating conversation. When that

didn't work, De Palma tried climbing a tree outside the doc's office to snap sneaky pictures of the lovebirds in the act. Finally he gave up on subtlety altogether and simply staged a commando-style raid on Dr. De Palma's compound. Armed with a .22 caliber rifle and a knife, De Palma broke into his dad's office demanding to know where the naughty nurse was. After a frantic search, he eventually found her cowering in a nightgown on the fourth floor. Mr. and Mrs. De Palma separated soon after. In 1980, De Palma used elements of this bizarre episode as the basis for his film *Home Movies*.

His work at home completed, De Palma left to attend Columbia University in New York City. He self-induced an asthma attack to avoid being inducted into the military during the Vietnam War. "I did have asthma, actually. But I really had a case when I went to the draft board. I could hardly breathe. I had taken everything in the world to make me . . . asthmatic." At age twenty-two, the fledgling filmmaker had his first serious run-in with the law. Distressed over a breakup with his girlfriend, he got drunk, stole a motorcycle, and started zooming through the streets of Manhattan. "Some cops pulled me over, and I was feeling a little self-destructive," De Palma recalls. "And I knocked one down.

> IT HASN'T BEEN ALL SEX AND GORE FOR BRIAN DE PALMA. THE DIRECTOR LEFT AN INDELIBLE MARK ON SCIENCE FICTION BY WRITING THE OPENING "CRAWL" FOR *STAR WARS*.

And they ran me down and shot me." Plugged once in the leg, De Palma spent the night in a hospital and several hours in jail. He ultimately pleaded guilty to grand larceny and assault and received a suspended sentence.

In the mid 1960s, De Palma started making experimental films in the style of the French new wave. Many starred one of his discoveries, Robert De Niro (or "Robert Denero" as he was billed in one early effort). One of their most successful collaborations, the 1968 antiwar comedy *Greetings*, was the first movie to receive an "X" rating for adult content. Although only the most dedicated downtown New York cinephiles can boast of having seen *Hi Mom!*, *Murder à la Mod*, or *Get to Know Your Rabbit* upon their release, the films did earn De Palma substantial indie cachet. Substantial Hollywood cash followed in the mid-seventies, as the auteur made the difficult transition to directing more mainstream fare. In 1976, the Stephen King adaptation *Carrie* was a huge hit and earned star Sissy Spacek an Academy Award nomination, and 1980's *Dressed to Kill* channeled the spirit of Alfred Hitchcock and helped revive Angie Dickinson's career. With their emphasis on gore, voyeurism, and transgressive sex, De Palma's early Hollywood films invariably profited from a lot of media scrutiny. The director became an easy target for public scolds and critics outraged by the amount of violence and nudity in American movies.

Never what you would call a consistent filmmaker, De Palma grew ever more maddeningly uneven in the 1980s, '90s, and into the new millennium. There were "popcorn movie" hits (*The Untouchables*, *Mission Impossible*) epic bombs (a misbegotten adaptation of Tom Wolfe's *Bonfire of the Vanities*), and scandalous oddities like the quasi-pornographic *Body Double* and the hyperviolent *Scarface*. Although De Palma may have shot his wad as a major director some time around the dawn of the Reagan era, he remains an artist of sufficient idiosyncrasy that moviegoers typically look forward with curious anticipation to his next big-screen project.

✳   ✳   ✳

MARTY, MEET BOB

Where would American movie history be without Brian De Palma? Besides making his own movies, he was the man who introduced Martin Scorsese to Robert De Niro, paving the way for one of the most fortuitous actor/director pairings of the 1970s, '80s, and '90s.

WHAT A KIDDER

In the early 1970s, De Palma had a passionate fling with actress Margot Kidder, who would go on to play Lois Lane in the *Superman* movie series. They were known for the frequency and intensity of their lovemaking—once going at it inside a closet at a friend's home. When they weren't having sex, they were matching wits across a chessboard. De Palma became obsessed with the game during the worldwide media frenzy over the Bobby Fischer–Boris Spassky chess match in 1972. He spent hours holed up in his Malibu beach house honing his game against producer Michael Phillips or screenwriter Paul Schrader. Eventually he taught Kidder how to play as well. Patience with the newcomer wasn't one of De Palma's virtues, however. Whenever Kidder made a move he considered unwise, he simply upended the board and dumped all the pieces in her lap.

WRITHE OF HER LIFE

Melanie Griffith fans can thank Brian De Palma for giving the actress her biggest break: the role of porn queen Holly Body in 1984's *Body Double*. To be fair, few actresses in Hollywood wanted to go anywhere near the role, which required them to simulate masturbation in front of the camera, so De Palma's choices were limited. For her audition, he asked Griffith to writhe suggestively for him. Whatever she did obviously piqued his interest, because he gave her the part and helped revive her flagging film career.

STAR MAN

It hasn't been all gore and sex for Brian De Palma. The director left an indelible mark on the science-fiction genre as well. In 1976, his good friend George Lucas asked him to audition and interview actors for an epic space opera he was making. The film turned out to be *Star Wars*. After the film was finished, Lucas came back to De Palma and asked him to help him write an opening "crawl" that would set up the events depicted in the movie. Thus, though he received no on-screen credit for his efforts, De Palma had a hand in composing one of the most famous roll-ups in movie history: "A long time ago in a galaxy far, far away . . . "

BOSS OF ME

De Palma wasn't the only big-time filmmaker to try his hand at directing a music video in the 1980s. Martin Scorsese lensed Michael Jackson's "Bad," of course, and Sam Peckinpah did what he could with Julian Lennon's execrable "Valotte." But De Palma may have scored the biggest coup of all when he helmed the clip for Bruce Springsteen's "Dancing in the Dark" in 1984. It was De Palma who came up with the video's simple but memorable concept: The Boss plucks a fan out of the crowd at one of his concerts and engages in an impromptu (if somewhat stiff and awkward) dance. The actress, Courtney Cox, went on to become a star on TV's *Friends*, the song went to number two on the *Billboard* charts, and De Palma received plaudits for the video. The only person who wasn't happy? Springsteen himself. He hated the clip, considering it contrived and phony.

Alice Guy-Blaché and Other Overlooked Women Directors

I t didn't start with Sofia Coppola—or Penny Marshall or even Yoko Ono. Women have been directing movies since the earliest days of the medium. Here are four pioneers on whose shoulders stand all subsequent female filmmakers.

ALICE GUY-BLACHÉ (1873–1968)
Major Films: *A Fool and His Money* (1912), *Matrimony's Speed Limit* (1913)
The world's first female film director, Alice Guy-Blaché was making pictures while D. W. Griffith was still figuring out how to crank the camera. From the time she completed her first movie in the late 1800s to the early 1920s, she directed more than 300 films and produced and wrote hundreds more. At her prolific peak she was churning out about two two-reelers a week. She was also one of the industry's first moguls. With her husband, Herbert Blaché, she founded Solax, the biggest pre-Hollywood studio in North America. A technical innovator, Guy-Blaché experimented with the integration of music and film and even developed some rudimentary special effects. With the advent of Hollywood and the demise of New Jersey as a moviemaking hub, she saw her fortunes decline and never made another movie after 1920.

LOIS WEBER (1881–1939)
Major Films: *The People Vs. John Doe* (1916), *The Blot* (1921)
Picking up where Alice Guy-Blaché had left off, Lois Weber became the first woman to direct a full-length feature when her big-screen adaptation of Shakespeare's *The Merchant of Venice* dropped in 1914. By that time, she already had a long list of shorts to her credit, and worked as an actress and writer to boot. Her specialty was the socially relevant melodrama. Over the years, she used film as a medium to address issues as varied as birth control, Christian Science, abortion, capital punishment, corruption in big busi-

ness, and racial intolerance. At the height of her fame, in 1916, she was one of the highest-paid directors in the world.

DOROTHY ARZNER (1900–1979)

Major Films: *The Wild Party* (1929), *The Bride Wore Red* (1937)

"There should be more of us directing," Dorothy Arzner once declared, and by "us" she could have been speaking of women or of male-identified lesbians who routinely dressed in men's suits and ties, for she was a member of both groups.

Arzner was the only woman director working during the golden age of Hollywood, in the thirties and forties. She made twenty films—including the first talkie ever made at Paramount—and helped launch the careers of Rosalind Russell, Katharine Hepburn, and Lucille Ball. Joan Crawford claimed that Arzner fell in love with her. So how did such an unconventional woman thrive for so long in Hollywood's male-dominated studio system? Simple: Her films made money. "I made one box-office hit after another," she said. "If I had a failure in the middle, I would have been finished."

IDA LUPINO (1918–1995)

Major Films: *Outrage* (1950), *The Hitchhiker* (1953)

As an actress, Ida Lupino was called "the poor man's Bette Davis." On becoming a director, she once joked, she morphed into "the poor man's Don Siegel." A femme fatale fixture of the film noir classics of the 1940s, she turned toward the end of that decade to making her own pictures, which were often just as compelling—if somewhat less polished—than those of her male contemporaries. Between 1949 and 1966, she directed nine films, the best of which is considered to be the minor noir classic *The Hitchhiker*. At the time, she was the only female director working in Hollywood. Assignments were scarce, even for an artist of her talents, however, and by the middle of the 1960s she was reduced to TV sitcom work. That's *the* Ida Lupino you see credited as the director of numerous episodes of *Bewitched* and *Gilligan's Island*.

WERNER HERZOG

SEPTEMBER 5, 1942–

NATIONALITY:
GERMAN

ASTROLOGICAL SIGN:
VIRGO

MAJOR FILMS:
AGUIRRE, THE WRATH OF GOD (1972), *FITZCARRALDO* (1982),
GRIZZLY MAN (2005)

WORDS OF WISDOM:

*"I SHOULDN'T MAKE MOVIES ANYMORE.
I SHOULD GO TO A LUNATIC ASYLUM."*

*I*n 1974, Werner Herzog learned that his good friend, film historian Lotte Eisner, was near death. Determined that she not pass away before seeing him one last time, he walked to her home in Paris—all the way from his home in Munich. Eisner was so delighted to see him she lived another eight years. The anecdote—one of many unbelievable but true stories about the famously eccentric German director—says a lot about the character of a man whose grandiose antics blur the line between visionary craftsman and monomaniacal whackjob.

The only director to make a feature film on each of the seven continents, Werner Herzog (real name: Werner Stipeti) grew up in virtual isolation from the rest of the world, in a remote mountain village in Bavaria, the son of an absentee German father and a doting Croatian mother. The mythmaking started early. Herzog has claimed that when he was just a few days old, he was nearly killed when the Allies bombed his village, causing a skylight in his nursery to shatter. He took the name *Herzog*, or "duke," in an effort to steel himself against what he has called "the overwhelming evil of the universe."

By the time the bombs stopped dropping, Herzog had started reading (his first book was a Marshall Plan–supplied edition of *Winnie the Pooh*). He spent most of the rest of his childhood wandering aimlessly through the mountains by himself. He never watched any films or television programs and did not use a telephone until he was seventeen years old. But the long, solitary walks gave him the imaginative sustenance to contemplate life as a filmmaker. A fifteen-page encyclopedia entry on how to make movies provided all the technical know-how he needed to get started. A 35-millimeter camera he stole from the Munich Film School supplied the means of production. His first seven films were shot using that camera. To finance his early work Herzog worked the night shift as a welder in a steel factory. Contrary to popular belief, he did not shoot films for America's National Aeronautics and Space Administration in the 1960s—or give up a promising career as a NASA scientist. He directed his first feature-length film, *Signs of Life*, in 1968.

International acclaim came quickly, with the release of *Aguirre, The Wrath of God* in 1972. A hallucinatory tale of Spanish conquistadors, filmed in the Peruvian rain forest and set to a pulsating Krautrock score, it was the first of his five successful collaborations with his one-time flatmate, the unhinged German actor Klaus Kinski. Their best films together dealt with a subject with which both men were well acquainted—monomania—with perhaps the finest example being 1982's *Fitzcarraldo*, about a crazed tycoon who tries to build an opera house in the middle of the Peruvian jungle. In recent years, Herzog has eschewed narrative films to concentrate on documentaries, such as the enormously successful *Grizzly Man*, which often take place in wild landscapes and follow subjects on a quest for a deeper level of reality that Herzog calls "ecstatic truth."

OLD SOFT SHOE

Never doubt a documentarian. That's a lesson Herzog learned the hard way, when he lost a bet to aspiring filmmaker Errol Morris and had to dine at

> DURING A 2005 INTERVIEW, WERNER HERZOG WAS SHOT BY A DRIVE-BY SNIPER WITH A HIGH-POWERED AIR RIFLE. UNFAZED, THE DIRECTOR CONTINUED HIS INTERVIEW AND DIDN'T EVEN BOTHER CALLING THE POLICE.

Chateau Timberland afterward. It all started in the late 1970s, when Morris was a philosophy student at the University of California, Berkeley, where Herzog was teaching. One day, Morris told Professor Herzog about a movie he was hoping to make about the denizens of a California pet cemetery. A skeptical Herzog was convinced no film on so obscure a topic could ever get produced, so he bet Morris that if his film premiered, he would eat his shoe. Amazingly, Morris's debut feature, *Gates of Heaven*, did get made—and opened to such widespread critical acclaim that Morris went on to a long and successful career as a documentary filmmaker. For Herzog, that left the little problem of paying up, which he was more than willing to do. Settlement of the bet was recorded for posterity in Les Blank's twenty-minute short film *Werner Herzog Eats His Shoe*. The film depicts Herzog cooking the eponymous shoe (a leather boot, to be precise), which he boiled for five hours in garlic, herbs, and broth in the kitchen of the trendy Bay Area restaurant Chez Panisse, under the supervision of celebrity chef Alice Waters. Herzog is then shown consuming the footwear (or part of it, anyway; he claimed he would not eat the sole, for the same reason that diners do not eat the bones of a chicken) in front of a rapt audience at the *Gates of Heaven* premiere.

KLAUS OF ILL REPUTE

Herzog has had a long and tumultuous relationship with Klaus Kinski, who starred in five of his films, including his masterpiece *Aguirre, The Wrath of God*. The two men originally met in the mid-1950s, when Kinski lived as a boarder in the Herzog family's apartment building in Munich. During this period, a teenaged Herzog got an up-close look at Kinski's irrational and outrageous behavior, which included physical assaults on critics and audience members who didn't like his stage performances and a two-day frenzy of autodestructive rage spent locked inside a bathroom. The clearly demented performer left such an impression on Herzog that he sent Kinski a copy of the *Aguirre* script in 1971, convinced that he was the perfect choice to play the deranged conquistador. He was right—Kinski's performance is mesmerizing—but the process of completing the film drove both men to distraction. Kinski accepted the part in a keening 3 A.M. phone call. "It took me at least a couple of minutes before I realized that it was Kinski who was the source of this inarticulate screaming," Herzog recalled. In a sense, Kinski and Herzog never stopped screaming at each other. The Peruvian jungle shoot was a nightmare. Kinski nearly split another actor's head open with a sword. He shot off part of an extra's finger because the man was making too much noise. And he constantly threatened to flee the production, prompting Herzog at one point to state his intention to shoot Kinski and then blow out his own brains with a rifle if he did not rejoin the cast and crew.

The volatile pair locked horns again in 1981 on the set of *Fitzcarraldo*. It was another tortuous jungle shoot, and once again it brought out the worst tendencies in both men. Herzog was completely out of control, according to Kinski, mistreating the cast—including the Amazonian Indian extras—and abusing every animal in sight. At one point, Herzog dispatched a llama to its doom on the Pongo River rapids. Cast and crew had to watch as the helpless beast got sucked into a whirlpool and died. Another time, Kinski was consigned to the helm of a steamboat and sent down the raging river. He barely escaped the llama's fate. A lumberjack working on the film had to saw off his own leg after being bitten by a poisonous snake. A plane carrying six members of Herzog's crew crashed into the mountains, killing all aboard. For his part, Kinski stomped around like a diva. His erratic behavior so terrified the natives that they offered to kill him to make life easier for everyone involved. Herzog declined their offer, but only because he needed his leading man to complete the picture.

Even when they weren't working together, Herzog and Kinski remained locked in a death grip of mutual antipathy. The frothing actor continued to deliver periodic tongue lashings to Herzog via telephone. After one such tirade, Herzog actually went over to Kinski's house with a can full of gasoline, intent on burning it down. He changed his mind only because he was afraid of Kinski's dog. "Every grey hair on my head I call Kinski," Herzog once quipped. As the actor grew older and lost some of his Teutonic good looks, Herzog mercilessly picked at the scab. "He's not aging well," he said of Kinski at one point. "The best thing to happen to his career is for him to die immediately."

Kinski was even more cutting when speaking about his erstwhile collaborator. Writing in his autobiography, *Kinski Uncut*, he unburdened himself of his true feelings about the director:

> Herzog is a miserable, hateful, malevolent, avaricious, money-hungry, nasty, sadistic, treacherous, cowardly creep. . . . He should be thrown alive to the crocodiles! An anaconda should strangle him slowly! A poisonous spider should sting him and paralyze his lungs! The most venomous serpent should bite him and make his brain explode! No—panther claws should rip open his throat—that would be much too good for him! Huge red ants should piss into his lying eyes and gobble up his balls and his guts! He should catch the plague! Syphilis! Yellow fever! Leprosy! It's no use; the more I wish him the most gruesome deaths, the more he haunts me.

WHAT A PRICK

Herzog is famously hard on his actors. (He reportedly made Christian Bale eat worms and maggots on the set of *Rescue Dawn* in 2007.) But he met his match when he pissed off a determined group of little people while shooting *Even Dwarves Started Small* on the Canary Island of Lanzarote in

1970. The bizarre film, which involves a revolt by little people confined on an island mental institution, was murder on everyone involved. One unlucky actor was run over by a van and accidentally set on fire. The others were so unnerved by the mayhem that Herzog had to plead with them not to abandon the set. He promised them that if they made it through the rest of the shoot without any further mishaps he would let them film him as he jumped naked into a cactus patch. The rest of the film went off without a hitch and, good as his word, Herzog took his flying leap into the spiny green yonder. "Getting out was a lot more difficult than jumping in," he said afterward.

A PASSION FOR POULTRY

It's fair to say that Herzog is more interested in chickens than any other major filmmaker. (And not just chickens, but monkeys, crabs, ski jumpers, auctioneers, dwarves, bears, boats, mountains, windmills, enchanted waterfalls, jellyfish, and people wearing aviator goggles also pop up again and again in his films. But poultry is his main source of phobia/fascination.) Chickens, roosters, and hens reappear in dozens of his films. Often they are depicted eating other animals, attacking or pecking at other birds, or engaged in bloody cockfights. Herzog has called chickens his "grand metaphor"—for what, he isn't sure. "Look into the eyes of a chicken and you will see real stupidity," he once said. "It is a kind of bottomless stupidity, a fiendish stupidity. They are the most horrifying, cannibalistic, and nightmarish creatures in the world."

IN THE LINE OF FIRE

Never let it be said that Werner Herzog wasn't willing to take a bullet for his art. Well, a pellet anyway. During a 2005 interview in Los Angeles to promote his film *Grizzly Man*, Herzog was shot by a drive-by sniper using a high-powered air rifle. The aforementioned pellet penetrated his jacket and lodged in a catalog Herzog had stuffed into his waistband. Unfazed (and uninjured), the director went right on with the interview. He even refused to call the police, for fear they would overreact, and chalked up the entire incident to "the folklore of L.A." Speaking about the shooting to muscle-bound punk icon Henry Rollins on his eponymous gabfest, Herzog remained nonplussed. "It's something very exhilarating for a man to be shot at with little success," he said.

MARTIN SCORSESE

NOVEMBER 17, 1942–

NATIONALITY:
AMERICAN

ASTROLOGICAL SIGN:
SCORPIO

MAJOR FILMS:
TAXI DRIVER (1976), *RAGING BULL* (1980), *GOODFELLAS* (1990)

WORDS OF WISDOM:

"MY WHOLE LIFE HAS BEEN MOVIES AND RELIGION. THAT'S IT. NOTHING ELSE."

Gang wars. Knife fights. Brutal beatings. They sound like scenes from a typical Martin Scorsese movie—and they are—but they're also scenes from his own childhood. When he was a boy, Scorsese would spend hours gazing out the window of his family's apartment in New York's Little Italy. That might sound romantic, but the street life tableaux he beheld were anything but. "I saw a great deal of physical, emotional, and psychological violence," he later recalled, "as well as various bodily functions and people having sex. Things like that tend to leave an impression on you."

And when he wasn't watching, Scorsese was being watched—or so he believed. While still a young child, he painted a pair of eyes on the wall of his bedroom. They represented the eyes of God or perhaps his own reproaching conscience. A thick sense of Catholic guilt—at the time he wanted to grow up to be a priest—coupled with a taste for the thug life were both the hallmarks of his early life and a powerful influence on the films he would one day create.

Scorsese was too frail to be a thug—he was so severely asthmatic he couldn't pet a dog without triggering a life-threatening attack—and too impure to hack it as a priest. He flunked out of the seminary before enrolling in the NYU film school. Working under the tutelage of an inspirational professor, Haig Manoogian, in 1967 he made a series of short films and a debut feature, *Who's That Knocking at My Door*. In 1972, the legendary schlockmeister Roger Corman hired him to direct *Boxcar Bertha*, a cheesy exploitation film about a pair of sex-crazed Depression-era train robbers. The shoot brought much-needed cash—but at the price of artistic integrity. John Cassavetes, the indie auteur whom Scorsese idolized, berated him for "wasting a year of your life making a piece of shit" and challenged Scorsese to start taking on more ambitious projects.

Taking the admonition to heart, Scorsese scored his artistic breakthrough with 1973's *Mean Streets*. It was the first of many collaborations with Robert De Niro and a searing evocation of life among the small-time hoods of New York

City. Box-office success followed in 1974 with *Alice Doesn't Live Here Anymore*, which earned Ellen Burstyn an Academy Award for best actress. At age thirty-two, Scorsese was now fully empowered to pick his own projects. The result was two undisputed masterpieces—1976's *Taxi Driver* and 1980's *Raging Bull*—that solidified his reputation in the top tier of American directors. It was also during this period that Scorsese's appetite for drugs and extramarital sex began to catch up with him. He cycled through four wives and a veritable mountain of cocaine. By the end of the seventies, his personal life had cratered, and his professional prospects were dimming as well. The advent of the blockbuster and the decline of auteurist cinema meant that Scorsese's intensely personal brand of filmmaking fall out of favor. He spent most of the 1980s trying to reestablish his commercial viability in the changing movie marketplace. The release of a third consensus masterwork, *Goodfellas*, in 1990 seemed to herald the end of that era and the dawn of a new one in which really great movies could actually make money.

Scorsese's subsequent output has been somewhat scattershot. *The Age of Innocence* (1993) and *Kundun* (1997) pleased critics but baffled longtime fans. The dreadful *Bringing Out the Dead* (1999) was a career low point, but 2006's *The Departed* earned him his first Best Director Oscar, capping his long run of unredeemed nominations at five. An increasingly elfin figure in his dotage, the one-time hard liver seems to have settled comfortably into his role as America's grandfatherly cinephile-in-chief.

THE AVIATOR

Scorsese has always been terrified of flying. For weeks before departing on an airplane trip, he monitors the weather forecast for the city he is visiting so he won't have to land during a storm. If it looks like there's going to be bad weather, he simply reschedules all his appointments and books a different flight. If he can't work out the weather patterns ahead of time, he refuses to get on the plane. (He once missed picking up an award for best director at the Cannes Film Festival for just that reason.) For decades, Scorsese also swore off flying on the eleventh of any month, part of a passel of separate numerological phobias based on the number eleven, which he considers unlucky. (He won't take flights whose numbers add up to eleven for instance, and refuses to stay on the eleventh floor of a hotel.) When he does board his

plane, Scorsese carries a lucky crucifix with him, which he clutches during takeoff. He also totes around a gold amulet to ward off evil spirits and wears a satchel of lucky charms around his neck.

SORRY, CHARLIE

Scorsese was offered the part of Charles Manson in the 1976 TV movie *Helter Skelter*, based on the best seller by Vincent Bugliosi. He turned it down, and the role of the wild-eyed psychotic killer went to Steve Railsback instead. That didn't stop angry members of the Manson family from sending Scorsese death threats for months afterward.

LOVE AT FIRST SIGHT

That Scorsese is no Adonis isn't exactly front page news. You don't get offered the part of Charles Manson based on your good looks. Still, the wee, ungainly asthmatic does have his female admirers. Take his longtime girlfriend of the 1970s, producer Sandy Weintraub. The first time she met him, she fell head over heels. "I thought Marty was just the cutest thing I

> **WHEN DID MARTIN SCORSESE REALIZE HE HAD A COCAINE PROBLEM? RIGHT AFTER HE CHECKED INTO A NEW YORK HOSPITAL WEIGHING 109 POUNDS, WITH BLOOD STREAMING FROM HIS EYE SOCKETS.**

had ever seen," Weintraub recalled later. "He was chubby and he had long hair and no neck, and was shorter than me." She immediately asked him out to dinner.

COCAINE BLUES

In the late seventies, Scorsese descended into a cocaine-fueled death spiral that nearly ended his life. He first started snorting the white powder for the creative jolt it provided. "At first you felt like you could make five films at once," Scorsese recalled later. "And then you wound up spending four days in bed every week because you were exhausted and your body couldn't take it." Regular consumption of alcohol and Quaaludes helped perpetuate this cycle of binge and crash. By the spring of 1978 Scorsese was a hopeless coke addict, jonesing for a toot at every opportunity. "No more coke, no more interviews," he told the assembled press at that year's Cannes Film Festival. When his supply ran out, he ordered a private plane flown into France from New York to bring him a fresh mound of blow. His behavior became volatile and erratic. At parties, he would fly into a rage at the drop of a hat, throwing glasses at people he believed had insulted him. He later confessed of having a death wish. He finally bottomed out that August, when he scored some bad coke that interacted with his asthma medication, causing massive internal bleeding. The drug so ravaged the diminutive director's system that he checked into a New York hospital with a near-zero platelet level and blood pouring out of his eye sockets. Doctors who examined him found he had shriveled to 109 pounds. Upon finally coming to, he discovered that his second wife had left him. With his life and career circling the drain, Scorsese finally found the determination to clean up his act.

LIZA WITH A ZZZZZZ

Cocaine does strange things to a man. In Scorsese's case, it drove him into the arms of Liza Minnelli. Near the nadir of his drug period, the director had a torrid affair with the brassy chanteuse on the set of the 1977 disaster *New York, New York*. Like Scorsese, Minnelli was married and heavily into drugs. She was also carrying on a simultaneous affair with ballet dancer Mikhail Baryshnikov. Not that Scorsese noticed. Most of the time, he was in too much of a narcotic stupor to know whom he was sleeping with. "I was making love to different women," he said later, "but I didn't find that very interesting."

SILENT TYPE

While filming the fight scenes in *Raging Bull*, Scorsese drew on an unusual source of inspiration: silent comedy. "The only person who had the right attitude about boxing in the movies for me," he once observed, "was Buster Keaton." Scorsese was particularly enamored with Keaton's 1926 comedy *Battling Butler*, in which the Great Stone Face plays a dandy whom a brutish pugilist suspects of having an affair with his wife. In Scorsese's film, a similar dynamic played out between the Joe Pesci and Robert De Niro characters.

BATS I CAN LIVE WITH

Despite having directed what many people consider to be the greatest boxing movie ever made, Scorsese is anything but a sports fan. "Anything with a ball, no good," he once pronounced.

DUBIOUS DISTINCTION

Scorsese's vivid depiction of the Chinese destruction of Tibet and the mistreatment of the Dalai Lama in his 1997 film *Kundun* came with a price. That year, the Chinese government named him one of the fifty people barred from ever entering Tibet.

STONED AGAIN

Scorsese is a huge fan of the Rolling Stones—and one of their songs in particular. The director has featured "Gimme Shelter" in three of his films: *Goodfellas*, *Casino*, and *The Departed*. His obsessive use of the classic 1969 track prompted Mick Jagger to quip that *Shine a Light*, the 2008 Stones concert film that Scorsese directed, was the first of his films *not* to include "Gimme Shelter" on the soundtrack. For the record, Scorsese, whose pioneering use of the "needle drop" helped revolutionize movie music in the 1970s, has also featured the Jagger–Richards chestnuts "Jumpin' Jack Flash" and "Monkey Man" at key moments in his movies.

WHO'S BAD?

Scorsese has generally fared well with his rock 'n' roll–themed projects. *The Last Waltz* and *Shine a Light*, his concert films for the Band and the Rolling Stones, respectively, were well received, and he directed a stylish video for ex-Band guitarist Robbie Robertson's 1987 single "Somewhere Down the Crazy River." But the one musical Scorsese film that probably won't be appearing in a Lincoln Center career retrospective anytime soon is "Bad," the eighteen-minute video he shot for King of Pop Michael Jackson in 1987. Jackson's producer Quincy Jones personally recruited Scorsese for the project, which is today considered an example of the worst excesses of the music-video genre. The film, which dramatizes the conflict between a fey prep-school boy named Daryl (Jackson) and a thug named Mini Max (Wesley Snipes), was written by acclaimed novelist and screenwriter Richard Price, who has subsequently disowned any involvement. "Everybody did their job," Price said of the misbegotten video in a 2008 interview. "Jackson is not a bad actor, and Scorsese, well, he's great. I wrote a really good eight-page script. Problem is that Michael Jackson is Michael Jackson . . . he looks like Minnie Mouse. And you forget the whole thing has to end with a song." A really, really bad song, as it turns out. Where's "Gimme Shelter" when you need it?

GEORGE LUCAS

MAY 14, 1944–

NATIONALITY:
AMERICAN

ASTROLOGICAL SIGN:
TAURUS

MAJOR FILMS:
AMERICAN GRAFFITI (1973), *STAR WARS* (1977)

WORDS OF WISDOM:

"IF YOU CAN TUNE INTO THE FANTASY LIFE OF AN ELEVEN-YEAR-OLD GIRL, YOU CAN MAKE A FORTUNE IN THIS BUSINESS."

T he director who would make his fortune telling tales of heroic deeds performed "a long time ago, in a galaxy far, far away" grew up in the most ordinary circumstances imaginable. The only son in a family of four children, George Walton Lucas Jr. grew up in the shadow of his domineering father, a prosperous office supplies salesman, in Modesto, California. A classic authoritarian personality, George Sr. ruled over his family with an iron fist. Sometimes it was clutching a razor. Every summer he made a point of shaving all of George Jr.'s hair off. He also made it quite clear he expected the boy to follow him into the stationery business. However, George Jr. wasn't biting. Despite all his efforts at trying to instill in his son the old-fashioned virtues of hard work and frugality, George Jr. "never listened to me," his father said. "He was his mother's pet. If he wanted a camera, or this or that, he got it. He was hard to understand. He was always dreaming up things."

Young George dreamt to escape reality. He was slight of build—"a scrawny little devil," his father once called him—and a frequent target of neighborhood bullies. One of their favorite pranks was to toss his shoes into the sprinkler. Incapable of fighting back, Lucas instead immersed himself in a fantasy world of superhero comic books and Saturday morning cartoons. When he grew older, he moved on to muscle cars. He spent countless hours cruising the streets of Modesto in a souped-up Fiat. The one day, shortly before his high school graduation, Lucas drove his mean machine smack dab into a walnut tree. He spent the next four months in the hospital and nearly died from his injuries. The brush with mortality proved to be a turning point in his life. Determined to break free of his father's yoke, Lucas resolved to pursue a career as a filmmaker. After two years of junior college, he enrolled in the prestigious USC film school.

After graduating in 1967, Lucas worked as a freelance cameraman and editor. A notoriously avid networker, he scored a series of sweet gigs: cranking the camera for legendary animation director Saul Bass, editing a United States Information Agency film about President Lyndon Johnson's trip to Asia, and directing a "making of" documentary about Francis Ford Coppola's 1969 feature *The Rain People*. The friendship he developed with Coppola would prove especially fruitful. Coppola's newly formed production company agreed to produce Lucas' directorial debut, the dystopic sci-fi epic *THX-1138*. Though the film bombed, it attracted a cult following, and established Lucas as a player in the emerging "New Hollywood." In 1973, Lucas parlayed that cachet into the chance to direct his first mass market feature, the surprise mega hit *American Graffiti*.

A cinematic love letter to his early sixties adolescence, and the nights Lucas spent racing cars up and down the streets of Modesto, *American Graffiti* took less than a month to film and enraged the studio chiefs at Universal (who, fearing it would be mistaken for an Italian film, at one point asked Lucas to change the title to *Another Slow Night in Modesto*). But it grossed more than $50 million on initial release and was nominated for five Academy Awards. From that point forward, Lucas was calling the shots in Hollywood.

The dream project the newly empowered director demanded the studio bankroll, of course, was *Star Wars*, a gussied-up re-imagining of the space opera serials Lucas had loved so much as a child. Written and produced under immense pressure—science fiction epics were box-office poison at the time—*Star Wars* went way over budget and drove Lucas to distraction. He lost weight and became so stressed out by the possibility of failure that he checked himself into the hospital midway through filming. But the film surpassed even the most optimistic commercial expectations and elevated Lucas from a successful director into a worldwide geek icon. His generous cut of the merchandising pie also made him one of Hollywood's wealthiest directors.

Lucas spent the next three decades sporadically writing and producing, occasionally in collaboration with his friend and fellow baby boomer Steven Spielberg. He used some of his *Star Wars* luchre to build his sprawling Skywalker Ranch in northern California and founded the enormously successful Industrial Light & Magic special effects company. But there were downsides to fame as well. Lucas's marriage to film editor Marcia Lucas collapsed in 1984—a casualty of his workaholic, control freak personality. He lost $50 million the in the divorce settlement. And a series of increasingly bizarre turkeys produced under his auspices—the ghastly *Willow* and *Howard the Duck* chief among them—took a toll on his artistic and commercial reputation. A new round of Lucas-helmed *Star Wars* films, released between 1999 to 2005, met with mixed critical reception, even among hardcore fans of the original trilogy. Though still treated with shaman-like reverence within the science-fiction fan community, Lucas is widely considered a shot wad by the larger universe of cinephiles.

SWEET SURPRISE

Hoping to evade combat duty during Vietnam, Lucas tried to enlist in the U.S. Air Force's Officer Candidate School. His goal was to be posted to a filmmaking unit that would keep him out of harm's way for the duration of the conflict. However, he was turned down because he had racked up too many speeding tickets. After briefly entertaining the idea of fleeing to Canada to dodge the draft, Lucas was inducted, but managed to avoid service when a routine military physical revealed he was diabetic.

YOU CAN'T ALWAYS GET WHAT YOU WANT

In the fall of 1969, twenty-five-year-old Lucas was hired by filmmakers Albert and David Maysles to work the camera at an outdoor concert by the Rolling Stones. It seemed like a sweet gig—until people started trying to kill each other. The event in question was the notorious Altamont Free Concert, during which an eighteen-year-old man named Meredith Hunter was stabbed to death in an altercation with members of the band's Hell's Angels security force. Sadly, Lucas' missed his big chance at capturing rock 'n' roll history on film. His camera jammed and he lost all his footage.

HE'S JUST NOT THAT INTO YOU

Lucas hates working with actors. He finds the casting process excruciating and prefers to let his underlings deal with the performers whenever possible. On the set of *American Graffiti* in 1972, Lucas sat down for a heart-to-heart talk with eighteen-year-old Ron Howard about the former child star's directorial aspirations. True to form, Lucas encouraged Howard to eschew live action in favor of animation. "It's great," he enthused. "It's just you and [the]

material. No actors!" Howard, who was by that time a grizzled show-business veteran and the future director of such hits as *Apollo 13* and *A Beautiful Mind*, came away from the exchange feeling a little puzzled. "It's our actor-director meeting," he later recalled, "and he's basically telling me he doesn't want to deal with me!"

FASTER, PUSSYCAT, ACT, ACT!

Although he generally avoids coaching his actors, Lucas is partial to one particular directorial exhortation. On the *Star Wars* set, he was known for incessantly instructing his cast to redo their lines, only "faster and more intense." It became such a joke that, when Lucas was stricken with a bout of laryngitis, the actors proposed getting him a sandwich board that read "Faster" on one side and "More intense" on the other.

> HERE'S THE ONE GEORGE LUCAS PRODUCTION YOU'LL NEVER FIND ON DVD: THE STAR WARS HOLIDAY SPECIAL FEATURED SUCH Z-LIST CELEBRITIES AS HARVEY KORMAN AND BEA ARTHUR.

LIGHT SABER DUEL

In 2001, in a legal maneuver worthy of Darth Vader, Lucas filed suit against a Buffalo, New York–based medical equipment company over its use of the term "light sabers" to describe a line of laser-guided surgical tools. Claiming that use of the name was "likely to result in loss of revenues to Lucasfilm and damage to its reputation," the litigious filmmaker asked a San Francisco judge to enjoin Minrad Inc. from using the moniker, which Lucas personally coined and had been using to sell light-up toy swords since 1977. The dispute was eventually settled out of court for an undisclosed amount.

USING THE FORCE

Always one to aim for the really big targets, Lucas also successfully sued foul-mouthed rapper Luther Campbell of 2Live Crew to stop him from raising the stage name "Luke Skyywalker." Petrified of losing his livelihood in the face of a Lucasfilm legal onslaught, Campbell agreed to rechristen himself "Luke" and drop all references to *Star Wars* mythology from his act.

ONE FOR THE GIPPER

The most unlikely target of the Lucasfilm legal machine? President Ronald Reagan. In the 1980s, Lucas sued to stop the then-commander-in-chief from using the term "Star Wars" to describe his anti-nuclear defensive shield. There was only one problem: The Reagan Administration never called it that, preferring the initialism SDI, for Strategic Defense Initiative.

BURN AFTER WATCHING

The harsh critical response to the last three *Star Wars* movies may not have fazed Lucas, but there's one project he's still too mortified to even discuss: the catastrophic two-hour *Star Wars Holiday Special* that aired on CBS television stations on November 17, 1978. Larded with misbegotten musical numbers, badly animated cartoons, and guest appearances by such Z-list seventies "stars" as Jefferson Starship, Harvey Korman, and Bea Arthur, the variety extravaganza has been disowned by *Star Wars* fans and repeatedly ridiculed in popular culture. When prodded by interviews, Lucas will only say it "does not represent my vision for *Star Wars*." He once confessed, "If I had time and a hammer, I'd track down every bootleg copy and smash it."

PAPER TIGER

He may be a master of special-effects technology, but when it comes to word processing, Lucas is decidedly old school. He prefers to do all his writing in longhand and will only use a number-2 pencil. The color of the paper is another object of compulsion. Lucas insists on blue-and-green-lined looseleaf paper and once reamed out his bookkeeper for procuring pads that weren't colored and lined to his specifications. When he gets writer's block, Lucas has a characteristically old-school way of dealing with the frustration: He literally tears out his hair, leaving little clumps of discarded fuzz in his wastepaper basket.

BEAUTY AND THE GEEK

In the mid-1980s, Lucas embarked on a long and stormy relationship with pop singer Linda Ronstadt. The seventies hitmaker was in the midst of a protracted career slump and had just come off a nasty break-up with up-and-coming comic Jim Carrey when the recently separated Lucas swept her off her feet. To most observers, it was an unlikely match—especially given Ronstadt's rock-star looks and Lucas' nebbishy demeanor. According to *People* magazine, when the lovebirds walked into a San Anselmo, California, drug store one day, the owner didn't even know who Ronstadt's companion was. "I just thought he was her houseboy," she said. Friends tried to warn Lucas the relationship was doomed: Ronstadt was notorious for cycling through lovers like chewed-up wads of bubble gum. But the smitten director remained ever hopeful. He took guitar lessons, exchanged his nerdy glasses for contact lenses, and even talked of building a honeymoon cottage on his Skywalker Ranch. Sadly, it was not to be. After about five years of on-and-off dating, the odd couple broke up for good.

BOOB JOB

Lucas is obsessed with detail. On the *Star Wars* set, his micromanaging extended to personally duct-taping Princess Leia's breasts. "No breast bounce in space," the director told actress Carrie Fisher as he flattened down her hooters. "No jiggling in the empire!" So why not a less restrictive form of upper body support? According to Lucas, if a woman were to wear a bra in a weightless environment, it would strangle her.

DAVID LYNCH

JANUARY 20, 1946–

NATIONALITY:
AMERICAN

ASTROLOGICAL SIGN:
AQUARIUS

MAJOR FILMS:
ERASERHEAD (1977), *BLUE VELVET* (1986)

WORDS OF WISDOM:

"THERE'S NO SUCH THING AS BAD WEATHER—JUST THE WRONG CLOTHES."

The poet laureate of the American grotesque, David Lynch grew up in a world strikingly similar to the placid small-town milieu depicted in so many of his movies— a place of "picket fences, blue skies, red flowers, and cherry trees," to use his own formulation. But like the characters in his films, the young David Lynch was always fascinated by the unseemly underbelly of things. "I studied ants and drew ammunition and pistols," he said of his principal childhood pursuits. The ants he found sucking the pitch oozing from the cherry trees that grew around his boyhood home. He drew the weapons because, well, he just thought guns were cool. Browning automatic submachine guns were a particular favorite.

No one seemed to find Lynch's hobbies the least bit alarming. His parents led a quiet, respectable life. His father was a research scientist for the U.S. Department of Agriculture. His mother was a language tutor. David was an Eagle Scout, and his troop even scored VIP tickets to the inauguration of President John F. Kennedy. The family moved around a lot, from Montana to Washington to Idaho to Virginia. As long as little David was just drawing guns and not actually blowing stuff up, Ma and Pa Lynch were content to let him be. Then he started blowing stuff up. A teenaged Lynch targeted his junior high school swimming pool with a homemade IED (building pipe bombs was another hobby), and the explosion shook windows five blocks away. Lynch was arrested and the incident made the local papers. Somehow, he still managed to finish high school.

· After graduation, Lynch traveled through Europe, and enrolled in various art schools, looking for a way to translate his skewed inner life into visual images. He hit upon the idea of using film, rather than paint, as his medium and began churning out shorts. For his first feature, he drew on his experiences living in the urban wastelands of the late 1960s to create the surrealist nightmare *Eraserhead*. One of the most celebrated "midnight movies" of the late seventies, the disturbing black-and-white freak show set the tone for much of Lynch's subsequent work. It also attracted the attention of funnyman-turned-producer Mel Brooks, who hired Lynch to direct his first commercial film, *The Elephant Man*, in 1980. That picture proved Lynch could adapt his aesthetic to a mass audience and earned him the first of his three Oscar nominations for best director.

In the 1980s, Lynch continued to forge an idiosyncratic path. He turned down offers to direct *Return of the Jedi* and *Fast Times at Ridgemont High*, but said yes to *Dune*, a woebegone adaptation of novelist Frank Herbert's sci-fi epic. The film flopped, but Lynch soldiered on with the low-budget *Blue Velvet*—arguably his masterwork—and the TV series *Twin Peaks*, which became an unlikely hit in the summer of 1990. His subsequent output has been sporadic, baffling, intermittently brilliant, and only rarely commercially successful—an almost perfect replication of the Stanley Kubrick business model. Away from the camera, Lynch has been more visible—though no less bizarre—than Kubrick. His extracurricular pursuits include marketing his own brand of organic coffee (called "David Lynch Signature Cup" and promoted under the tagline "It's all in the beans") and preaching the gospel of transcendental meditation, which he has practiced faithfully since 1973.

WOLF AT THE DOOR

Lynch's college roommate was Peter Wolf, lead singer for the J. Geils Band. The unlikely pair first met in late summer 1964, as they gathered around the "roommates wanted" bulletin board on their first day of classes at the Boston Museum School of Fine Arts. Wolf (real name: Peter W. Blankfield) had been crashing at the local YMCA and was looking for someone to share an apartment. Lynch had a place, but there was a catch: They'd have to sleep in a bunkbed. (For the record, Wolf took the top, Lynch took the bottom.) It didn't take long for the unusual arrangement to unravel. Lynch's crib was infested with cockroaches, and both he and Wolf were clinically depressed. They spent all their time together arguing about art. (Lynch was a fan of abstract expressionism, whereas Wolf preferred the German variety.) Wolf also annoyed Lynch by being constantly late with his rent and playing Thelonious Monk records day and night. "David was a very mellow, very kind guy," Wolf later recalled. "But the days we spent together, we were all in a deep shadow of gloom. It was a very nihilistic period." Eventually Lynch kicked Wolf out, claiming he was "too weird" to live with.

IT'S ALWAYS SLUMMY IN PHILADELPHIA

Lynch has a somewhat complicated relationship with the city of Philadelphia, where he studied painting from 1965 to 1969. "I've said many, many, many unkind things about Philadelphia," he once admitted, "and I meant every one." Elsewhere Lynch called the city "a very sick, twisted, violent, fear-ridden, decadent, decaying place" and derided it for being "filled with violence, hate and filth." His evident distaste for Philly may have something to do with the old real estate agent's saw: location, location, location. During his sojourn in the city, Lynch lived in an old industrial neighborhood near the corner of 13th and Wood. His apartment was across the street from a greasy spoon and catty-corner to the morgue. He spent most of his idle moments gazing out the window at the body bags as they were being cleaned. "The area had a great mood," he remembered years later. "Factories, smoke, railroads, diners, the strangest characters, the darkest nights." He was robbed twice, had his car stolen and his windows shot out, and recalled a child getting shot to death and lying on the street for five days. "I felt like I was constantly in danger. But it was so fantastic at the same time." Despite—or perhaps because of—its squalor—the Philadelphia of the late 1960s became an important source of inspiration for Lynch, who often includes images of urban blight in his films. "I just have to think of Philadelphia now, and I get ideas," he has said. "I hear the wind, and I'm off into the darkness somewhere."

DOG DAYS

Before he started practicing transcendental meditation, Lynch was full of anger—and so was his dog. For nearly twenty years, he channeled the residue of all that pent-up aggression into a comic strip entitled "The Angriest Dog in the World." The strip featured crude, static drawings of the titular canine, accompanied by surreal captions reflecting a decidedly downbeat worldview. "The humor in the strip is based on the sickness of people's pitiful state of unhappiness and misery," Lynch has remarked. "But it thrills me." It also thrilled readers of various alternative newspapers until 1992, when "The Angriest Dog" was unceremoniously put to sleep. Lynch has recently revived it as an occasional Web comic.

BOY GENIUS

A fanatic about order, Lynch ate lunch at the same restaurant—Bob's Big Boy in Los Angeles— every day for seven years. He embarked on the bizarre ritual during the filming of *Eraserhead* in 1977, after discovering that consuming massive quantities of sugar helped spur his creativity. Every day at 2:30 P.M. (or "Bob's Time," in Lynch's parlance), after the afternoon rush had cleared, Lynch would boogie on down to the Big Boy and order a chocolate shake and as many as seven cups of coffee loaded with the sweetener he called "granulated happiness." The ensuing sugar rush was so intense that Lynch found himself writing ideas for films on napkins. "Many, many things came out of Bob's," he later remarked.

FUN WITH ANIMALS

Lynch has an interesting hobby, one that would make Henry "Eraserhead" Spencer sit up and take notice: He dissects animals for fun. The unusual avocation first took hold after a veterinarian kindly gave him a dead cat as a present. Lynch took it home and promptly cut it open. Then he stuffed the

> **DAVID LYNCH LIKES TO UNWIND BY DISSECTING CATS, MICE, FISH, AND CHICKENS. AFTER CUTTING THE CARCASSES INTO PIECES, HE PHOTOGRAPHS AND DISPLAYS THE RESULTING MONSTROSITY.**

remains inside a bottle, where rigor mortis set in and the frozen beast became lodged forever, like a feline Cutty Sark. Lynch soon began dissecting other animals, "to study the textures," as he put it. After he has cut the carcasses into pieces, he likes to stitch them back together, stretching the skin and internal organs on wooden planks. He then photographs the resulting monstrosity, which he calls a "kit," likening it to a model airplane assembled from parts. Over the years, Lynch has fashioned kits out of cats, mice, fish, chickens, and, in one unfortunate instance, a duck. The duck kit "didn't turn out too well," he admits. "There were so many parts, and it didn't quite catch the details of the small parts."

STYLE MAVEN

With his impossibly high hair and perpetually buttoned-up shirts, Lynch has fashioned an iconic look that is the envy of other contemporary directors. The snug collar, he explains, came out of his own sense of insecurity. "I felt too vulnerable with the top button opened," he has said, "especially with a wind on the collarbone. That was something that really disturbed me. And I liked that tightness around the neck." The finger-in-the-socket hair is just something he was born with, he says. "It is the way it is, sort of does what it wants to." For a time, Lynch tried covering it up. He claims he wore a ten-gallon cowboy hat at all times for six years, in an homage to the Westerns of his childhood. "I love forties movies when everyone wore a hat," he says. "Now there are no more hats, and that's a real shame."

OUT OF ODOR

If you're ever invited to a party at Lynch's place, it's best to bring your own dish. The oddball auteur doesn't cook, nor does he allow any cooking on the premises. The smell of cooking food disturbs him, especially the way it seeps into everything in his home. "So I eat things that you don't have to light a fire for," he says. "Or else I order a pizza. The speed at which I eat it, it doesn't smell up the place too bad."

ANT MAN

As anyone who has seen *Blue Velvet* can tell you, Lynch is intrigued by insects. Ants, in particular, fascinate him: He says they are "tireless workers. So if you get a project that they can do, they'll do it. And there's no questions asked. No unions." Calling himself an "ant wrangler," Lynch enjoys devising novel ways to coax the little creatures to come out and play with him. One time he fashioned a makeshift human head out of cheese and turkey and mounted it on a coathanger. He stuffed the orifices with scraps of turkey and left the tasty totem out in his kitchen for the wee beasties to devour. Over the course of four days and nights, ants began climbing all over the head and completely picked it clean.

OLIVER STONE

SEPTEMBER 15, 1946–

NATIONALITY:
AMERICAN

ASTROLOGICAL SIGN:
VIRGO

MAJOR FILMS:
PLATOON (1986), *WALL STREET* (1987), *JFK* (1991)

WORDS OF WISDOM:
"I LOVE FILM, BUT THE FILM BUSINESS IS SHIT."

You could plug Oliver into New York and he could power the city for two weeks," said actor Gary Oldman. "Hyperkinetic" doesn't begin to describe the Academy Award–winning director of *Platoon, JFK*, and half a dozen other politically charged, polarizing films. Stone says he stopped taking cocaine in the early 1980s, but his frantic affect and outspoken espousal of all things conspiratorial evoke someone who's been mainlining the stuff on a daily basis for decades.

It didn't have to end in a haze of hash smoke and half-baked JFK assassination theories. William Oliver Stone (or "Bill Stone," as he used to like to style himself, thinking his middle name made him seem too effeminate) was in fact a child of privilege. His father, Louis Stone, was a prosperous New York City stockbroker—the model for the character or Gordon Gekko in *Wall Street*. Grumpy and emotionally distant, Louis Stone never showed affection to Oliver, preferring to greet his son with a chilly businessman's handshake rather than a hug or kiss. Stone's mother, Jacqueline, was little better, spending her days flitting about the Manhattan arts scene. Childhood, Stone remembers, "was continual abandonment."

Left to his own devices, Stone sought refuge in creative endeavors. He wrote stories, plays, and sketches and enlisted his cousins to act in them. He even charged admission to the performances. "Oliver was the leader, and his cousins did the work," his mother once remarked. "Oliver likes to have it his own way." At age fourteen, Stone was sent off to boarding school in Pennsylvania. While there, his parents divorced. Upon learning of his father's infidelities, Stone came to a critical realization: Nothing is as it seems on the surface. The conspiratorial worldview that would later infuse some of his best-known films was set.

After a desultory year at Yale University, Stone dropped out of college and headed off to teach English in Vietnam. Upon returning to the United States, he was bored and devoid of direction, so less than two years later he again set off for Southeast Asia, less than two years later—this time as an infantryman in the U.S. Army. Within a few months, idealistic Private Bill Stone found himself transformed by his combat experiences into a self-described "jungle animal"—hooked on drugs and the high he got off killing without consequences. It was a journey he would later chronicle in his semi-autobiographical masterpiece *Platoon* in 1986.

Stone returned from the war a bitter, angry man. "It was Amerika with a 'k'," he said of the country he no longer recognized. "I would have joined the Black Panthers if they'd asked me. I was a radical, ready to kill." Seeking a way to channel his rage, he enrolled in New York University's film program, where he studied under Martin Scorsese. He graduated in 1971, worked as a cab driver and a Xerox messenger to support himself, and slowly built a name for himself in the movie business. After years of grinding out scripts, he finally hit it big, winning the 1978 Academy Award for best adapted screenplay for *Midnight Express*.

In 1981, Stone tried his hand at directing a Hollywood feature. The schlock horror movie *The Hand* starred Michael Caine as a comic-book illustrator (!) whose disembodied hand starts killing people. Stone himself had a cameo as one of the victims. Amazingly, the film did not kill off his directing career as well, and he went on to score critical and commercial hits with *Platoon*, *Wall Street*, and *Born on the Fourth of July* in rapid succession. The 1990s brought *JFK*, the first of Stone's hallucinogenic political biopics, as well as the similarly themed *Nixon* and *The Doors*. These films, along with 2008's *W.* and his outspoken support of Fidel Castro and Hugo Chavez, have earned Stone a reputation in the press as a left-wing crackpot, wiling to play fast and loose with the facts in pursuit of advancing his ideological agenda. Certainly his enthusiastic advocacy of drug use has done little to endear him to America's right wing, which pegs him just below Michael Moore on its axis-of-evil filmmakers.

OLIVER STONED

Stone maintains that he kicked his longtime cocaine habit cold turkey in 1981, by temporarily relocating to France while writing the script for *Scarface*. That doesn't mean he gave up on *all* drugs, however. He's been a recreational user of marijuana and hashish and still extols the virtues of hallucinogens to anyone who'll listen. "I like ayahuasca [a natural psyche-delic long used by South American natives]," he has said. "And I liked LSD, and I liked peyote." He loves LSD so much, in fact, that he once spiked his own father's wine with the stuff. "I just wanted to destroy him," Stone re-members. "I wanted to shake his head up." Louis Stone quickly realized he had been dosed and identified his son as the culprit. "But he was cool about it," Stone says. The old man spent the next several hours swinging from a tree limb in the family garden, hallucinating about African women and drums. A soothing snack of milk and cookies eventually brought him back down to planet Earth.

In 1993, while driving around the New Mexico desert in a rented van scouting locations for *Natural Born Killers*, Stone once again shared a little something from his personal stash—passing out psychedelic mushrooms to producer Jane Hamsher and various members of his crew. Trouble nearly en-sued when the band of middle-aged stoners came upon a police roadblock. A quick-thinking Stone hustled Hamsher inside a Kentucky Fried Chicken and escaped into the men's room, where he presumably flushed his fungus. "When I returned to the parking lot," Hamsher wrote in her memoir of the shoot, "I looked to the field next door and saw Oliver running back and forth with his suede bomber jacket spread wide to catch the wind. 'Oh, good,' I thought. 'That'll throw the cops off.'"

NOT SO SMART

In the early nineties, Stone had a near-death experience after taking an over-dose of an amino acid "smart drug." Instead of taking two teaspoons, the nor-mal dose, he took two *tablespoons*—more than enough to kill a man of his size. Stone promptly passed out at his desk, but his personal assistants—who were used to his occasional blackouts—didn't bother to call 911 for several hours, until his breathing became shallow. Paramedics arrived and had to defibrillate the zonked-out auteur. When Stone still failed to wake up, he was transported to the nearest emergency room, where his stomach was pumped until he slowly came to his senses. Stone woke up to find a nurse holding his penis, trying to make him urinate into a cup. "I gotta pee! I gotta pee!" he shrieked, unaware of where he was or how he had gotten there. "One minute I was in my office," Stone later recalled, "and the next I was naked in the hospital with [a] woman in white whom I'd never seen before, holding my penis and yelling at me to pee in her hand. It was strange." Eventually Stone had to be sedated and then gradually reacclimated to life on this planet before he was allowed to leave the hospital.

SMUGGLER'S BLUES

Stone's drug use has occasionally gotten him in trouble with the law. In November 1968, less than two weeks after returning from Vietnam, he was arrested at the U.S./Mexico border for possession of two ounces of Vietnamese marijuana. He was taken into custody and thrown into a San Diego jail on federal smuggling charges. After two weeks spent sleeping on a filthy floor waiting for a visit from a public defender who never came, Stone was finally allowed to make a phone call. He rang up his father and gave him the good news/bad news scenario: "I'm out of Vietnam, but I'm in jail." A mortified Louis Stone contacted a lawyer, who managed to get his son's case dismissed and his record scrubbed clean "in the interest of justice."

Success did little to curtail Stone's penchant for carrying his stash. In June of 1999, the director was busted again, this time for possession of hashish, meprobamate (a muscle relaxant), and fenfluramine and phentermine, the component parts of the drug fen-phen, an erstwhile weight-loss tonic now banned by the FDA. He was picked up by cops while driving under the influence near his home in Beverly Hills. As part of a plea bargain with prosecutors, Stone agreed to undergo drug counseling—although given his outspoken advocacy of drug use, it's not sure just who was counseling whom.

BREAKING POINT

Stone's 1993 divorce from his wife, Elizabeth, was a messy affair—brought on in part by his penchant for conducting messy affairs. Their twelve-year union disintegrated after he carried on numerous flings with other women, all without his wife's knowledge. Elizabeth Stone finally learned the truth about her husband's infidelities when she read an interview he had given to *Elle* magazine, in which he mused about the male impulse toward promiscuity, with an accompanying photo spread that showed him cavorting with Australian supermodel Elle Macpherson. Convinced that her husband must be cheating on her, she read his diary. In it, he described in graphic detail his dozens of extramarital affairs over the years. She promptly filed for divorce.

PARTY ANIMAL

Robert Downey Jr. once observed that "a Saturday night with Oliver Stone is

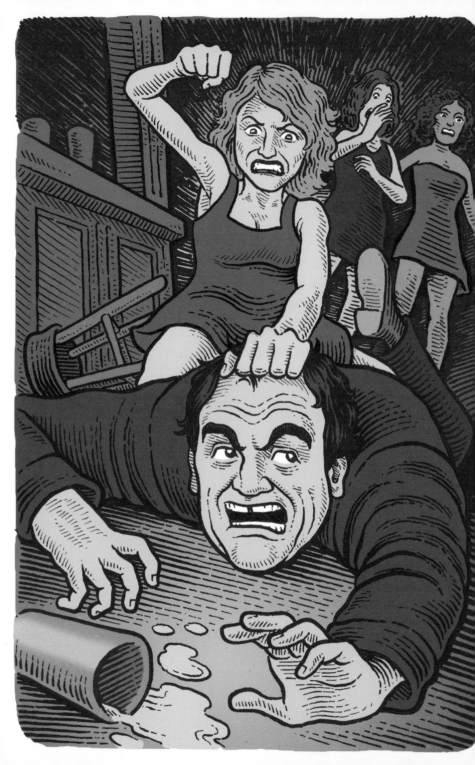

basically pagan Rome, 26 A.D." The drug-addled director is one of the hardest partiers in Hollywood and whose revels have an unfortunate tendency to climax in violence and property damage. While attending a party in Los Angeles, a plastered Stone broke through his hostess's bathroom door while she was on the toilet, screaming, "What kind of dump is this? Don't you have a door that works?" The wrap party for Stone's movie *W.* ended in a bar brawl, with actors Josh Brolin and Jeffrey Wright pepper-sprayed and tased by cops in Shreveport, Louisiana. And during production of *Any Given Sunday*, Cameron Diaz physically assaulted Stone when she found him flirting with another woman in a bar. "I'm not one of your groupies," the aggrieved actress cried. "It looks like a harem in here!" When Stone told her to "stop acting like white trash," Diaz jumped on his back and began buffeting him about the head. "Get this crazy bitch off me!" the Oscar winner wailed. The next night, the two were at it again, partying together in another club.

OLIVER STONE ONCE ADMONISHED CAMERON DIAZ TO "STOP ACTING LIKE WHITE TRASH" AFTER SHE LEAPT ON HIS BACK AND BEGAN PUMMELING HIM.

DON'T CRY FOR ME—JUST GET ME OFF THE PICTURE!

Before chronicling the life of the Lizard King, Jim Morrison, in *The Doors*, Stone tried to collaborate with another sexually provocative pop icon— Madonna. His original plan was to follow up *Born on the Fourth of July* with a big-screen adaptation of Andrew Lloyd Webber's musical *Evita*, starring the Material Girl as Eva Perón. The abrasive director and the headstrong pop star were an oil-and-water combination from the start. Madonna insisted on rewriting some of Webber's songs, to the composer's consternation, then requested that Stone give her script approval. Calling her demands "meaningless" and a personal insult to him as a director, Stone torpedoed the deal. "I just said, 'Well, we have nothing to talk about, do we?' She left. . . . " The director then sought Meryl Streep for the role, but she asked for too much money. In the end, Stone fled the accursed project and made his Doors biopic instead. *Evita* eventually did get made, by director Alan Parker, with Madonna in the title role. When the film opened,

Stone was blistering in his appraisal of her performance. "The thing about Eva Perón was that she was a hooker and a saint," he sniffed. "Madonna could do the hooker, but not the saint." Ever since, Stone has never missed an opportunity to take a shot at "Her Madgesty."

"Madonna—she's like toilet paper," he once observed. "She's on every magazine cover in the world. Devalued."

TONE DEAF

Long considered an oracle of 1960s counterculture, Stone is widely praised for his use of popular music in his films. But as producer Jane Hamsher reveals in her book *Killer Instinct*, an account of the making of *Natural Born Killers*, he actually knows little or nothing about rock 'n' roll. When they attended a concert by the legendary lead guitarist for the Rolling Stones, Hamsher was shocked to discover that Stone "barely knew who Keith Richards was." When Hamsher presented the director with a mix tape containing the Cowboy Junkies' rendition of the Velvet Underground classic "Sweet Jane," Stone was surprised to learn it wasn't an original composition. "There's another version?" he asked. And during a dinner with erstwhile Genesis frontman Peter Gabriel, Stone seemed almost totally in the dark about who *he* was. In fact, the only time Stone grew animated about rock music came when he told Gabriel about his lifelong dream to have sex with Jefferson Airplane singer Grace Slick.

SITTING PRESIDENT

Stone's George W. Bush biopic, *W.*, may have bombed at the box office, but it wasn't for lack of an innovative marketing campaign. Lionsgate executive Tim Palen devised an Internet banner ad featuring a photo of Josh Brolin as George W. Bush sitting on a toilet in the manner of Rodin's *The Thinker*. Entitled "Sitting President," the ad enraged Stone, who thought it trivialized his film and made him look like a jackass. He immediately nixed the concept. Palen was undeterred. Convinced that the film's marketing campaign "needed some *teeth*," he took his case to one of the film's producers, Moritz Borman, who advised him to run the ad—and not tell Stone. The director didn't find out about "Sitting President" until *W.* had already opened—and been flushed by critics and audiences alike.

STEVEN SPIELBERG

DECEMBER 18, 1946–

NATIONALITY:
AMERICAN

ASTROLOGICAL SIGN:
SAGITTARIUS

MAJOR FILMS:
JAWS (1975), *E.T.: THE EXTRA-TERRESTRIAL* (1982),
SCHINDLER'S LIST (1993)

WORDS OF WISDOM:

"ONCE A MONTH THE SKY FALLS ON MY HEAD, I COME TO, AND I SEE ANOTHER MOVIE I WANT TO MAKE."

The most straitlaced of the "Easy Rider, Raging Bull" generation of American directors, Steven Spielberg came to filmmaking via an appropriately wholesome route: the Boy Scouts. He made his first film, an 8-millimeter Western called *The Last Gunfight*, as means of fulfilling the requirement for a photography merit badge. In those days, he used his three younger sisters for a crew, financed his work using the proceeds from his neighborhood tree planting business, and charged admission to his "screenings"—hiring one sister to pull double duty running the popcorn concession. When a bully began tormenting him on the playground, he pacified the boy by offering him the lead role in a World War II epic he was filming.

There were a lot of bullies in those days—more than he could possibly cast. As a child, Spielberg used filmmaking as a means of escaping the horrors he endured at school. "I was skinny and unpopular," he says. "I was the weird, skinny kid with acne. . . . I never felt comfortable with myself, because I was never part of the majority." The other kids nicknamed him "the retard" after he lost a footrace with a boy who was mentally challenged. Once, during biology class, Spielberg was forced to leave the room after nearly fainting at the sight of a dissected frog. He stood out in the hall with the other queasy students. "They were all girls," he remembers. Spielberg's own father, an electrical engineer, was so appalled by his spinelessness and indifferent performance in school that he barely spoke to him. So the boy lost himself in the world of homemade movies.

By age fourteen, Spielberg was making forty-minute shorts, and by age sixteen he had completed his first science-fiction feature, a two-hour UFO invasion extravaganza called *Firelight*. In 1965, he took a tour of the Universal Studios lot and ingratiated himself with the head of the editorial department. Told he couldn't hang around the lot any longer without a pass, he took to showing up at the gate every morning with his father's briefcase, pretending to work there. "There was nothing in it but a sandwich and two candy bars," Spielberg said. "So every day that summer I went in my suit and hung out with directors and writers and editors and dubbers." Like a cinephile version of George Costanza, he started squatting in one of the empty offices, even forging his name in the building directory: Steven Spielberg, Room 23C.

His grades weren't good enough to get him into USC, so Spielberg briefly attended California State University at Long Beach instead. That ended the day Sid Sheinberg, Universal's head of TV production, offered him a seven-year contract to direct for television. Spielberg was twenty years old. "I quit college so fast, I didn't even clean out my locker," he later said. He landed gigs directing segments of *Columbo* and *Marcus Welby* and honed his craft. His first theatrical feature, 1974's *The Sugarland Express*, capped a remarkably meteoric rise for the self-taught director, who won praise from critics for his technical virtuosity even as the film itself bombed at the box office. Commercial success was just one movie away, however, when 1975's *Jaws* became a worldwide megahit and helped usher in the era of the big-budget blockbuster.

A precocious motormouth with an infectious enthusiasm for movies, Spielberg became the biggest star in an age of celebrity directors. More approachable than George Lucas, less of an *artiste* than Martin Scorsese, he pleased crowds with a string of genre hits: *Close Encounters of the Third Kind*, *Raiders of the Lost Ark*, and the heartwarming sci-fi fable *E.T.: The Extraterrestrial*. When he tried his hand at more "serious" fare, like *The Color Purple* and *Schindler's List*, he won the critical approval that typically eluded directors of so-called popcorn movies. The latter film, a harrowing true-life tale of the Holocaust, earned Spielberg his first Academy Award for best director. He scored a second for another high-minded World War II film, *Saving Private Ryan*, in 1998.

Spielberg's personal life hasn't been nearly as messy as those of some of his contemporaries. Too much of a nerd to get heavily involved in drugs, he has faltered only when his all-consuming interest in movies got in the way of his real-world relationships. His on-again, off-again romance with actress Amy Irving collapsed during the making of *Close Encounters of the Third Kind* in 1977. (Spielberg confided to a friend that when Irving started crying over his lack of affection he felt like telling her, "I'm fucking my movie!") They eventually reconciled, married, and divorced in 1989. In the settlement, Irving was awarded $100 million after the judge voided a pre-nup Spielberg had hastily scrawled on a napkin. It was one of the costliest celebrity splits in history. Undeterred, Spielberg tried marriage again, with actress Kate Capshaw, in 1991. They have seven children.

"Steven Spielberg is so powerful," comedian Robin Williams once observed, "he had final cut at his own circumcision!" A long string of box-office hits (and very few bombs) will do that for you. The rare director whose work pleases critics as well as the masses, Spielberg has carved out a special place in the pantheon of American middlebrow cinema—as a sort of kindly uncle of directors who moviegoers know is never going to touch them in an inappropriate or discomfiting manner.

THE SPIELBERG STALKERS

For such an ungainly man, Spielberg has attracted an unusual number of crazed stalkers—each with a peculiar agenda:

> In 1997, a disturbed Iranian immigrant tried to pass himself off as Spielberg's nephew. The twenty-seven-year-old celebrity-obsessed man, Anoushirvan D. Fakhran, began calling himself Jonathan Taylor Spielberg and enrolled under that name in a Catholic high school in Fairfax, Virginia. Authorities were alerted by Spielberg's personal security firm. Fakhran was arrested on child pornography charges and eventually convicted of forgery.

> In 1998, a man named Jonathan Norman was arrested and charged with felony stalking after showing up at Spielberg's Pacific Palisades mansion carrying what police described as a "rape kit": handcuffs, razor blades, duct tape, nipple clamps, chloroform, a box cutter, and a stun gun. Authorities also seized a notebook containing photos of Spielberg, his wife, and their seven children. In the ensuing trial, it emerged that the deranged intruder intended to rape Spielberg while his bound and gagged family watched. Norman was sentenced to twenty-five years to life in prison.

In 2002, Spielberg had to secure a restraining order to keep a thirty-year-old Canadian loon named Christopher Richard Hahn from pestering him at his DreamWorks compound in Studio City, California. After trespassing on the lot more than twenty times, the man attempted to break into Spielberg's office in a futile effort to break into movies. When police finally arrested him, he gave them a false name and claimed to have been an extra in the film *Ocean's Eleven*.

Later that same year, Spielberg had to obtain yet another restraining order—this time to keep an insane woman named Diana Louisa Napolis away from his home and office. Napolis, a paranoid, claimed that Spielberg and his wife, Kate Capshaw, were part of a Satanic cult that had implanted a microchip in her brain in hopes of controlling her. "To state the obvious," Spielberg said in a court statement, "I am not involved with any form of manipulating Ms. Napolis's mind or body through remote technology or otherwise." The woman was later committed to a state mental hospital.

GOOD COMPANY

Anyone who has observed Spielberg's rapid-fire speaking pattern and knows of his compulsive fixation with film history has probably already guessed the obvious: The director suffers from Asperger's Syndrome, a mild form of autism which leads to obsessional interests. Over the years, many other high-functioning creative types have also had Asperger's, including one-time Monkee Peter Tork, Pokemon creator Tajiri Satoshi, and "Cars" songster Gary Numan.

DIRECTING MOMMIE DEAREST

In 1969, Spielberg got his first big break as a filmmaker: directing the pilot episode for the TV horror anthology series *Night Gallery*, hosted by Rod Serling. The experience almost turned into a career-ending disaster, however, thanks to temperamental star Joan Crawford. The sixty-five-year-old Hollywood legend schemed to get Spielberg fired from day one, forcing Serling to intervene on his behalf. When Spielberg asked her out to lunch to patch things up, Crawford refused. "I'm not going to be seen in public with you," she told the then twenty-three-year-old director. "People will think you're my

child." Crawford's method-acting pretensions also irked Spielberg. Playing a wealthy blind woman who gets the chance to regain her sight for a few hours, Crawford insisted on meeting Spielberg at her New York City penthouse while wearing a blindfold to get into character. "She went lurching around the apartment," Spielberg remembers. "I was terrified." After a rough beginning, the two mismatched collaborators did manage to forge a *modus vivendi*. Spielberg coaxed a serviceable performance out of his alcoholic star by strategically placing cue cards all over the set (she kept forgetting her lines). And though the finished episode stunk Spielberg did win Crawford's respect. During an on-set visit with a reporter for the *Detroit Free Press*, Crawford pointed to Spielberg and said, "Go interview that kid, because he's going to be the biggest director of all time!"

GARLIC TOAST

Although not usually thought of as a playa, Spielberg did sow a few wild oats in his younger days. Before settling down, he enjoyed flings with female celebrities Victoria Principal and Sarah Miles. One of his most high-profile conquests was sitcom actress Valerie Bertinelli, whom he briefly dated in the

STEVEN SPIELBERG HAS ATTRACTED AN UNUSUAL NUMBER OF CRAZED STALKERS, INCLUDING A WOMAN CLAIMING HE HAD SATANIC POWER AND A MAN WIELDING NIPPLE CLAMPS.

early 1980s. The cute-as-a-button star of *One Day at a Time* auditioned for the part of Indiana Jones's ex-lover in *Raiders of the Lost Ark*. She was all wrong for the part, but Spielberg saw something he liked and sent her flowers the next day, along with a dinner invitation. Soon, sparks were flying. "We went out a few times . . . and did more," Bertinelli later revealed. Their love match wound up fizzling for the oddest of reasons: Spielberg's pathological distaste for garlic. "I was making dinner for him one evening and I was getting ready to chop up the garlic and he saw it," Bertinelli recalls. "He said, 'No, no, no, no garlic!' I went, 'Really? OK.' "In my head I'm thinking, 'I can't be with someone that can't eat garlic.'" It wasn't long before the object of many a 1970s adolescent's desire rebounded into the arms of an artist more amenable to Italian cuisine: guitarist Eddie Van Halen.

THE SUM OF ALL FEARS

"I think we survive on our fears," Spielberg once said. He should know. His catalog of phobias is almost Woody Allen-esque in scope and includes insects, rats, snakes (the inspiration for *Indiana Jones*), and water (he has a recurring nightmare about his house being swallowed up by waves and refuses to go in the ocean because, he says, "there are sharks out there"). The director is also terrified of elevators, convinced he will get stuck between floors and die in one someday. He had his production offices built on two floors so that he would never have to use one, and has been known to conduct business meetings in a lobby so that he'll never have to take one. Whereas elevator phobias are fairly common, Spielberg also has one pathological dread that almost no one shares: fear of furniture with feet. "I wait for them to walk out of the room," he says.

RADIO FREE STEVEN

In a 1979 interview with pasty-faced pop-art scenester Andy Warhol, which aired on a New York City public access channel, Spielberg admitted that when he was a child he could receive radio broadcasts through the fillings in his teeth. During the same conversation, Spielberg also revealed that he once ate a transistor given to him by his father, an electrical engineer: "I can remember the day my father brought home a transistor and said, 'Son, this is the future.' So I put it in my mouth and swallowed it. . . . My father didn't understand why." Neither do we, Steven, neither do we.

Stephen King and Other People Who Had No Business Directing Movies

Some people should never be allowed near a camera. Yet they go there anyway. Their reasons remain a mystery. Here are four "directors" whose misguided efforts give well-intentioned amateurs a bad name.

NORMAN MAILER

Whatever you think of him as a writer—and some find his style overheated and bombastic—you can't deny that being a big-time literary author was Norman Mailer's true calling. He certainly wasn't cut out to be a director. Although his early, experimental films, like *Maidstone* and *Wild 90*, have undergone a reappraisal by the art-house crowd in recent years, one's opinion of these heavily improvised vanity projects largely depends on one's opinion of Mailer himself. One of the purest narcissists in the history of cinema, Mailer, in the words of his cinematographer D. A. Pennebaker, "has the idea he can look at a camera and take it away from the person who's running it, as if he's got the control and is photographing himself." By the time of 1987's *Tough Guys Don't Dance*—a woebegone self-adaptation of his own novel about an alcoholic man who finds a severed head in his marijuana stash—Mailer had made the wise decision to remain offscreen. This time he let Isabella Rossellini, magician Penn Jillette, and a past-his-sell-date Ryan O'Neal do his dirty work for him. The multiple Golden Raspberry–nominated travesty is highlighted by a scene cinephiles have dubbed "the worst line reading ever"—in which O'Neal reads a letter informing of his wife's infidelity and responds with a flat, affectless delivery of the deathless line: "Oh man, oh god, oh man, oh god, oh man, oh god!"

STEPHEN KING

Not content with being the most famous writer on the planet, Stephen King has doggedly pursued careers in other areas of entertainment. He launched his "acting" career playing an illiterate hayseed in 1982's *Creepshow* and regularly plays rock 'n' roll gigs with his all-star author jam band, the Rock Bottom Remainders. But by far the most egregious of his attempts to break away from the typewriter was his misguided decision to direct the big-screen adaptation of his short story "Trucks" in 1986. Retitled *Maximum Overdrive*, the strange film about big rigs who turn evil and start killing the residents of a North Carolina town starred Emilio Estevez, voice of Bart Simpson Yeardley Smith, and King himself in an uncredited cameo. The master of horror must have realized how ridiculous his macabre tale of trucks gone bad looked on screen, because he amped up the camp value and set it all to an eardrum-rattling hard-rock soundtrack. Even that couldn't save it. After years of complaining about what directors like Stanley Kubrick were doing to his novels, King had finally risen to his level of incompetence. Calling his first directorial effort a "moron movie," he pocketed his Golden Raspberry nomination for worst director and promised fans he'd never again set foot behind the camera.

WILLIAM SHATNER

There's nothing wrong with actors directing movies. There's nothing wrong with *Star Trek* actors directing movies. Leonard Nimoy—TV's Mr. Spock—did an admirable job lensing *Star Treks III* and *IV*, for example. But something about *William Shatner* taking the helm for *Star Trek V* in 1989 just felt wrong—to critics, the show's fans, and even his fellow cast members, who reportedly hated their egomaniacal costar. "Oh my God," actor George "Mr. Sulu" Takei was said to have intoned when he learned that Captain Kirk would be taking the Con. "What are we going to do now?" As it turned out, the other actors' worst fears were well founded. On the set, Shatner was imperious, condescending, and more than a little manic. "He thought that by talking fast it would speed up the schedule," observed Nimoy. "But you couldn't understand a word he was saying." It didn't help that the inexperienced director (whose previous work had been confined to the television screen) was handed a $30 million budget, more than a third of which he plowed into special effects. As a consequence, *Star Trek V* was plagued by cost overruns, labor disputes, and production snafus, such as the unexplained disappearance of more than $60,000 worth of costumes. Reviewers panned the final product, and audiences fled from the bloated spectacle in droves. *Star Trek V* ended up making about half as much as the previous films in the series. Shatner was never invited to direct another installment and has since done very little work behind the camera. *Star Trek II* screenwriter Harve Bennett may have summed up the experience best: "Directing multiple episodes of *T. J. Hooker* just did not prepare Bill Shatner for the wide screen's demands."

THE BEATLES

Some rock stars can make movies. Headbanger Rob Zombie has become a respected director of violent horror films. Even Madonna didn't totally embarrass herself with her 2008 debut *Filth and Wisdom*. Others, however, shouldn't quit their day jobs. No one is clamoring for Bob Dylan to take up the reins again after seeing his bizarre 1978 feature *Renaldo and Clara*. And I think we're all "in agreeance" that Limp Bizkit frontman Fred Durst should stick to spitting rhymes in the aftermath of his 2007 dud *The Education of Charlie Banks*. But by far the worst of the rock legends turned auteurs were the biggest rock legends of them all, the Beatles. After making two successful pictures with British filmmaker Richard Lester, the members of the Fab Four elected to "co-direct" their third feature, *Magical Mystery Tour*. That basically entailed getting stoned and turning on the camera. The resulting incoherent mess—set aboard a psychedelic bus and anchored to the floor by several of the group's worst songs ("Flying," anyone?)—baffled Beatlemaniacs when it first aired on British TV in December 1967. Unlike other LSD-inflected chestnuts of the era, like the Monkees' *Head*, it has not grown in stature since.

The Beatles' first certified flop, *Magical Mystery Tour,* was so agonizingly awful that Paul McCartney issued a public apology for its existence.

PEDRO ALMODÓVAR

SEPTEMBER 24, 1949–

NATIONALITY:
SPANISH

ASTROLOGICAL SIGN:
LIBRA

MAJOR FILMS:
WOMEN ON THE VERGE OF A NERVOUS BREAKDOWN (1988),
ALL ABOUT MY MOTHER (1999), *TALK TO HER* (2002)

WORDS OF WISDOM:

"CINEMA IS A VAMPIRE LOVER. IT DOESN'T LET YOU DO OTHER THINGS."

I wasn't a normal child," Pedro Almodóvar has said. That will come as no surprise to anyone who's seen one of his movies, which celebrate the outrageous and are invariably populated by some combination of transsexuals, bullfighters, assassins, rapists, gay dentists, and big-breasted porn stars.

Growing up in La Mancha, Spain (home of Don Quixote), Almodóvar loved to read, watch movies, and avoid playing with the other boys. In an early indication of where he was headed, he preferred to spend recess discussing the life and legacy of chesty 1950s screen queen Ava Gardner. "Even though I didn't know all that well who she was, I knew that she had had fifteen husbands, and that amused me more than playing." His father, who could barely read and write, worked as a muleteer—a man who delivers barrels of wine and olive oil by mule—and was generally baffled by Pedro's, shall we say, unconventional character. He regarded his son as an alien and would occasionally question his paternity.

Almodóvar was closer to his mother, a creative and nurturing woman saddled with the stultifying life of a 1950s rural Spanish housewife. "She was extremely intuitive and had great initiative and a sense of humor," Almodóvar later recalled. He has cited her as a major influence on what is generally considered one of his great strengths as a filmmaker: his ability to create fully developed, well-rounded female characters. He rewarded her later by casting her in cameo roles in several of his films prior to her death in 1999.

Early on, Almodóvar showed great promise as a writer. When he was ten, he won a prize for an essay about the immaculate conception—a choice of topic that undoubtedly won him brownie points with the priests at his Catholic boarding school. For a time, his parents even held out hope that Pedro might one day don the collar himself. But it was not to be. That essay turned out to be the high point of Almodóvar's religious education. Around the same time, he first started questioning his faith. He reached a deal with God in which he gave the deity exactly one year to manifest himself in his life. "He didn't, so I reached the conclusion that I was agnostic," Almodóvar later reported. Being an eyewitness to several incidents of sexual abuse by priests didn't help either. Nor did his growing awareness of his own burgeoning homosexuality.

As soon as he finished high school, Almodóvar left home and moved to the Spanish capital. "La Mancha is a very macho, chauvinistic society," he has said. "I saw very clearly that my life had to be in Madrid." His parents disapproved. His father even threatened to send Spain's fearsome federal police force, the Guardia Civil, to bring him back, but to no avail. Arriving in Madrid at the height of the 1960s countercultural revolution, Almodóvar immersed himself in the city's artistic underworld. Lacking the funds for college, he supported himself by selling books and jewelry in the Madrid flea market and eventually landed a steady job working as a clerk for Spain's state telephone company. He would remain in this position for more than a decade, using the money he earned to bankroll his nascent filmmaking career. (If you've ever wondered why there are so many telephones in Almodóvar's early films, that's the reason.)

From 1972 to 1978, Almodóvar made almost a dozen short films. Most were ribald sex comedies, shot with a Super-8 camera, embryonic versions of the kind of features he would create throughout the 1980s. Peopled by wild and colorful characters from the fringes of Spanish society, these early films scandalized bourgeois audiences—not to mention the Catholic church—but won him an appreciative cult following. Commercial success finally came in 1988, with the release of *Women on the Verge of a Nervous Breakdown*, a more mainstream work featuring two of the players from his repertory company, Antonio Banderas and Carmen Maura. It was nominated for an Academy Award for best foreign film.

His ticket punched, Almodóvar continued to shock, titillate, and surprise adventurous moviegoers throughout the 1990s and beyond. *Tie Me Up! Tie Me Down!* was slapped with an X rating in the United States. *All About My Mother* signaled a shift to more mature subject matter. *Talk to Her* put straight male characters front and center for the first time, earning Almodóvar some of his most effusive critical praise and scoring him an Oscar for best original screenplay. Though occasionally derided for a lack of range and his predilection for outré subjects, Almodóvar seems content to let mainstream audiences come to him. "Critics have realized," he says, "that whatever I do, it is authentic."

* * *

THE ODD FATHERS

Dispatched by his parents to a Catholic boarding school when he was eight years old, Almodóvar got an up-close look at the kind of rampant pedophilia that would scandalize the Church in the early 2000s. Although Almodóvar himself was never abused, he knew of plenty of other children who were. As a consequence, he developed an extreme physical fear of priests. One of the things that bothered him most was being forced to kiss the priest's hand whenever he came to visit the students. A disgusted Almodóvar refused to do so and would run the other way whenever a collared cleric came around. "But there was one priest who would seek me out and he'd stand in front of me, stick his hand out and force me to kiss it," the director later recalled. "And then after I'd kissed it, he'd grab my hands and hold them tightly until I ran away. So even this I do remember as being somewhat abusive." Almodóvar remembers one priest so debauched that he assembled a "harem" of about twenty boys. He was eventually found out and transferred to another school.

TRANNY BOY

Priests he can live without, but there's one group of sexually ambiguous individuals whom Almodóvar wholeheartedly endorses: transexuals. "[They] are a slap in the face of the idea that God creates people," the director has said. "What they do is change their nature." Not surprisingly, gender benders play an outsize role in Almodóvar's films. "If you put a transsexual into a story dramatically as a narrative element it is very powerful because it changes all the other characters and is a challenge to them all."

LA LUNATIC

Almodóvar's early years in Madrid were one of his most creatively fertile periods—and one of his most bizarre. He contributed articles and X-rated comic strips to underground newspapers and periodicals such as *Star*, *Vibora*, and *Vibraciones*. He wrote a soft-core photonovel about a tampon mogul embroiled in a love triangle. And he donned a wig, black eyeliner, and fishnet stockings to serve as lead singer of a cross-dressing punk-rock duo, Almodóvar & McNamara, with his friend Fabio de Miguel—better known by his nom de drag "Fanny McNamara." (Their show-stopping number was entitled

"Suck It to Me.") Perhaps most oddly of all, Almodóvar created a female porn-star alterego, Patti Diphusa, whose outrageous "memoirs" he submitted weekly to the newspaper *La Luna*.

POP OFF

In the early 1980s, Almodóvar's strange affect and track record of directing experimental 8-millimeter films earned him the appellation "the Spanish Andy Warhol." Around that time, he got a chance to meet his namesake when the pasty-faced pop artist staged an exhibition at his home in Madrid. At the afterparty, when Warhol asked him why he was called that, Almodóvar speculated it might be due to his penchant for casting transvestites. The two men didn't exactly hit it off. Although Warhol took lots of photos of Almodóvar—part of his overall fascination with snapping pictures at parties—he refused to paint Almodóvar's portrait on the grounds that he wasn't yet famous enough.

IN HIS YOUTH, PEDRO ALMODÓVAR DONNED A WIG, BLACK EYELINER, AND FISHNET STOCKINGS AS THE LEAD SINGER OF A CROSS-DRESSING PUNK-ROCK DUO.

WOODY'S WAY

Sex, frequent and exuberant, plays a big part in Almodóvar's films. (One of his early features even bore the title *Fuck, Fuck, Fuck Me Tim*.) So it's somewhat surprising to learn that he claims to have had only three lovers in his life. This might be due to a reluctance to commit. Almodóvar eschews emotional entanglements and prefers long-distance relationships. "I'm with Woody Allen on this one. I'd say with lovers it's always best to live in different flats and, if possible, in different cities."

SISTER RAY

The next time the Almodóvar Fan Club throws a party, they might not have to hire a caterer. Celebrity chef Rachael Ray is a huge fan of the Spanish filmmaker. She took future husband John Cusimano to see *Talk to Her* on their first date. To commemorate the occasion, the perky gastronome keeps a framed poster for *Talk to Her*—signed by Almodóvar—on the wall in their home. Ray even named a chicken dish after her favorite director. Her "Chicken for Almodóvar" has a decidedly Spanish flavor, consisting of chicken topped with garlic, onions, green olives, pimentos, golden raisins, and toasted almonds and served over saffron rice.

RACQUET MAN

He's not much of an athlete, but Almodóvar is officially obsessed with one sport: women's tennis. "What both fascinates me and terrifies me in tennis is the fact that the players work in front of the public and the public's response to their work is so immediate," the director says. "I find that attractive because it's precisely what doesn't happen to me when I work." Describing himself as a "nationalist," Almodóvar once ranked Spain's Aranxta Sanchez as his favorite tennis player, with Monica Seles a close second.

BLINDED BY THE LIGHT

There's a reason Almodóvar is often photographed wearing dark sunglasses—and it has nothing to do with wanting to look cool for the camera. For many years, the director has suffered from piercing, painful migraine headaches accompanied by a severe sensitivity to light, or photophobia. The chronic condition, which Almodóvar inherited from his father's side of the family, flared up in a big way in 2007, after a particularly grueling publicity tour promoting his 2006 film *Volver*. Stricken by a fresh round of nearly uninterrupted headaches, Almodóvar spent the next several months laid up at his home in agonizing pain. He consulted neurologists and underwent various treatments, to no apparent effect. "I couldn't read or watch DVDs or type on the computer," he confessed on his personal blog. Undaunted, he vowed to turn his experience into his next cinematic masterpiece. "It's strange that no one has yet made a film about migraine," he wrote, "a mysterious and terrible illness with a name that sounds like a plague of spiders."

THE COEN BROTHERS

JOEL COEN
NOVEMBER 29, 1954–

NATIONALITY:
AMERICAN

ASTROLOGICAL SIGN:
SAGITTARIUS

ETHAN COEN
SEPTEMBER 21, 1957–

NATIONALITY:
AMERICAN

ASTROLOGICAL SIGN:
VIRGO

MAJOR FILMS:
FARGO (1996), *THE BIG LEBOWSKI* (1998), *NO COUNTRY FOR OLD MEN* (2007)

WORDS OF WISDOM:
"THE MOVIE PEOPLE LET US PLAY IN THE CORNER OF THE SANDBOX AND LEAVE US ALONE. WE'RE HAPPY HERE."

Like Frick and Frack, Change and Eng, or Tweedledee and Tweedledum, Joel and Ethan Coen have become inextricably linked in the public mind. There have been other sibling filmmaking tandems—Peter and Bobby Farrelly and Andy and Larry Wachowski come to mind—but none have projected quite the same symbiotic vibe as the gangly film geek brothers from St. Louis Park, Minnesota. In fact, it's become increasingly impossible for anyone but the most dedicated cinephile to distinguish between the two men. Be honest: Off the top of your head, can you remember which one's married to Frances McDormand? I rest my case.

The entity that would come to be known as the Coen Brothers was born between 1954 and 1957 in a predominantly Jewish suburb of Minneapolis. The Coens' parents also shared the same career—they were academics at nearby colleges. And they, it seems, were able to tell their children apart. Joel was the outgoing one, whereas little brother Ethan was quiet. Early on, Joel developed a penchant for pranks and schemes. One day he and a friend dissected a chicken on Rena Coen's ironing table. "At that point we thought, 'Well, Joel might be interested in medicine,'" Mrs. C later recalled. The less audacious Ethan took no part in the chicken gutting. "He was in his own world," his mother remembers.

With Joel leading the way, the brothers started raising cash to fund their various projects. They mowed lawns, sold ice cream in the summertime, and even published a neighborhood newspaper, *The Flag Avenue Sentinel*, which they sold door-to-door for two cents a copy. In high school, they hit upon the idea of channeling their creative energies into moviemaking. They watched Truffaut's *The 400 Blows* with their cinema class, and that was fine as far as influences go, but the films that really inspired them were the ones they watched at home: Tarzan movies, the Hercules series starring muscleman Steve Reeves, breezy sixties sex comedies like *Pillow Talk* and *That Touch of*

Mink, anything with Jerry Lewis, Tony Curtis, or Doris Day. The brothers also took inspiration from the live-action Disney movies of the period, such as *The Love Bug* and *That Darn Cat*.

One summer they decided they should make their own films. Using money saved from cutting lawns, they purchased a Vivitar Super-8 camera and started "exploring the studio space," to quote a phrase. Their first brainstorm was simply to shoot whatever was showing on the TV screen at the moment and call it a movie. Then they graduated to filming their own feet. Eventually they reconciled themselves to the idea of narrative and started creating homemade remakes of the films they saw on TV. Early efforts in this vein included *Zeimers in Zambia*, a reimagining of the 1966 jungle adventure movie *Naked Prey*, starring their neighbor Mark "Zeimers" Zimering (and Ethan as a native brandishing a spear); and a remake of *Lassie Come Home* entitled *Ed, A Dog* with Ethan as the leading lady (clad in his older sister's tutu) and Zeimers once again playing male lead, outfitted in a Cub Scout uniform and yarmulke. There followed the originals *Lumberjacks of the North*, *Froggie Went A-Courtin'* (featuring scenes of road-killed frogs and toads); *Henry Kissinger—Man on the Go* (shot on location at the Minneapolis airport); and what was perhaps their magnum opus, *The Banana Film*, about a man with an unusual talent for smelling bananas. Originally designed to serve as visual accompaniment to the Frank Zappa album *Hot Rats*, it again starred Zeimers and gave him a chance to throw up on camera.

It would be fair to call both Coens nontraditional students, so it's no surprise their parents sent them away to a nontraditional educational institution. Simon's Rock College in Great Barrington, Massachusetts, was a fully accredited college for students who want to take college courses before graduating high school. Both Coens attended, graduated, and then briefly went their separate ways. Joel attended NYU film school, where he did little to distinguish himself. "I was a cipher there," he later recalled. "I sat at the back of the room with an insane grin on my face." A professor at NYU remembered him as the guy who was "very quiet, seemed self-possessed, and smoked a lot." After that fizzled out, he sought work as a production assistant in industrial films, including the enthralling *How to Buy a Used Car*. Director Barry Sonnenfeld hired him to work on one such project, but later realized his mistake, calling Coen "the worst PA I ever worked with. He got three parking tickets, came late, and set fire to the smoke machine." Editing seemed to suit Coen better, and he soon found a more productive outlet as an assistant editor on low-budget

horror movies, including *Fear No Evil*, about a high school student possessed by demons, and *The Evil Dead*, directed by his friend Sam Raimi. Joel Coen and Sam Raimi have a very brief cameo as gun-toting security guards in the 1985 spy comedy *Spies Like Us*.

While Joel was cutting his teeth in the movie business, Ethan was getting a more conventional education at Princeton University, where he majored in philosophy and generally devoted himself about as assiduously to his studies as his brother had. Ethan even quit school at one point and had to apply for readmission. When he missed the deadline for submitting his application, he informed school officials that he had lost his arm in a hunting accident. They readmitted him on the condition that he first be cleared by a psychologist. Somehow, Ethan managed to graduate. His senior thesis was a forty-one-page essay entitled "Two Views of Wittgenstein's Later Philosophy."

In 1979, Ethan moved to New York City and reunited with his brother. He took a job as a statistical clerk at Macy's, inputting the data that went onto the tags on men's pajamas and bathrobes, and spent his free time writing for the TV cop drama *Cagney & Lacey*. Together, the Coens began cranking out scripts.

FINISHING EACH OTHER'S SENTENCES, WEARING THE SAME DRAB CLOTHING, AND SMOKING THE SAME BRAND OF CIGARETTES, THE COEN BROTHERS ARE NEARLY IMPOSSIBLE TO TELL APART.

Their early efforts included a screwball comedy called *Coast to Coast*, about a Chinese plot to clone Albert Einstein, and *The XYZ Murders*, a collaboration with Raimi that involved a pair of rat exterminators turned hit men. By far, their best screenplay was a neo-noir thriller called *Blood Simple*.

To get the film made, the brothers shot a three-minute trailer and came up with an innovative way to secure financing. Joel returned to Minneapolis, walked into the office of Hadassah—a Jewish philanthropic organization—and asked for "a list of the hundred richest Jews in town." The brothers then took their trailer to each one, raising the bulk of the $855,000 budget from sixty-eight individual investors, each of whom contributed $5,000. They paid their crew a pittance and shot the movie in eight weeks.

Released in 1984, *Blood Simple* was a sleeper hit and helped usher in the era of independent cinema. With the 1987 comedy *Raising Arizona*, the brothers broadened their appeal without sacrificing any of the stylistic flourishes that so endeared them to the indie audience: ironic humor, extensive use of homage to classic film plots and characters, and jittery hyperactive camerawork. Little changed stylistically over the next two decades, as the siblings embarked on a long march toward mainstream acceptance marked by huge strides forward (the multiple Oscar winners *Fargo* and *No Country for Old Men*), short steps backward (the unwatchable *The Hudsucker Proxy* and the anodyne *Intolerable Cruelty*), as well as curious detours like the cult hit *The Big Lebowski*, an antic mash-up of film noir and stoner comedy that befuddled critics at the time of its release but has since attained masterpiece status. Although their choice of projects remains too idiosyncratic to guarantee consistent box-office performance, the Coens seem to have attained a level of respect within the film community sufficient to ensure that they can keep making their type of movie—without having to hit up wealthy Minnesota Jews for money—well into the foreseeable future.

And for those keeping score at home, Joel Coen is the one who's married to Frances McDormand.

PEAS IN A POD

Known to their friends as "the boys," the Coens do little to dispel the myth that they are essentially one creature hatched out of the same egg. They are known for finishing each other's sentences, wearing the same drab clothing (jeans and T-shirts), even smoking the same brand of cigarettes (Camel Lights). They also have something of a private language. In Coenspeak, a "Miles" is the muffled sound someone on the other end of a movie telephone conversation makes; "hubcaps" are the echoes left by on-screen sound effects; and an "ambassador" is a gesture or bit of dialogue that reveals a character's motivation. While filming *Miller's Crossing*, the brothers also got into the habit of calling the camera viewfinder "Little Elvis," after Elvis Presley's nickname for his penis. When they finished filming for the day, they announced that "Elvis has left the building."

COMMERCIAL INTERRUPTIONS

For indie darlings, the Coens sure aren't shy about shilling for corporate America. Their portfolio of ad work includes one TV commercial for the Gap (featuring Dennis Hopper and Christina Ricci sitting beside a pool playing chess), two for the Honda Accord, and a 2002 Super Bowl ad for tax-preparation behemoth H&R Block. Set to the tune of "Tax Man" by the Beatles, the spot resulted in a huge uptick in sales for the firm—which presumably redounded to the brothers' benefit. Not that they did it for the money, of course. "We have always been fascinated with the mysteries of the tax code," the brothers explained—apparently with a straight face—"and with the people who struggle so mightily to plumb its depths."

YES MEN
John Turturro has an unusual nickname for the Coens. He calls them "the Yeah Yeahs" for their strange habit of ending every sentence with "heh heh" or "yeah yeah" in the manner of Beavis and Butthead.

SHARE'S FAIR
The Coens split the credit on all their films—with Joel billed as the director and Ethan as the producer—although they actually work jointly on every aspect of the production. (They edit the films together using the pseudonym Roderick Jaynes.) When asked why they came up with this arrangement, Joel attributed it to his being three years older and thirty pounds heavier than Ethan. "I can beat him up, so I get to direct," he quipped. But the real inspiration came from the 1965 comedy *Boeing-Boeing*—one of the brothers' favorite films—in which the names of top-billed stars Jerry Lewis and Tony Curtis rotate on an axis during the opening credits.

GOLDEN BOWL
There are a lot of unsettling elements in the Coens' 2007 Oscar winner *No Country for Old Men*—none more so than Javier Bardem's hair. The severe bowl cut Bardem sported as methodical killer Anton Chigurh was simultaneously terrifying and ridiculous—and 100 percent the Coens' idea. They drew inspiration from a photograph of a barfly circa 1979, when the movie is set. "That bowl is fantastic," Joel Coen told an interviewer after the movie came out. "We just copied it." After initially expressing reservations about the 'do—which he feared might inhibit his sex life—Bardem eventually came to accept it. He feels it may even have enhanced his performance."The haircut was really doing the job," Bardem said, "so you don't have to act the haircut; the haircut is acting by itself."

SPIKE LEE

MARCH 20, 1957–

NATIONALITY:
AMERICAN

ASTROLOGICAL SIGN:
PISCES

MAJOR FILMS:
DO THE RIGHT THING (1989), *MALCOLM X* (1992)

WORDS OF WISDOM:

"WHAT'S THE DIFFERENCE BETWEEN HOLLYWOOD CHARACTERS AND MY CHARACTERS? MINE ARE REAL."

A tiny man filled with rage, Shelton Jackson Lee was appropriately nicknamed "Spike" by his mother. He obviously believes he has some special claim on that pugnacious moniker, since he sued the cable television network Spike TV for infringing on his implied trademark in 2003. ("People don't realize that I'm a brand," Lee railed, "and all the goodwill that I have invested in it can be contaminated by Spike TV." The two sides later settled out of court.) It was one of many high-profile battles Lee has initiated over the years against enemies real and imagined. "People think I'm this angry black man walking around in a constant state of rage," Lee once complained to an interviewer. If only he had consulted the voluminous public record of personal put-downs, charges of conspiracy, and allegations of racism he has amassed through the decades, he might understand why. Is it any wonder a major magazine once ran a profile of him under the headline "Spike Lee Hates Your Cracker Ass"?

Although he's closely identified with the borough of Brooklyn (where he hasn't lived in more than a decade), Lee was actually born in Atlanta, Georgia. His mother, a teacher, and his father, a jazz musician, provided him with an artistic education and comfortable middle-class upbringing, particularly after they moved to the Italian American neighborhood of Cobble Hill, Brooklyn. Lee inherited some of his trademark tenacity from his dad, who so revered traditional instrumentation in jazz that he refused to play an electric bass—even though it cost him lucrative studio gigs.

Lee himself seemed destined for a musical career, at first, until he picked up an 8-millimeter camera during his sophomore year at Morehouse College. He spent the entire summer of 1977 shooting New York street scenes, interweaving images of disco dancers with those of ordinary citizens beleaguered by a citywide blackout and the ongoing terror of the Son of Sam killer. He would eventually edit that footage into his first short feature, *Last Hustle in Brooklyn*. Now convinced he wanted to be a professional filmmaker, Lee enrolled in the prestigious NYU film school.

As one of the school's few black students, Lee found it easy to stand out from the herd of aspiring Scorseses. His first-year project, a parody of D. W. Griffith's *Birth of a Nation*, put racial consciousness-raising at the heart of his aesthetic agenda. His next film, a 45-minute film about an inner-city barbershop called *We Cut Heads*, won a student director's academy award. But the acclaim brought little in the way of money, and Lee found himself working at a small production company until he could scrape together enough money to make his first feature, *She's Gotta Have It*, in 1985. That film cost less than $175,000 to make and pulled in $7 million at the box office. Lee was now a bona fide independent filmmaking sensation. What's more, his winning performance in the film, as motor-mouthed Knicks fan Mars Blackmon, heightened his public profile and led to a lucrative endorsement deal with Nike.

Suddenly rich, Lee struggled through the inevitable sophomore slump—the misbegotten musical *School Daze*—but found his true voice with 1989's *Do the Right Thing*, a panoramic examination of racial tensions in one Brooklyn neighborhood on the hottest day of the summer. It earned Lee an Academy Award nomination for best original screenplay. The diminutive director continued to explore issues of race, class, and the merits of violent vs. nonviolent social change in subsequent films, such as *Mo Better Blues*, *Jungle Fever*, and *Malcolm X*. This last represented Lee's high-water mark at the box office. His more recent work has struggled to find a mass audience, and critics have generally taken more kindly to his politically charged documentaries, like *Four Little Girls* and *When the Levees Broke,* than to less-than-inspired narrative features such as *Summer of Sam*, *Bamboozled*, and *She Hate Me*.

✳   ✳   ✳

MO' BETTER HOUSES

Despite pretensions of being a man of the 'hood, Lee has cultivated a lifestyle more suited to a wealthy white hedge-fund manager than a scrappy independent filmmaker. Married to a former corporate lawyer, he sends his children to school at a posh private academy. He no longer even lives in Brooklyn, preferring to reside in a lavish palazzo-style townhouse on Manhattan's Upper East Side, which he purchased from artist Jasper Johns for $4.75 million. The Lees also maintain a second home on Martha's Vineyard.

BAT MAN

Lee is infamous for instigating feuds with other celebrities—many of which seem to originate at the Cannes Film Festival, for some reason. (In the future Lee might want to avoid the festival, or at least keep away from its open bar.) One of the earliest instances of Spike Behaving Badly came in 1989, when an irate Lee let loose on German director Wim Wenders—then serving as a judge at the festival—for not awarding the Jury Prize to *Do the Right Thing* and for labeling Mookie, the protagonist of Lee's film, as "unheroic." "Wim Wenders had better watch out," Lee warned, "'cause I'm waiting for his ass. Somewhere deep in my closet I have a Louisville Slugger bat with Wenders's name on it."

GUN RAMPAGE

Another of Lee's Cannes Jobs came in 1999, at the expense of legendary actor turned National Rifle Association president Charlton Heston. While at the festival promoting *Summer of Sam*, the diminutive director jokingly suggested that Heston should be assassinated. "Shoot him with a .44 Bulldog!" Lee railed, referencing the model handgun used by the Son of Sam serial killer. In a letter to the *Los Angeles Times*, Heston excoriated Lee for his remark—and provided a history lesson. "When Lee was still in diapers," he wrote, "I was working with Dr. Martin Luther King to break down the racist code in the Hollywood technical unions that denied blacks any place behind the cameras, paving the way for young filmmakers like Lee."

WATCH YOUR LANGUAGE

There's nothing like a catfight between two indie darlings. In the mid-1990s Lee and Quentin Tarantino went at it over Tarantino's promiscuous use of the word "nigger" in his screenplays. "I'm not against the ["n"] word, and I use it," Lee told *Variety*. "But Quentin is infatuated with the word. What does he want to be made? An honorary black man?" Tarantino responded by belit-

tling Lee's box-office performance—and the 5' 5" director himself. "Lee would have to stand on a chair to kiss my ass," Tarantino told shock jock Howard Stern. Later, when Samuel L. Jackson intervened in the dispute on Tarantino's behalf, Lee attacked *him*, likening the *Pulp Fiction* star's defense of Tarantino to "the house negro defending the Massa."

MILLION DOLLAR BABIES

Jumping ugly on the unimposing Tarantino was one thing, but Lee really should have thought twice before taking on Dirty Harry. In 2008, Lee started flapping his gums (yet again) at the Cannes Film Festival, where he was supposed to be promoting his World War II dud *Miracle at St. Anna*, but seemed strangely preoccupied with trashing Clint Eastwood's vastly superior film *Flags of Our Fathers*. Accusing Eastwood of deliberately excluding black soldiers from his depiction of the Battle of Iwo Jima, Lee boasted that his movie would correct the historical record. "That was his version," Lee bragged. "The negro soldier did not exist. I have a different version." An irate Eastwood responded by saying that Lee should "shut his face" and insisted that the racial composition of the fighting forces in his film was historically accurate. Un-

> SPIKE LEE DOESN'T ARRIVE AT KNICKS AND YANKEES GAMES IN A LIMO JUST TO FLAUNT HIS POSH LIFESTYLE. THE CELEBRATED DIRECTOR FROM BROOKLYN HAS NEVER LEARNED HOW TO DRIVE.

bowed, Lee shot back: "[Eastwood] is not my father and we're not on a plantation. . . . He sounds like an angry old man." The childish verbal jousting went on in the press for weeks, until Lee called a truce, using mutual friend Steven Spielberg as an intermediary.

POOR RELATION

It's not just white directors who grind Lee's gears. The tiny auteur also attacked fellow African American filmmaker Matty Rich, whose 1991 indie feature *Straight Out of Brooklyn* bore an unmistakable resemblance to some of Lee's own early films. In interviews, Lee derided Rich as "Matty Poor" and ridiculed his lack of formal training. "He knew nothing about film. He was ignorant to film grammar. That type of thinking, not just Matty Rich, but where black people equated being down, being real, and being black with just being stupid, you know that shit has got to stop. Where if you're intelligent, and you speak well, and you go to school, then you're considered [trying to be] white. [Matty Rich] used to say 'Spike Lee, he went to college. He went to college. I'm from the streets!' That's just some ignorant shit, man. We've got to stop that stuff. It's ignorant."

BAGGER OFF!

Will Smith is another African American icon Lee isn't shy about criticizing. When Smith played Matt Damon's oracular caddy in the 2000 golfing feature *The Legend of Bagger Vance*, Lee charged the film with whitewashing the reality of race relations in depression-era south. Mocking the movie as *Driving Mr. Damon*, he told an audience at Harvard University: "In real life, black men were being castrated and lynched left and right. With all that going on, why are you trying to teach Matt Damon a golf swing?" Some industry insiders saw a less high-minded motivation behind Lee's diatribe. They claimed he was still stewing over Smith's decision to have white filmmaker Michael Mann direct the 2001 Muhammad Ali biopic *Ali* instead of him.

THE BLUEST EYE

Whoopi Goldberg found herself on the receiving end of yet another Lee tirade when she committed the unpardonable sin of wearing blue contact lenses. A seething Lee excoriated her for trying to look white. Not one to back down from a fight, Goldberg shot back: "I would caution Spike Lee to think about his own feelings about being black. . . . People do this whole trip about black; I'm not interested in that. My answer to Spike is I hope everything goes well. But stay off my eye color because if I want to change it, I will."

IT'S A CONSPIRACY!

And don't get Lee started on the Jews. When an interviewer remarked that Lee stood a good chance of winning an Academy Award for his 1997 documentary *Four Little Girls*, a powerful examination of the events leading up to a 1963 Birmingham church bombing, Lee went ballistic. Pointing out that his principal competition was a movie about the founding of the state of Israel after World War II, Lee railed: "When the film is about the Holocaust and one of the producers is a rabbi and it comes from the Simon Wiesenthal Center, there are not many sure things in life, but that was a sure thing when you consider the makeup of the voting body of the Academy of Motion Picture Arts & Sciences. I'd have rather been the New York Knicks in the fourth quarter, down ten points, a minute left in the United Center, than have the odds we faced of winning the Oscar against the Holocaust film."

A SIMPLE "NO COMMENT" WOULD HAVE SUFFICED

A *New York Post* reporter once telephoned Lee to inquire about rumors that the director's epic biopic *Malcolm X* was running over budget. Although he refused to confirm or deny the reports, Lee did offer up his candid opinion of the right-leaning tabloid: "The *Post*," he raged, "is a "motherfucking racist rag and I hate it!"

HIS ARSENAL

Everyone knows that Lee is a huge basketball fan. He can often be seen courtside at New York Knicks games, waving a towel and occasionally trash talking with players on the opposing team. The pint-sized auteur has also been known to show up at New York Yankees games in the South Bronx (often inexplicably wearing a Dodger jersey). Fewer people are aware that Lee is also a big fan of European soccer—a "Gooner," to be precise, otherwise known as a supporter of the English Premier League club Arsenal. Lee attended his first Arsenal match in London in 2003 and has since amassed a huge collection of Arsenal jerseys, which he's known to wear on the set of his films. According to the UK newspaper *The Guardian*, the director has expressed an interest in casting former Arsenal star Thierry Henry in one of his movies and has developed a penchant for using the word *bollocks* during his visits to Britain.

CITY SLICKER

That limo ride to Knicks games must be costing Lee a fortune. The wee moviemaker from Brooklyn has never learned how to drive a car.

QUENTIN TARANTINO

MARCH 27, 1963–

NATIONALITY:
AMERICAN

ASTROLOGICAL SIGN:
ARIES

MAJOR FILMS:
RESERVOIR DOGS (1992), *PULP FICTION* (1994)

WORDS OF WISDOM:

"THE AUDIENCE AND THE DIRECTOR, IT'S AN S&M RELATIONSHIP, AND THE AUDIENCE IS THE M."

Quentin Tarantino's is the classic American success story: hyperactive video store geek with an encyclopedic knowledge of cinema borrows plot points and characters from obscure foreign films and assembles them into cool-looking English-language movies whose unexpected popularity instantly transforms him into an international celebrity. He gets to hang with the Wu-Tang Clan, who call him "Q. T."

Okay, so maybe that's not the way Horatio Alger wrote it. But it's the way Tarantino would have written it, if some unknown dude in Hong Kong had written it first. Tarantino's life story actually begins before he took a job at Video Archives in Manhattan Beach in 1985, although that's hardly the most interesting part. Named for Quint Asper, the character Burt Reynolds played on *Gunsmoke* (some sources say Quentin Compson, the suicidal hero of William Faulkner's *The Sound and the Fury*), Tarantino endured a rather desultory Southern California childhood—raised by a single mom, for whom he composed a story every Mother's Day that ended with her dying horribly.

He dropped out of school in the middle of ninth grade and briefly held a job working as an usher in the local porn theater, the Pussycat Lounge, before landing at Video Archives. That gig was to last five years and prove more conducive to Tarantino's dream of becoming an actor. The future Oscar winner was the Stephen Hawking of video clerks—a motormouthed savant whose wide-ranging knowledge of movie history was so impressive that one of his fellow clerks actually committed suicide out of fear he would never be able to live up to Tarantino's potential. When he wasn't dazzling customers with his understanding of early 1970s grindhouse, Tarantino spent much of his time there looking for his big break: cold-calling Hollywood producers asking for work or posing as a journalist to score interviews with A-list directors like Brian De Palma.

Along the way, his focus shifted from acting to writing and directing. In 1985, at age twenty-two, he wrote his first screenplay, the unfortunately titled *Captain Peachfuzz and the Anchovy Bandit*. Sadly, it never saw the light of day, although Tarantino's next script, *True Romance*, sold and was eventually made into a film in 1993 by director Tony Scott. By that time, Tarantino had started his roll, selling *Natural Born Killers* to Oliver Stone and directing his own script for 1992's *Reservoir Dogs*. Those three films, released over the course of three years, established Tarantino's reputation in Hollywood and within the burgeoning indie film community. After fending off offers to cash in and direct the crowd-pleasers *Men in Black* and *Speed*, Tarantino then cemented his hipster cred with 1994's *Pulp Fiction*, a dizzyingly entertaining mélange of situations, characters, and bits of dialogue borrowed from other films and pop-culture sources. Although some derided the director as a plagiarist (he claimed he was just paying homage), and cowriter Roger Avary groused that he was denied proper credit for his contributions, audiences didn't seem to care. The film was a critical and commercial smash, revived John Travolta's moribund movie career, and earned Tarantino an Oscar for best original screenplay. As evidence of *Pulp Fiction*'s enduring impact, a DVD of the film was later discovered lying around one of Saddam Hussein's palaces following the U.S. invasion of Iraq.

In the aftermath of *Pulp Fiction's* success, Tarantino became a worldwide celebrity—the "George Gobel of filmmakers," as one producer put it, famous for being famous. His subsequent output has been somewhat scattershot: the disappointing *Jackie Brown*, the visually thrilling *Kill Bill*, as well as 2009's long-delayed, much-anticipated *Inglourious Basterds* (yes, that is how he spells it), a genre-changing World War II epic/spaghetti Western Tarantino had been promising and failing to unleash on audiences since 2001. Through it all, Tarantino has remained eminently quotable, an invariably entertaining late-night talk-show guest with a laptop's worth of material about his various and sundry Hollywood feuds, sexual peccadilloes, and opinions on every subject—from why he hates the Who to how much he loves Cap'n Crunch. If Q. T. didn't exist, it seems clear, someone (possibly Ringo Lam) would have to invent him.

DOG DAYS

During his lean years working as a video clerk, Tarantino would take almost any gig offered to him—as long as it was even tangentially connected to the entertainment industry. In 1987, that meant serving as a production assistant on has-been muscleman Dolph Lundgren's workout video *Maximum Potential*. Director John Langley hired Tarantino for the job, which entailed scooping dog feces off the front lawn of the house where the video was being shot. "As a P.A., Quentin was always bashing into nightstands and babbling at everybody," Langley later recalled. "He's quite a talker and loves to get into debates about film. My partner would say, 'Fire that kid. He doesn't know what the hell he's doing.'"

THE MAN WHO WOULD BE KING

Four years before hitting the big time with *Reservoir Dogs*, Tarantino scored his first big break in show business, playing an Elvis impersonator on a November 1988 episode of *The Golden Girls*. The geriatric sitcom was then wheezing through its fourth season, and Tarantino was a struggling actor desperate for work—any work—to keep him solvent while he honed his craft. After learning that the show was looking for twelve Elvis impersonators to appear as guests in a wedding scene, Tarantino's agent pitched him to the casting director as "Elvis meets Charles Manson." Unlike the other Elvises (Elvii?), Tarantino wore his own clothes to the shoot. "I was the real Elvis," he later told *Playboy* magazine. "Everyone else was Elvis after he sold out." Though he ended up looking more like Smiths frontman Morrissey than the King of rock 'n roll, he did get to harmonize alongside the other Presley pretenders to Don Ho's *Hawaiian Love Chant* and stay on the good side of temperamental star Bea Arthur. "[She's] fine after she's had her morning coffee," Tarantino recalled. For his work, the future Academy Award winner received residuals totaling more than $3,000 over the course of a year. "Every time I was running out of money, I'd get a check for $100 or $200 or $300," Tarantino marveled. "It was so great—now I understand why people do this."

GOING MEDIEVAL ON HIS ASIAGO

He may have written the original screenplay for *Natural Born Killers*, but when it comes to dishing out violence, Tarantino is no Mickey Knox. In October 1997, the irascible director turned a posh West Hollywood Italian eatery into his own personal fight club when he assaulted *Natural Born Killers* producer Don Murphy inside the restaurant Ago. According to eyewitnesses, Tarantino sucker-punched Murphy—who had slammed him in a tell-all book about the making of the Oliver Stone film—as he ate lunch at the trendy eatery, a well-known haunt of Tinseltown dealmakers. "I don't

think either of these guys had a clue how to fight," commented another diner on the melee, which spilled over to the maitre d' station and culminated with Tarantino standing over a simpering Murphy and repeatedly punching him in the head. Sheriff's deputies were called in, but by the time they arrived the brawl had already broken up. Murphy subsequently sued Tarantino for $5 million. In the suit, Murphy blamed Tarantino for breaking the band on his wristwatch and forcing him to miss a month of work while tending to his injuries. For his part, Tarantino called the beat down a "misunderstanding," although he took to the airwaves just days later to crow about it on the *Keenan Ivory Wayans Show*. "I really think I slapped some respect into the guy," he told *Variety*.

QUENTIN, THE LOVE GOD

So is Tarantino more a lover than a fighter? Not really—if his early erotic experiences are any indication. The first time he had sex, when he was sixteen years old, Tarantino ejaculated prematurely. "I think I came the second dick hit pussy—voom," he confessed to an interviewer. Subsequent

QUENTIN TARANTINO SCORED HIS FIRST BIG BREAK IN SHOW BUSINESS BY PLAYING AN ELVIS IMPERSONATOR ON *THE GOLDEN GIRLS*. HE WORE HIS OWN CLOTHES TO THE SHOOT.

forays proved more fruitful—though no less unsettling. When he was seventeen years old, Tarantino had intercourse with a prostitute—in his mom's bed while she was out buying groceries. At some point, the young videostore clerk hit upon the idea of actually asking women out on dates, with little success. Perpetually broke, Tarantino occasionally slept in his car, a dilapidated Honda Civic. As a result, he rarely showered and reeked to high heaven. To compensate for these shortcomings, he developed some innovative pick-up strategies. One of his favorites was to tell an attractive female patron there was a problem with her membership, and then show her that she was identified as "Dreamgirl" in the store's computer system. On one occasion, he asked out another would-be conquest for a picnic lunch—in the video-store parking lot.

HOGG HEAVEN

An inveterate pop-culture junkie, Tarantino collects lunch boxes and board games based on old TV shows, including *I Dream of Jeannie* and *The A-Team*. One of his prized possessions is a *Dukes of Hazzard* board game from 1981 that challenges players to compete in a "wild race" to Uncle Jesse's farm. In a way, the *Dukes* fixation is a nod to Tarantino's beginnings in show business. As a young man, he studied acting with James Best, who played Sheriff Rosco P. Coltrane on *The Dukes of Hazzard* from 1979 to 1985.

JAILHOUSE DORK

A self-styled outlaw, Tarantino has had numerous brushes with the law—all for petty offenses one might expect someone intent on posing as a criminal to commit. When he was fifteen years old, the wannabe badass was arrested for shoplifting a copy of Elmore Leonard's novel *The Switch* from a neighborhood K-Mart. (The book later provided the inspiration for Tarantino's film *Jackie Brown*.) As an adult, Tarantino was jailed on three separate occasions for failing to pay his parking tickets. The first time was a gas, he reported: "I learned some great dialogue." The second and third incarcerations—not so much. By the time of his third stint in the crapper, Tarantino had racked up more than $7,000 worth of fines. He was confined for more than a week. "After the first time, the bloom was completely off the rose," he recalled. "The last time I was there for eight days, and it was really hell."

CEREAL KILLER

Tarantino and Jerry Seinfeld have more in common than you might think. They both appeared on cheesy 1980s sitcoms (Tarantino on *The Golden Girls*, Seinfeld on *Benson*); they're both known for writing dialogue in which characters free associate about food, movies, comic books, and all aspects of popular culture; and they both love cereal. Seinfeld's well-stocked kitchen cabinets on his eponymous sitcom were the stuff of legend, of course, but who knew the director of *Pulp Fiction* had such a craving for Kellogg's? "Breakfast cereal is one of my favorite foods," Tarantino has said, "because it's so easy to fix and it tastes so incredibly great. Cap'n Crunch is, of course, the creme de la creme." Although his heart resides with the old classics, Tarantino does make room for some more contemporary takes on the cuisine. "The best of the newfangled cereals, far and away, was Bill and Ted's Excellent Cereal," he told *Playboy*. "It was fantastic. It was like a particularly terrific Lucky Charms."

IT'S PAT, MOTHERF*CKER!

According to published reports, Tarantino did an uncredited rewrite of the screenplay for *It's Pat*, the 1994 turkey based on comic Julia Sweeney's long-running *Saturday Night Live* character, Pat Riley, an irritating office worker of indeterminate gender. Tarantino seemed curiously invested in the project, which he worked on around the same time he was writing the script for *Pulp Fiction*. "What I love about the character is that Pat is so fucking obnoxious," he has said. "To tell the truth, I don't know what Pat is. But I know what I want Pat to be: I want Pat to be a girl."

T.M.I.?

In a 2004 interview with *Rolling Stone* magazine, Tarantino revealed that he once seriously considered sawing off his own finger. "The knife wasn't poised," he said, "but I did have it out." He also announced his official policy on submitting to anal rape in a penitentiary—as if anyone had asked. "If I went to prison, I would *not* be butt-fucked," the director declared. "Let's say it's Mike Tyson. I can bite his lip off. Bite his nut sack off. I could rip it open. Those are the things that I could do. And I would do them."

PLAYING FOOTSIE

Although he denied it for years, documentary evidence now confirms what Tarantino watchers have suspected for a long time: The garrulous director has a raging foot fetish. Anyone still seeking evidence in this case is advised to consult the multiple shots of Uma Thurman's bare tootsies in both *Pulp Fiction* and *Kill Bill*, the scene in *From Dusk Till Dawn* in which Tarantino slurps tequila off of Selma Hayek's foot, numerous paparazzi photographs of Tarantino with his lips around the toes of an unseen female, and Tarantino's own admission during a 2008 film festival Q&A with director John Waters that he has "an affection for that appendage." In his tell-all memoir *Hollywood Animal*, screenwriter Joe Eszterhas revealed that his manicurist told him about Tarantino's proclivities—and that Tarantino had once sucked Cameron Diaz's toes for pleasure. Actors on the set of *Kill Bill* reported that Tarantino spent so much time filming their feet he could have made a whole other movie using those shots alone. In 2006, a good-humored Tarantino appeared as a celebrity judge on a special foot fetish edition of Tyra Banks's *America's Next Top Model* entitled *America's Next Top Foot Model*.

SELECTED BIBLIOGRAPHY

Amende, Carol. *If You Don't Have Anything Nice to Say, Come Sit Next to Me*. New York: Macmillan, 1994.

Anger, Kenneth. *Hollywood Babylon*. San Francisco: Straight Arrow Books, 1975.

Bach, Steven. *Leni: The Life and Work of Leni Riefenstahl*. New York: Alfred A. Knopf, 2007.

Baxter, John. *Buñuel*. New York: Carroll & Graf, 1994.

Baxter, John. *Fellini: The Biography*. New York: St. Martin's Press, 1993.

Baxter, John. *Mythmaker: The Life and Work of George Lucas*. New York: Avon Books, 1999.

Bergan, Ronald. *The Coen Brothers*. New York: Thunder's Mouth Press, 2000.

Bergman, Ingmar. *The Magic Lantern: An Autobiography*. New York: Viking Penguin, 1988.

Biskind, Peter. *Easy Riders, Raging Bulls: How the Sex-Drugs-and-Rock 'n' Roll Generation Saved Hollywood*. New York: Simon & Schuster, 1998.

Brody, Richard. *Everything Is Cinema: The Working Life of Jean-Luc Godard*. New York: Henry Holt and Company, 2008.

Charyn, Jerome. *Raised by Wolves: The Turbulent Art and Times of Quentin Tarantino*. New York: Thunder's Mouth Press, 2006.

De Baecque, Antoine and Serge Toubiana. *Truffaut: A Biography*. New York: Alfred A. Knopf, 1999.

D'Lugo, Marvin. *Pedro Almodóvar*. Urbana and Chicago: University of Illinois Press, 2006.

Eyman, Scott. *Print the Legend: The Life and Times of John Ford*. New York: Simon & Schuster, 1999.

Farrow, Mia. *What Falls Away*. New York: Doubleday, 1997.

Fine, Marshall. *Bloody Sam: The Life and Films of Sam Peckinpah*. New York: Donald I. Fine, 1991.

Frayling, Christopher. *Sergio Leone: Something to Do with Death*. London: Faber and Faber, 2000.

Galbraith, Stuart IV. *The Emperor and the Wolf: The Lives and Films of Akira Kurosawa and Toshiro Mifune*. New York: Faber and Faber, 2001.

Hamsher, Jane. *Killer Instinct: How Two Young Producers Took on Hollywood and Made the Most Controversial Film of the Decade*. New York: Broadway Books, 1997.

Lee, Spike (as told to Kaleem Aftab). *That's My Story and I'm Sticking to It*. New York: W. W. Norton & Company, 2006.

LoBrutto, Vincent. *Martin Scorsese: A Biography*. Westport, CT: Greenwood Publishing Group, 2008.

LoBrutto, Vincent. *Stanley Kubrick: A Biography*. New York: Penguin, 1997.

Louvish, Simon. *Cecil B. DeMille: A Life in Art*. New York: St. Martin's Press, 2008.

McBride, Joseph. *Frank Capra: The Catastrophe of Success*. New York: St. Martin's Press, 2000.

McCarthy, Todd. *Howard Hawks: The Grey Fox of Hollywood*. New York: Grove Press, 2000.

McGilligan, Patrick. *Robert Altman: Jumping Off the Cliff*. New York: St. Martin's Press, 1989.

Meade, Marion. *The Unruly Life of Woody Allen*. New York: Simon & Schuster, 2000.

Mosley, Leonard. *The Real Walt Disney*. London: Futura Publications, 1985.

Pollock, Dale. *Skywalking: The Life and Films of George Lucas*. New York: Harmony Books, 1983.

Riordan, James. Stone: The Controversies, Excesses, and Exploits of a Radical Filmmaker. New York: Hyperion, 1995.

Rodley, Chris (editor). Lynch on Lynch. London: Faber and Faber Ltd., 1997.

Salamon, Julie. The Devil's Candy: The Bonfire of the Vanities Goes to Hollywood. New York: Bantam Doubleday Dell, 1991.

Sandford, Christopher. Polanski: A Biography. New York: Palgrave Macmillan, 2008.

Sanello, Frank. Spielberg: The Man, The Movies, The Mythology. Dallas, TX: Taylor Publishing, 1996.

Schickel, Richard. D. W. Griffith: An American Life. New York: Simon & Schuster, 1984.

Schickel, Richard. Elia Kazan: A Biography. New York: HarperCollins, 2005.

Schneider, Stephen Jay. 501 Movie Directors. Hauppauge, NY: Barron's Educational Series, 2007.

Schumacher, Michael. Francis Ford Coppola: A Filmmaker's Life. New York: Crown Publishers, 1999.

Spoto, Donald. The Dark Side of Genius. New York: Da Capo Press, 1999.

Straus, Frederic. Almodóvar on Almodóvar. London: Faber and Faber Ltd., 1995.

Thomson, David. Rosebud: The Story of Orson Welles. New York: Vintage Books, 1996.

Trimborn, Jurgen. Leni Riefenstahl: A Life. New York: Darrar, Straus, and Giroux, 2002.

Weddle, David. If They Move . . . Kill 'Em! The Life and Times of Sam Peckinpah. New York: Grove Press, 1994.

Weissman, Stephen M. D. Chaplin: A Life. New York: Arcade Publishing, 2008.

INDEX

irreference \ir-'ef-(ə-)rən(t)s\ *n* (2009)

1 : irreverent reference
2 : real information that also entertains or amuses

How-Tos. Quizzes. Instructions.
Recipes. Crafts. Jokes.
Trivia. Games. Tricks.
Quotes. Advice. Tips.

Learn something. Or not.

VISIT IRREFERENCE.COM
The New Quirk Books Web Site